WHERE TO CRUISE

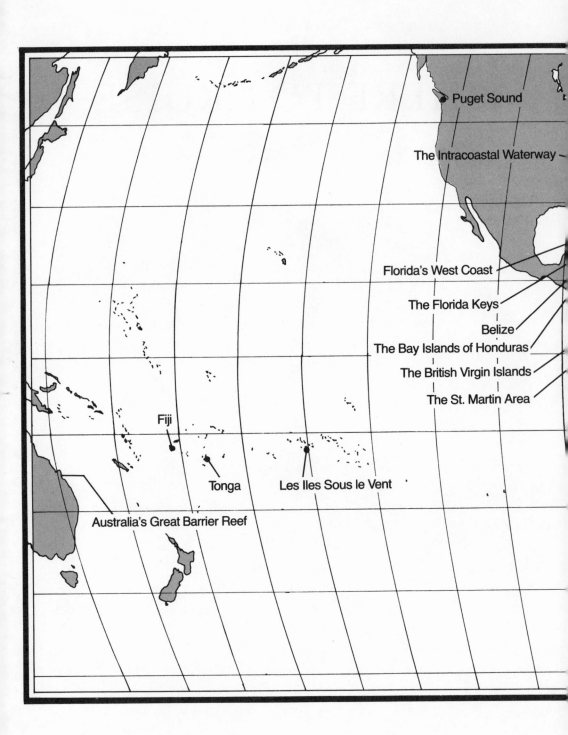

Puget Sound

The Intracoastal Waterway

Florida's West Coast

The Florida Keys

Belize

The Bay Islands of Honduras

The British Virgin Islands

The St. Martin Area

Fiji

Tonga

Les Iles Sous le Vent

Australia's Great Barrier Reef

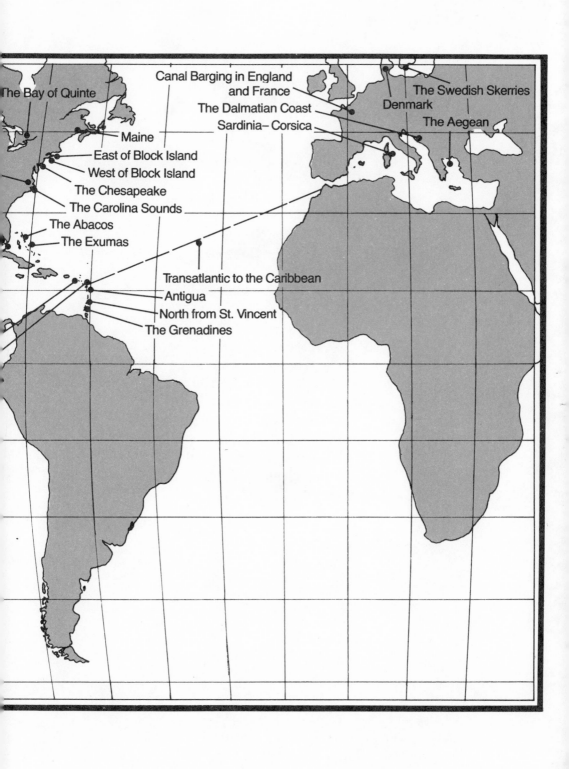

The Bay of Quinte

Canal Barging in England and France

The Swedish Skerries

Denmark

Maine

The Dalmatian Coast

Sardinia–Corsica

The Aegean

East of Block Island

West of Block Island

The Chesapeake

The Carolina Sounds

The Abacos

The Exumas

Transatlantic to the Caribbean

Antigua

North from St. Vincent

The Grenadines

Bill Robinson

WHERE TO CRUISE

W·W·NORTON & COMPANY

NEW YORK   LONDON

Library of Congress Cataloging in Publication in Data
Robinson, Bill, 1918–
    Where to cruise
    I. Yachts and yachting—Directories.   I. Title
GV813.R563   1984   979.1'025   83-13489

First published as a Norton paperback 1991

ISBN 0-393-30796-4

W. W. Norton & Company, Inc.
500 Fifth Avenue, New York, N.Y. 10110
W. W. Norton & Company Ltd
10 Coptic Street, London WC1A 1PU

2 3 4 5 6 7 8 9 0

Contents

Preface   9

PART I   NORTHERN UNITED STATES   11

East of Block Island   13
West of Block Island   25
Maine   32
The Chesapeake   43
The Carolina Sounds   53
The Bay of Quinte   60

PART II   EUROPE   69

Denmark   71
The Swedish Skerries   80
Canal Barging in England and France   89
Sardinia–Corsica   99
The Dalmatian Coast   109
The Aegean   119

PART III   THE PACIFIC   131

Puget Sound   133
Fiji   143
Les Iles sous le Vent   151
Tonga   160
Australia's Great Barrier Reef   170

PART IV   SOUTHWARD   181

The Intracoastal Waterway   183
Florida's West Coast   192

The Florida Keys   201
The Abacos   208
The Exumas   215

PART V   THE CARIBBEAN   227

Transatlantic to the Caribbean   229
Belize   240
The Bay Islands of Honduras   247
The Grenadines   255
North from St. Vincent   264
Antigua   275
The St. Martin Area   287
The British Virgin Islands   297

Brunelle under flasher

Mar Claro

Tanagra

Preface

In my more than 25 years on the staff of *Yachting* and more than 50 years of going cruising whenever the occasion presented itself, I have had the rare opportunity to visit most of the world's best cruising areas. Because of this, I am frequently asked questions about them, both by people who hope to get there themselves and by those who are simply curious and perhaps want to make comparisons with areas with which they are familiar.

Remembering these questions, I am reporting here on the best of those areas. There are no negative reports (Delaware Bay is definitely *not* included), though I have tried to tell of drawbacks when they exist, and different areas have naturally served well under different circumstances. Some of the material has previously been reported in *Yachting* and other books, but in different form, as all the chapters are newly written; there are no reprints or scissors-and-paste jobs here.

The boats used were many and varied, often loaned by bareboat companies, and many more cruises were taken in our own three boats, namely, the *Mar Claro,* a 24-foot Amphibi-Ette trailable light displacement sloop with outboard auxiliary power and convertible canvas hood over the cabin, which we owned from 1958 to 1967; *Tanagra,* a Morgan Out Island 36 center-cockpit, diesel-powered sloop (1973–1978); and *Brunelle,* our current boat, a CSY 37 cutter, also diesel powered, with aft cockpit. We base her in the British Virgin Islands, and our adventures in getting her there were chronicled in my last book, *South to the Caribbean.* None of those stories are duplicated here, but more recent cruises are.

Areas I have missed that should rightfully have been included had I been there are the Bras d'Or Lakes, Baja California, and the North Channel of Lake Huron, and my only acquaintance with the Indian Ocean has been at 35,000 feet, from which point it looked like almost any other ocean. I have not included addresses and prices of charter companies and other such data, because much of it tends to be out of date by the time the book appears in print. The best place for finding up-to-the-minute information is in the classified pages of boating magazines (with *Yachting* naturally preferred!).

I hope this recounting of my adventures, mostly shared with my wife, Jane, will provide information and inspiration for those who would like to try all or some of the areas, or who would at least like to dream about them in front of the fire.

And what is my favorite area? Read on and find out.

Rumson, New Jersey

Part I

NORTHERN UNITED STATES

East of Block Island

East of Block Island, between Narragansett Bay and Cape Cod, lie some of the best and most popular cruising waters to be found anywhere in the world. In an area about 70 by 35 miles just north of the 41st parallel is an area of islands, sounds, bays, ponds, and coves that provides a perfect summer cruising ground. The first time I wrote an article about cruising in this area, I called it "Where Cruising Was Invented," as this stretch of Southern New England waters combines almost every kind of attraction one could want in a temperate climate. No limpid tropical waters and no rockbound, pine-clad coast, but reliable breezes, mostly from the southwest, attractive old towns reeking of atmosphere from Colonial and whaling days, miles of beaches, bayberry-covered moors, sandy cliffs, tricky tides and shoals, and a wide choice of harbors. Located, as it is, so close to the crowded cities and suburbs of the New York–Boston corridor, it has become so popular that one of the drawbacks now is overcrowding in the better harbors. Also, there is fog to contend with, as well as occasional three-day northeasters, and hurricanes have been known to happen, but none of these outweigh the very real charm of a cruise through these waters. Since 1932 I have been there a dozen or more times, and I still get back there as often as possible. Of all the cruises we have taken there, my favorite has to be one in our 24-foot Amphibi-Ette sloop Mar Claro in the summer of 1968. On it, we managed to see more ports and experienced a more typical gamut of weather conditions than on any of the other visits.

13

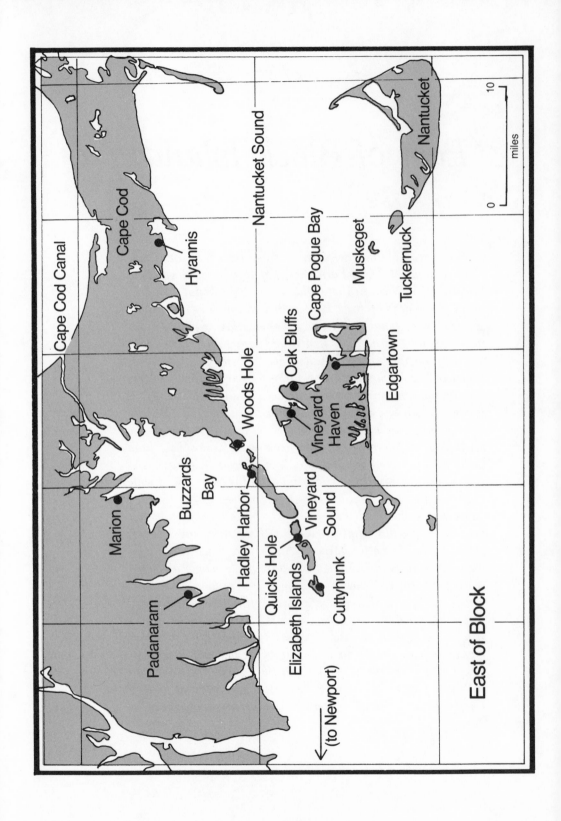

Cape Cod Canal

Cape Cod

Hyannis

Nantucket Sound

Woods Hole

Oak Bluffs

Cape Pogue Bay

Vineyard Haven

Muskeget

Edgartown

Tuckernuck

Nantucket

Marion

Buzzards Bay

Padanaram

Hadley Harbor

Quicks Hole

Elizabeth Islands

Vineyard Sound

Cuttyhunk

(to Newport)

East of Block

miles

0   10

We had gone to sleep under a wide, starry New England sky, lying in sleeping bags on the planking of a pier, with our cruising ketch on one side and a nest of commercial fishing boats on the other, as a soft, salty breeze drifted in from Nantucket Sound. It was a shock to wake up in cold, predawn mist to the odd perspective of a pair of sturdy legs in rubber boots straddling my head. The fishing boats were already on their way out, and a man handling the dock lines was standing right over me.

This vivid boyhood memory from my first cruise, the highlight of a summer at Camp Viking on Cape Cod, stays with me as a symbol of the atmosphere and the feel of cruising in the islands off the cape. There were too many campers for the bunks on the camp's 36-foot ketch, *Viking*, and we had spread our sleeping bags on the pier planks at Lake Anthony, the tiny harbor of Oak Bluffs on Martha's Vineyard. Somehow the memory of the stars above as we drifted off to sleep and the foggy mystery of the morning, with the strange sight above me on awakening, the smell of fish in the air, and the restless chuffing and spitting of the fishing boat engines, has always evoked New England cruising. It brings back the mix on the breeze of sandy shores, bay-berry, salt water, and fish, the special quality of sunlight through a smoky sou'wester, the heft of a northeaster over gray-green, white-capped water, and the extra sparkle in the air on a day of fresh breeze and bright sunlight.

I have returned to these waters many times over the intervening years, and each experience has been a renewal, a sense of the most pleasant kind of déjà vu of the feelings and sensations to which I first awoke on that boyhood cruise, the experience that sent me on to a lifetime of cruising wherever and whenever I could find the opportunity. No one has ever straddled my ears in a pair of fishing boots again, and Lake Anthony is not the most romantic of harbors. I have only been in it once since then, but the special excitements of the *Viking* cruise started a long chain reaction.

On my most recent cruise in these waters, 50 years later, we surged up Vineyard Sound before the same kind of sou'wester into which *Viking* had plowed coming out of Cape Cod Canal into Buzzards Bay,

Nantucket Harbor

and as we rounded West Chop and beat into the anchorage at Vineyard Haven, the smell of the island on the puffy breeze and the glow of the late afternoon sun on the yellow bluffs were all very familiar and reassuring. True, there were many more buildings on the shore and hundreds and hundreds more boats everywhere you looked, but the verities were still there.

Of the 15 or so cruises I have taken in southern New England, all of which had their moments, the one that covered the area best and during which I experienced the widest range of its moods and atmosphere was a first postwar visit in *Mar Claro*. This ended a hiatus of almost 25 years during which the war and raising a family had taken precedence. Not since 1938 had I been able to cruise there, although I had taken some flying visits to shore vacations on Nantucket, where I had spent 10 boyhood summers. The 1938 cruise was a month-long adventure between my junior and senior years in college, when, not being able to foresee just how much cruising I would be able to do as an editor of *Yachting* in the then distant future, I took the summer off on a last fling. Instead of getting a job, I chartered a 26-foot sloop for $105 (including the agent's commission) for the month of August and headed for Nantucket like a homing pigeon, with a classmate as crew.

It was a typical college boy cruise of girl chasing, moderate hell raising, and most of the nautical mistakes in the book, but it confirmed the excitement of the *Viking* cruise I had taken six years earlier and the very real charms of the area.

The *Mar Claro* venture was the product of a later era in that Jane and I trailed her there instead of taking the time for the 200-mile passage from home port in New Jersey. Trailing had an added advantage. The day we arrived at Marion, Massachusetts, on Buzzards Bay, intending to launch at the local boatyard, a storm heavy enough to be dignified by the code name Brenda, but not heavy enough to be a hurricane, made us keep the boat secure on her trailer while local skippers fretted over their moorings.

Behind Brenda came a gorgeous clearing northwester, and we had a fine day's sail with friends on a bay alive with sail, as everyone was making up for the Brenda-bound day in port. We had two August weeks ahead of us, and we covered the area well in a crisscrossing pattern that took us west to Newport, back through Buzzards Bay again, and out to Nantucket and the Vineyard before heading back for Marion and the trailer.

The jaunt to Newport was to pick up our daughters, Martha and Alice, then in their early teens, who had been visiting relatives in the area. The next day the northwester saw a morning of near-calm, as it died away to a whisper, leaving us adrift on a glassy bay. Soon a darkening approached across the glittering water from the Elizabeth Islands, marching off to the southwest on the sharp horizon, and a gentle breeze

Cuttyhunk's barren, windswept hills

from that direction gave us a lazy sail down the Elizabeths to Cutty-hunk—not a smoky sou'wester of the kind the bay is famous for, just a pleasant little sailing breeze over bright blue water. We had the bay almost to ourselves except for a parade of scallop draggers heading offshore from New Bedford through Quicks Hole. Cuttyhunk's hill, highest in the islands, caught the afternoon sun as we neared it and joined a parade of sail into the landlocked anchoring basin. This was before Cuttyhunk's development as the most popular cruising harbor in Southern New England, but even at that time it was jammed with boats by mid-afternoon, and we had to squeeze our way into a small area to anchor.

A soft night, with the breeze gently riffling through the rigging and the light of a half moon flooding the anchorage, was ideal for cockpit sitting and breathing in the atmosphere, but it also meant, with the breeze continuing to blow, that the weather would change by morn-ing, which it did. The southerly was now freighted with fog misting over Cuttyhunk's gray houses and swirling around the boats at anchor. We were due in Newport, 20 miles away, and we headed out into the fog with perhaps a half mile of visibility.

Fog does not mean calm in these waters, and the breeze continued to swing into the southwest and strengthen in moisture as the day wore on. *Mar Claro* enjoyed windward work, and she made good weather of it, plowing into the increasing chop and lowering visibility. By the time we picked up the moan of the horn at Brenton Reef, 200 yards was about as far as we could see, and we felt our way buoy to buoy into a snug marina berth at Newport.

We rendezvoused with the girls, who immediately talked us into a movie, and it seemed appropriate, with the wet wind moaning over-head and the sea fog swirling through Newport's narrow streets, that the movie was Alfred Hitchcock's *Psycho*. Jane and I were almost as scared as the girls on the spooky walk back to the boat.

The sou'wester was still with us in the morning, and the sun, a lemony balloon in the murk, had burned the fog off to about half a mile of visibility, filling the air with a whitish glare and reflecting dully on the gray waves. This was a smoky sou'wester at its most typical, with plenty of weight in the wind, and we were glad we were heading before it back to the islands. It was a swift, lurching sleigh ride, with the steep chop rising up astern and sliding under us, and we were alone in a misty void rushing eastward.

Younger daughter Alice was a bit prone to seasickness in those days, and we had given her half a Dramamine before starting out, to be safe. The Dramamine knocked her out like a sleeping pill, and she knew nothing of the exciting sail or the arrival for a lunchtime stop off the lovely curve of beach on Nashawena in Quicks Hole. She was still out cold when we secured at anchor, so I picked her up by the shoulders and shook her gently. She opened her eyes, and I said, "Would you like a swim?"

She nodded yes, with a smile, but as soon as I let go of her shoulders, she went limp and prone again, and it was impossible to get her up until mid-afternoon, when she was quite put out at all she had missed. At least she hadn't been seasick. By then we were heading across Buzzards Bay for Padanaram on the mainland, following the New York Yacht Club cruise, which had made a brave spectacle sweeping through Quicks under spinnakers while we sat at anchor and enjoyed the parade.

A late-afternoon thunderstorm, which we watched move along the shore as we came in from the bay, brought another weather change, as a fresh, gray northeaster swept in behind it in mid-evening, considerably shaking up the rafted NYYC fleet at the end of an evening of interyacht festivities.

This was another facet of New England weather that could easily be expected, and it made for a different atmosphere on board, as we bundled up in foul weather gear and had a fast, spray-flinging reach across Buzzards Bay to Woods Hole, even managing to sail through that notoriously tricky and narrow tide race against the 4-knot current that pulls big buoys under the surface as it shoulders its way between Buzzards Bay and Vineyard Sound.

Perhaps it was the mood of the weather and the sense of being confined on board that led at Woods Hole to a couple of those little contretemps that spice up family cruising. We were at a marina berth and

I was typing a syndicated newspaper column I was then producing, balancing my typewriter on a tiny little table atop the pipe that contained *Mar Claro*'s centerboard pennant. Alice, who was fishing from the pier, came running below, proudly displaying a tiny fish she had hooked, still wriggling in her hand.

"Look, Daddy! Look what I caught," she cried.

"Wonderful, Alice," I said, interrupting my typing.

"Where shall I put it?"

"Throw it back. You can't keep it," I said.

"What?" she wailed, and an argument ensured, with me increasing in adamancy in proportion to Alice's growing petulance.

"Look, I said no!" I yelled, throwing up my hands in an angry gesture, which knocked my typewriter off its perch. It clattered to the cabin sole with a crash that banged it out of true and ended its effectiveness for the rest of the cruise. The argument subsided into an angry truce (after the fish was returned to the deep), but I was still a bit testy the next morning when we wanted to get away for a fairly early start. In the interest of speed, we decided to have breakfast ashore at a lunch counter on the pier, but older daughter Martha, who was in a perpetual I-have-to-do-my-hair stage at the time, was still fussing on board when the rest of us went to the "greasy spoon."

It so happened that the counterman was about as dumb and uncooperative as anyone I have ever seen and seemed totally unable to fill any order more complicated than a fried egg. We had gone through all sorts of difficulties trying to get an order placed, when Martha flounced in, hair neatly done, and took the seat we had saved for her.

"I'll have an Egyptian peephole," she announced brightly to the open-mouthed counterman, while the rest of us howled in glee.

Somehow the laugh over Martha's Egyptian peephole (an egg put in a hole in bread and fried) restored the family goodwill (she got a fried egg like the rest of us), and we had a fine though damp sail in the still blowing northeaster through the wicked tidal races off East and West Chop and into Edgartown's picturesque but crowded harbor. Edgartown is the Vineyard's showplace, a town of lovely old houses and tall trees dating from whaling prosperity, with a modern veneer of Lily Pulitzer chic, boutiques, and a very active social life.

We had friends ashore and a guest card at the yacht club, but the main delight of our stay there was a day of exploration in Cape Pogue Bay on Chappaquiddick Island. Later to become nationally known through Ted Kennedy's misadventures, this island is separated from the Vineyard by a narrow channel, crossed by a small ferryboat, and forms the eastern side of Edgartown Harbor, where it opens out into an anchorage area and extends southward into Katama Bay.

Not much more draft than *Mar Claro*'s 2-foot-4 can get through the narrow tidal cut into Cape Pogue Bay, and we had its long string of beaches, shining white under the sun, and its broad, calm water all to ourselves on a day of almost no breeze. We drifted around for a while, then anchored for lunch while the girls splashed in the shallows and hunted shells along the shore, and the world was a million miles away. Terns and gulls, wheeling and squeaking overhead, were our only companions.

Another day of being alone took us on to Nantucket. It was a morning of soft sunlight and hazy horizons, not really smoky weather, as we reached away from Cape Pogue in a moderate sou'wester on the direct shortcut to Nantucket across the flats. The deep draft route makes a dogleg out to the eastward around Tuckernuck shoal, but our draft made it possible for us to sail over the shoal, past the remote islands of Muskeget and Tuckernuck. The area is not charted, so it was eyeball navigation, and soon we were alone on empty, pale green water as Cape Pogue faded into the haze, and low, sandy Muskeget, barely 6 feet high, had not yet shown up.

It was dreamlike sailing in a void, and I became a bit too dreamy, failed to keep eyeballing carefully, and suddenly we nudged onto sand, with the tide setting up a gurgle as it swirled around our now stationary bow. *Mar Claro*'s draft and light displacement made it easy for us to get off. The girls all hung over the leeward bow, I sheeted the sails in tight, and she heeled enough to sail clear. After that I was a bit more careful, and soon we could see Muskeget's pale sands and low dunes off to starboard and the yellow bluffs of Tuckernuck, topped by a few rambling, gray-shingled cottages, looming up ahead.

Isolated Tuckernuck, with just the few summer cottages, some fishermen's shacks, and no harbor large enough for more than a small motorboat, is a New England Bali Hai, a never-never land I had been fascinated by for years as it sat silhouetted against the sunset on Nantucket's western horizon. It was like peeping into a secret world to range along its eastern shore a few hundred feet off the beach, enveloped in the scent of sand flats and bayberry on the soft breeze.

Soon it had slipped astern and we were in charted waters again, off Eel Point at Madaket, Nantucket's western tip, and sightseeing the much more civilized scene of the impressive cottages along the bluff. Rounding between the jetties at the harbor entrance, we beat toward Brant Point, the cottage-lined sandpit that encloses the inner harbor, through a typical Nantucket-at-its-best scene of small sailboatss flitting about, many with the colored sails of the Rainbow Fleet, as Beetle Cats are called here, on a bright blue and white afternoon of perfect breeze and sparkling sun. Cruising yachts were arriving in a parade, the boxy ferry to Woods Hole shouldered its way past the small craft, flags flew briskly in front of the cottages on Brant Point, and the sun glinted off the gold dome of the Unitarian church, the town's most prominent landmark. This was nostalgia with all the trimmings for me.

The whole visit was an exercise in nostalgia as we spent a couple of days covering the island moors in a rental car while I pointed out landmarks of my youth to the family. These ranged from the view from the cliff overlooking the harbor, to Sankaty Light, the beach at Surfside, the Hidden Forest, and the stately homes of the whaling captains beneath the elms on upper Main Street. Only in the town area near the waterfront, where the daily "pickle boats" from Hyannis unloaded hordes of trippers, was there a noticeable change in Nantucket's atmosphere. More recently, this area has undergone extensive development, including a mammoth marina. This was long needed, as there was almost no place for yachts to tie up, and the 6-mile stretch of harbor northeastward to Wauwinet could raise a wicked chop in a northeaster. Even with the big marina, space is always at a premium at the height of the season, with reservations having to be made well in advance to get a berth.

While we were sightseeing by car, a foggy, damp southerly gusting close to 30 would have made a poor sailing day, and it was replaced on the morrow by one of those rare days of a New England summer, a clear northeaster. Great Point Light, the white spire at the very northeastern tip of the long sandy string of dunes stretching north from Wauwinet toward Cape Cod, stood out sharply against the clear horizon as we reached out between the jetties and set off on the 30-mile passage to Vineyard Haven at a splashy hull speed.

Vineyard Haven is the friendliest harbor in the area despite its limited capacity, and the chance to eat ashore and take in a movie appealed to the girls. From there, a quiet night at Hadley Harbor tucked away deep in the heart of Naushon, the largest Elizabeth Island, wound down the cruise, which ended in a swift sail back across Buzzards Bay to the trailer in a drizzle of rain.

We had seen just about all the weather moods this area usually produces in the summer. We had not been to every port, but we had renewed acquaintance with our favorite ones, and we had reaffirmed that this is one of the truly fine cruising areas to be found anywhere. It has lured us back many more times.

West of Block Island

Over the years, operating from a base on the North Jersey Coast, I have tended to look on Long Island, both on its south shore and on the Long Island Sound side, as something of an obstacle in the way of getting to favorite grounds further to the eastward, and yet, harking back, I remember some of the best days of sailing we have ever had getting through these waters. Western Long Island Sound, a base for as many boats as any similar-sized area anywhere, is a crowded rat race, and truly just a corridor to the eastward for the cruising sailor, but the eastward half of the Sound is something else again, with some attractive harbors and not as much crowding. The south shore, dominated by shallow, breezy Great South Bay, is a strong contrast to the Sound, and the "fishtail" area at Long Island's eastern end is a little world by itself, well worth a cruising visit. Very often Block Island, off by itself at sea, miles east of Long Island, is the turnaround point for a cruise in these waters, whose charms, not as highly publicized as those of Maine or the islands off Cape Cod, are well worth investigating. It was in Mar Claro that we did most of our passages here, and a trip that ended up as a circumnavigation of Long Island was perhaps the most memorable one.

Long Island Sound has never been a favorite cruising area of mine. It is too crowded and too calm, and I have always looked on it as a mere avenue to the eastward from home base in New Jersey. Sometimes we have had pleasant sailing in working our way through it, but

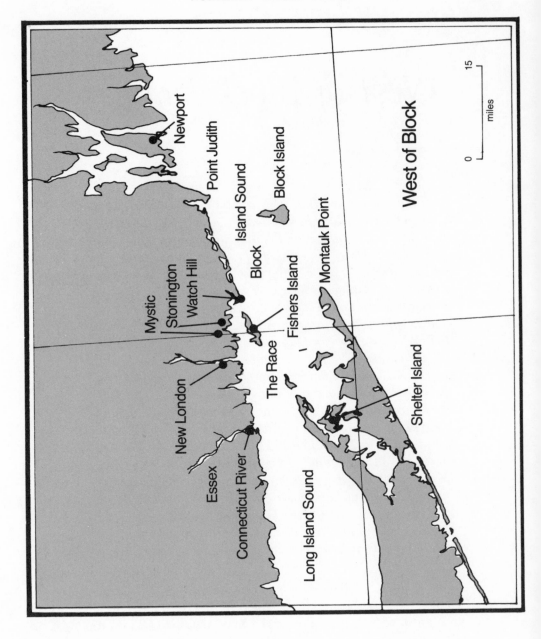

more often it has been a case of powering over windless water rolled by the wakes of a thousand powerboats. The south shore of Long Island is even less conductive to cruising, with its succession of shallow bays and tide-ripped inlets.

Despite this, I do have some happy memories of the area. There was the first time we took *Mar Claro* cruising and made Sandy Hook to Bellport, Long Island, over 50 miles, in one swooping mad rush of a sail before the typical afternoon sou'wester that gusts in across Great South Bay. It was gusting up to 30 and strong enough to dismast a couple of Star boats racing at Bellport, and it was an exhilarating passage as an introduction to a new boat.

Another time, we headed eastward from Sandy Hook to Montauk in the ocean, had a fine, walloping reach until mid-evening along the south shore of Long Island, and then had to power for 19 hours with our 6-horsepower outboard over an oilily calm, fog-bound sea—with one fuel stop at Shinnecock Inlet, a weird experience that has stayed with me.

The Sound was the first place we ever took our children cruising, when they were ages 3 to 8, in a borrowed 36-foot Alden yawl. The sailing was not spectacular, but the sense of change and adventure for the kids, and the way they took to it, had its own rewards. It was the kind of cruise where a trip ashore for an ice cream cone in the evening twilight at Cold Spring Harbor was cause for wide-eyed wonderment for the children; and it was a lasting memory for us of having fun with them.

I have raced on Long Island Sound in everything from a flat calm, anchored in a tide rip with a thousand flies bedeviling the boat, to a howling cold-front northwester laced with snow squalls, with very few of what I would call straight, plain good sails, and cruising has had about the same percentages. There have been a few exceptions though. One was a sail from Block Island to Sachem Head, Connecticut, over 50 miles, in *Mar Claro* before a sparkling, clear, fresh northeaster, a day of perfect sailing that we have used ever since to gauge others.

Although western Long Island Sound, with its jammed harbors and lack of wind, has been an almost total loss in my book, once you get east of New Haven, where the Sounds widens out, civilization is more widely dispersed, and the wind tends to be a bit more cooperative, the chances for good cruising are better.

This brings us to the cruise in these waters that I remember most pleasantly: the first time I ever took Jane cruising. It was soon after the war, and family life was in that stage where a harassed mother needs to get away from diapers, formulas, and visits to the pediatrician (who advised taking such a cruise as a break for Mom). Fortunately, grandparents were cooperative, and we chartered the 25-foot gaff-rigged cutter *Sea Myth* out of Essex, Connecticut, for a week of poking around eastern Long Island Sound. Incidentally, the cost for the week was what I had paid for a month's charter of a similar boat on our cruise to Nantucket in 1938. And what would it cost now?

The Connecticut River, with the ports of Essex, Old Lyme, and Old Saybrook and a wonderful tree-lined bywater called Hamburg Cove just up the river from Essex, gives on a cruising area of great potential in the number of harbors and their proximity. As in all other cruising areas near population centers, it has suffered of late from the usual overcrowding, but the elements are all there. Drawbacks include the swift tidal currents in the river itself and in and out of Long Island Sound, through the area at its eastern end, known as The Race, and a certain lack of reliability in the breeze system. This is nowhere near as big a factor as further west in Long Island Sound, and a pleasant breeze riffles in from the sea on a good percentage of summer afternoons.

This wide choice of harbors close together was one reason I chose the area for initiating Jane into cruising, as I did not want to subject her to any hard chances until I could tell how the initiation was taking. She had never been in a sailboat before we were married. Horseback riding was her main sport, and she had spent summers on a small pond in the fastness of the Catskills at a place called Hartwood. She had been brought up to hunting and freshwater fishing, but saltwater delights were totally new to her. A one-day sail together in a Baby Rainbow on wartime leave in Nantucket and a day sailer on Biscayne Bay in Miami the last year of the war was the extent of her experience.

I had not cruised in a sailboat since 1938, but I hoped that my two

Great Salt Pond, Block Island, with fog lying offshore

years of sea duty in command of a navy subchaser would prevent any recurrence of some of the errors I had made on that cruise, like mistaking Block Island for Point Judith. With the immortal last words, "This compass must be wrong," I had gone all the way outside of Block Island on a night passage from Vineyard Sound to Long Island Sound to find us seaward of Montauk Point in the open Atlantic in the morning, about 20 miles out of position. Fortunately, this time we had a pleasant sou'wester for a starter and fetched across to Plum Gut—where, mercifully, there was a fair tide through its millrace—for a first night at Dering Harbor.

Dering Harbor is a graceful cove on the north side of Shelter Island, which sits between the two halves of Long Island's fishtail at its eastern end. The sunset was scenic, the breeze was soft, and, as dusk fell and

29

we sat in the cockpit looking at the riding lights of the other yachts wavering across the water, I felt the first day had been a success.

There is a wide choice of harbors here. Greenport, just across from Dering Harbor, is a busy commercial port with shopping opportunities, and the Montauk side of the fishtail has Three Mile Harbor and Montauk Harbor. There are a few creeks and coves on Peconic Bay, west of Shelter Island, and Block Island is a tempting target off to the eastward. Years later we were to have an exciting sail in zero fog and a 20-knot breeze from Montauk to Block Island in *Mar Claro*, but I felt it would be wiser to stick to protected waters for this cruise. On the north side of The Race, there are Fishers Island West Harbor, Watch Hill, Stonington, Mystic, and New London. Obviously, we would not make them all in a week.

When we headed out to Montauk the next day, by way of contrast we had a damp northeaster that brought the foul weather gear out for a good brisk sail, and a swordfish dinner ashore at Montauk was a fitting reward. The fishing fleet there was a sight to behold as we walked around the docks in the evening.

Crossing back to the north through The Race the next day, with the weather once more sunny and pleasant, I made one of those errors that dampened Jane's enthusiasm for a while, the first time she had not been happy. She had coffee on the stove, which was not gimbaled, as we neared The Race, and I had failed to warn her that there was a bobble of sea ahead in the tide rip. With the first lurch there came an anguished cry from below, and I learned, in rather vehement terms, that the coffee had spread itself all over the bunk.

Things had calmed down by the time we reached Fishers West for a quiet night among the glossy yachts there, and Stonington, with its crowded harbor of fishing boats and yachts and the very New Englandy atmosphere of its narrow streets and old houses, made an interesting contrast the next night.

All in all, everything had seemed to go well despite the spilled coffee, and this was finally confirmed as we drifted back toward Essex in a lazy southerly and bathing suit weather. *Sea Myth* was making enough headway for there to be a pleasant swish and gurgle along her water-

line, but everything else seemed still and serene, the water was a pleasant blue, the clouds were puffy, and the sun was hot on our skins.

I was at the tiller, and Jane, who had been reading and knitting,
which she does for most of her waking hours, had let the needles drop,
and the pages of the book riffled idly, unread. She was not asleep
though, as I could see that her eyes were open.

"What are you thinking about?" I asked idly.

"Nothing," she answered, with a slow smile. "Absolutely nothing."

And I knew that the cruise was a success.

Maine

No other cruising area develops fanatic devotees like the 200-mile-long raggedly indented coast of the state of Maine. No matter how dedicated these devotees are, no one can take in every anchorage among Maine's myriad coves, bays, rivers, thoroughfares, and passages in a lifetime of cruising, so vast is the choice. A lifetime of cruising in Maine would be confined to about three months a year at the most, as mid-June to mid-September is about all the time that can be counted on at 45–46° north latitude. In addition, most cruises are inevitably interrupted by fog, perhaps for only a few hours if you are lucky, but perhaps for a week or more at a time. The Gulf of Maine is a perfect fog factory, since its waters remain cold throughout the summer. Hot air from the great land areas to the west drifts out over this cold water and results in condensation. We had one week of cruising in Maine, with only four hours of sailing because of fog.

The dedicated Maine cruising addict also has had to accept the fact that his favorite waters are becoming more and more crowded, but this is only in contrast to the splendid isolation that could be found there in seasons past. Compared to the waters south of Cape Cod, or to the Virgin Islands, Southern California, or Puget Sound, it is still possible to "get away from it all" amid Maine's dramatic scenery of pines and rocks.

Would there be fog?

That is always the question on a Maine cruise. We had experienced

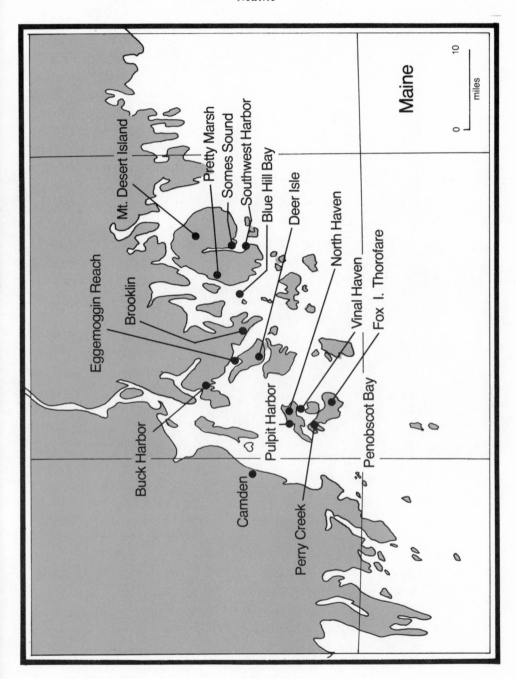

Maine

0   10

miles

Pretty Marsh
Somes Sound
Southwest Harbor
Mt. Desert Island
Blue Hill Bay
Deer Isle
North Haven
Eggemoggin Reach
Brooklin
Vinal Haven
Fox I. Thorofare
Buck Harbor
Pulpit Harbor
Penobscot Bay
Camden
Perry Creek

A Friendship sloop, off Friendship

fog on every previous cruise, and it was logical to expect some more this time, even though it was late August. Normally late summer is the best time to avoid the ever-present threat of fog in Maine, so we had our fingers crossed. This was a special cruise in that my all-girl crew consisted of three generations: Jane, Martha and Alice, and Martha's seven-year-old daughter Julie. It was to be Julie's first cruise that she would remember—we had had her on *Tanagra* in the Bahamas for a week when she was four months old—and we did not want to spend it fog bound in a harbor.

Alice, who is the charter broker for the John Alden Company in Boston (and who had gotten over her childhood need for Dramamine), had arranged the charter of the Morgan OI33 *Flying Gull* for her own vacation and wanted to make it a family cruise. I was never quite sure whether she or I was skipper, but this was one time when a "committee" seemed to work all right in operating a cruise.

Gull was well suited to our needs. First of all, she was the least expensive boat available that gave us enough room. I knew that she would be an adequate sailer for cruising, having raced against the design in *Tanagra* in some all-OI regattas our local dealer used to sponsor. The OI41 has given the whole range of OI boats a reputation for poor performance, because it was designed for comfort, roominess, and shallow draft, admittedly sacrificing windward ability; but the other models perform well on all points of sailing. With her high freeboard, lack of sheer, and contoured hull, the 33 did seem a bit out of place in Maine's tradition-bound waters (one crusty native took a long look at her and drawled, "Gawd offal lookin', ain't she," in his best Maine twang), but we were aboard her, not looking at her, and she served us well.

We boarded her on a Sunday afternoon in Camden, a Penobscot Bay yachting center that makes a joke out of Maine's reputation for isolated anchorages and lack of crowding. I have seldom seen a busier place or a higher concentration of boats than that shoehorned into Camden's tight little inner harbor, and something seemed to be going on aboard every one of them. Dominating the scene were big "dude cruise" schooners, the restored workboats (and replicas) that make weekly cruises as head boats out of Camden. Sunday is turnaround day for them, as a new band of individual ticket buyers replaces last week's bunch. Rafted together in twos and threes at several floats, with oversize pennants and ensigns flying, they would almost seem to fill the harbor by themselves, but dozens of yachts were tucked around them like so many ducklings hovering near their mother. All the shore facilities in Camden are served by floats because of the 10-foot tidal range, and *Gull*'s owner had managed to obtain some temporary space at one marina float for us to load our gear.

The utilitarian side of Maine

We had barely finished when two large, fuel-guzzling powerboats loomed alongside, obviously of more interest to the marina than we were, and we moved a few feet out into the center of the harbor to raft at one of the many mooring floats. These are an ingenious solution to Camden's crowding, as they accommodate a great many boats in a small area. Only a very few boats could anchor here because of the scope needed in the tide range. Everything is controlled by harbor masters, and the outer roadstead, which is somewhat exposed and rolly, has a lot of mooring buoys.

The NYYC cruise had disbanded here the day before, and the familiar red and blue burgee was in evidence on many of the glossiest yachts in the multitude. All in all, it was a fascinating floating boat show and a lively, colorful scene in the bright afternoon sunshine and southerly breeze riffling in through the harbor mouth. As evening chill descended and we rowed the few feet ashore to elbow our way into one of the busy restaurants, I wondered about fog developing from the sudden temperature change, but the night remained clear and starry.

The morning was clear, windless, and hot as soon as the sun made itself felt. The cloudless sky had a soft, milky aspect to it, and my first reaction was to gaze seaward looking for that low, gray line of fog bank on the horizon, but it was not there. Powering out in a parade of departing boats, we were on a flat, gray mirror, and the dude schooners up ahead of us had dutifully put up their sails. (After all, these *are* windjammer cruises, aren't they, Mabel?) They hung motionless over their wavering reflections and I naturally had to come up with "as idle as a painted ship upon a painted ocean" from "The Rime of the Ancient Mariner."

"What's that, Grampy?" Julie wanted to know, and her mother and aunt laughed at me, recalling the time I had once looked out the window when putting them to bed when they were about her age and said, "Oh. 'The moon is a ghostly galleon' tonight." Explanations of that quote kept them up a precious 15 minutes longer and resulted in a tradition of poetry readings at bedtime, starting, of course, with Alfred Noyes' "The Highwayman," source of the galleon quote.

We were headed in a casual, roundabout way toward Mount Desert Island, a rhumb line of 33 miles to the eastward, but a zigzag of much more than that through the maze of islands in between. In many areas this would be a one-day passage, but within that 33 miles, which took us about 70 miles to negotiate, there were several dozen anchorages from which we could choose. Obviously, with a week at our disposal, we would end up with nothing more than a small sampling.

When faint zephyrs from the south broke the sheen of the sea with dark splotches, we killed the motor and made sail, drifting peacefully along in the vagrant puffs. We had decided to head for Pulpit Harbor on North Haven, and just before we got there the afternoon sea breeze came whistling up the bay and gave us a brisk burst of sailing for the last half mile to the entrance. Pulpit, which branches out into several arms, has perfect protection and a choice of anchorages. Ashore, rolling farm fields alternate with stands of pine, and farmhouses and summer cottages dot the scenery here and there. We chose Minister Creek, hard to starboard, where a couple of locally based auxiliaries rode to moorings off a compound of summer cottages nestled in the pines. Later two other cruising boats came in, and one of them, *Klee*, was a Valiant 40 we had rendezvoused with in St. Martin, Martinique, and Tortola over the previous two winters of Caribbean cruising, so we enjoyed one of those pleasantly unexpected reunions cruising sailors run into in all parts of the globe.

Later we were glad we had chosen Minister Creek's snug surroundings, only a couple of hundred yards wide. Clouds built over the sunset, bringing a dash of rain, and then behind them a strong cold-front northwester swept in with its Canadian air as a reminder that autumn was on its way. It sang a high-pitched song in the rigging all night while *Gull* shuddered and quivered in the gusts.

It had moderated by morning, a crisp, clear day with a 40s nip in the air, and the breeze was just right for a circuitous bit of running and reaching around the southern tip of North Haven and back into Fox Island Thorofare. There was plenty of traffic, including a handsome gaff-rigged charter schooner headed the other way. The North Haven town waterfront was busy, with small boats skimming through the mooring area. By now the sun's warmth had overcome the Canadian chill and windbreakers came off. It was only early afternoon, and we had covered all of 12 miles, but there was a good anchorage near at hand and Julie wanted to do some exploring.

After passing the town, we hooked back 180° to starboard into lonely Perry Creek, another beautifully protected spot with more trees and fewer houses than Minister Creek. For a while it was ours alone, but a couple of other boats drifted in before sunset on the last breath of the northwester. Julie had a chance to practice a newly learned skill, rowing, and the girls explored along the rocky shore for a bit. Julie had saved her allowance for a binge on the cruise and persuaded her mother that North Haven looked like a good spot to spend it, so they took off in the dinghy under outboard, only to return with the news that the store had closed 10 minutes before they got there and not even an ice-cream cone was to be had in town.

The influence of the high-pressure area was still with us for another day of crystal-clear air, with that wonderful piny tang drifting over us and sparkling waters stretching away to the sharply etched horizon when we sailed out of the Thorofare into East Penobscot Bay. Here we turned north and reached up toward Eggemoggin Reach, threading our way through the islands. There was a noon lull in the westerly as the sun warmed, but soon after we drifted into the entrance to the reach, a fresh afternoon southerly swept in across Deer Isle. Eggemoggin Reach is a straightaway channel about 11 miles long and 1 mile wide, running northwest and southeast between the mainland and Deer Isle, and it is justly famous as a great stretch of sailing water.

A reaching breeze, smooth water, and graceful scenery is about all a cruising sailor could ask for, and we reveled in the perfect conditions, slipping along as part of a two-way parade of curved sails and glittering bow waves. This was Maine at its very best. At Brooklin, after a 24-mile day's run, we picked up the Cruising Club of America mooring maintained in Northwest Cove by Past Commodore Alan Bemis. His summer home, a unique stone "castle," stands high above the cove and the mooring of his classic 43-foot Herreshoff yawl *Cirrus* built in 1930. She and *Gull* formed a sharp contrast as representatives of the vastly different eras of wooden and fiber glass boats.

The southerly had spelled the departure of our high-pressure system, and the morning was a gluggy, cloudy one of no wind. My immediate instinct was to look for fog, but there was none in evidence as we powered out of Eggemoggin Reach and started north up Blue Hill Bay toward Pretty Marsh Harbor on Mount Desert Island. We were alone on the wide, still waters, and once a slight westerly zephyr drifted in and we switched to sail, helped by a fair tide, the silence was

Somes Sound, Mt. Desert

unbroken. Islands with crazy names like Smutty Nose, West Barge, East Barge, Ship, Trumpet, Moose, and Hardwood slipped by until we eased into Pretty Marsh under clearing skies and the slanting golden glow of late afternoon.

Pretty Marsh is a big harbor, but we were the only visiting boat on a night of starry stillness, and thoughts of fog receded. We now had a flat fair weather pattern, with calm mornings and afternoon sea breezes. Life aboard had been relaxed and easy, with Scrabble games the major entertainment at night, and the only "friction" was that Julie and I had built up a local joke that she was always in the head whenever I wanted to use it. With three accomplished cooks aboard, we were eating very well.

We were also in home waters of a sort, as Martha and Julie had lived on Mount Desert for several years. Pronounced like the last course of a meal, not the Sahara, probably because it was originally named by French explorers, it is the largest island on the Maine Coast, with the highest mountains, and its Cadillac Mountain at 1532 feet is the highest point on the Atlantic Coast between there and Mexico. It also has the only "fjord" on the U.S. Atlantic Coast, Somes Sound, which almost splits the island in two as it gashes northward between the scenic grandeur of Mount Desert's mountains.

A light northerly sent us south from Pretty Marsh on a cool, clear morning to round the southwest tip of the island at Bass Harbor, where the afternoon southerly found us and gave us a fast reach over Bass Harbor Bar and into Western Way. After the isolation of Perry Creek and Pretty Marsh, we were back in traffic again. A steady stream of boats was headed in and out of the multiharbor complex that leads to Somes Sound—Manset, Southwest Harbor, and Northeast Harbor. From a mooring off the Henry R. Hinckley Co. we could have dinner ashore and a visit and showers at the home of Julie's other grandmother, Gwen Hinckley, and there was finally a store where Julie could splurge with that saved-up allowance. Southwest was not as busy and crowded as Camden, and it has a great deal more room, but there was plenty of activity on all sides.

This was turnaround point, and the passage westward started in another morning calm. We were past Bass Harbor and entering Blue Hill Bay when the southerly darkened the water and sent us on another fast reach up Eggemoggin. It was cool and salty, and the bay was alive with dancing whitecaps before we swooped into the Reach's flat water and sped onward to Buck Harbor at its western end for our longest day of 28 miles.

Buck Harbor is small, rockbound, and very crowded, since many local boats base there, but we were able to pick up a courtesy mooring of the yacht club and found some former neighbors from New Jersey, who have retired there, for a pleasant visit ashore. They were highly enthusiastic about Maine retirement and produce most of their own food on their small farm, which they find both rewarding and economical.

This was our last stop, as it was back to Camden for turn-in on the morrow, and, almost forgotten in the week of clear sailing, there it was the next morning: fog.

The hills surrounding the harbor were enveloped in it and it hovered just at the tops of the masts of the larger boats. Its salty tang filled the air, and while we had breakfast, I did some extra careful checking of charts, courses, and distances. There was one stretch down Penobscot Bay of 8 miles with no buoys to check, and the thought of it nagged at me a bit while we were getting underway. On the legs out of the harbor and the entrance to Eggemoggin Reach, we checked courses and speeds between buoys very carefully and were all set to meet the expected challenge Maine traditionally throws at you.

But we never had to. After all the careful figuring, the fog never came down to the surface. There it was, about 100 feet up, but surface visibility was several miles, and we had no trouble with landmarks, powering down the bay into chill wind and a slap of sea. We had to turn the boat in at 1300, and to cap the cruise nicely, the sun began to burn through the overcast as we passed Mouse and Goose Islands and turned to starboard between Lasell and Saddle Islands for the last 5-mile reach westward into Camden. Instead of groping our way through the chilly gray stuff, we shed windbreakers for a last warm sunny reach into port. We had experienced that real rarity, a fog-free week in the heart of Maine's great cruising waters.

The Chesapeake

This storied bay, 200 miles from mouth to headwaters, has also surrendered its reputation for isolation and solitude to the great growth in cruising activity. On a fall Sunday off Annapolis, it is difficult to find the water for the sails swarming on it, and the main yachting centers like Annapolis, Oxford, Georgetown, Gibson Island, and the Hampton Roads area are chockablock with boat-filled marinas. Like Maine, though, there are enough gunkholes to poke into to absorb much of this pressure, and the choice of anchorages is so wide as to be tough on decision making for a cruise of a week or two. Again, as in Maine, no one could be expected to cover all of them in a normal lifetime of cruising, though there is a bit more time each season, which can be stretched from early May to mid-November. The drawback here is that mid-summer is not ideal for cruising, owing to light winds, heat waves, frequent thunderstorms, and, in some years, an excess of jellyfish. There isn't always an afternoon sea breeze to stir things up because of the Chesapeake's inland position. To make up for it, spring and fall tend to be gorgeous, with a soft, relaxing climate, pleasant breezes, and nature at its most benign. The low, rather featureless shoreline is still attractive in its trees, farm fields, and graceful old houses, and there is always that feeling of poking around a bend or into the mouth of another creek to see what delights are hidden there, mixed with open water sails out on the bay itself.

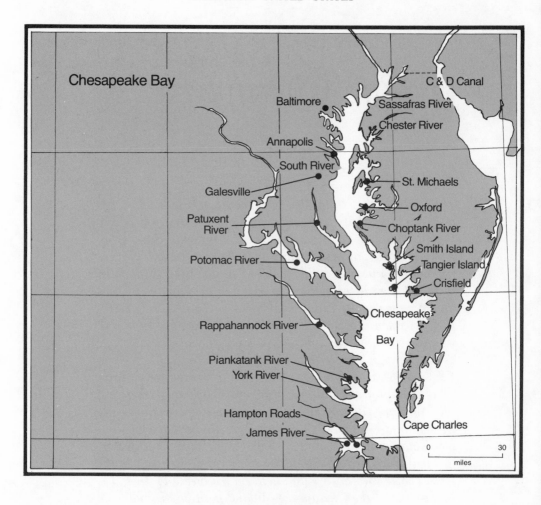

Chesapeake Bay

C & D Canal

Baltimore

Sassafras River

Chester River

Annapolis

South River

St. Michaels

Galesville

Oxford

Patuxent
River

Choptank River

Smith Island

Potomac River

Tangier Island

Crisfield

Chesapeake

Rappahannock River

Bay

Piankatank River

York River

Hampton Roads

Cape Charles

James River

0   30
miles

The Chesapeake

October is the month for the Chesapeake. We have cruised it in several other months, but all its charms come together in that early fall weather of hazy sunshine and slowly turning foliage, while great flights of geese, their vee patterns wavering and and billowing as they look for places in which to settle, sweep in from the north. In flight, their communications drift down like the distant baying of dogs, and at night their chatter fills the stillness in myriad coves and harbors.

Our first cruise in a chartered 25-foot sloop out of Galesville in 1947 was an October one, with the lazy days of sun, which glinted more on the water in its lower orbit across the southern sky, interrupted by the blast of one cold-front northwester. It was a delightful introduction to the Chesapeake's charms, and we have been coming back as often as possible, though sometimes in the spring. We learned one lesson in a late June cruise a few years after the first one. The first days were pleasant, with good sailing in adequate breezes, but a heat wave moved in before the cruise was over, stifling the breeze, bringing out mosquitoes, and generating wild thundersqualls at the end of each day's breathless bakeout. We had the children with us, and the final crusher for them was that there were too many jellyfish to allow swimming.

On that cruise we learned a trick that has since been helpful in similar situations. We found that the best place to be was near the mouth of a river, preferably behind a low point or spit of land. The slight difference in temperature between the open bay and inshore waters and fields would set up the faintest stir of air. In the shade of a cockpit awning this would make life moderately bearable.

On one May cruise, when we were ferrying a Columbia 50 from Norfolk to the Chesapeake and Delaware Canal, a strong northeaster developed rapidly soon after we left Norfolk, and the usually placid bay was a welter of short, steep, breaking waves when we tried to plug our way northward out of Hampton Roads. We took refuge just in time in the Back River near Langley Field, even though we had no local chart. We trusted that the buoys meant what they said, and we did have the *Waterway Guide* to help us. By the time we wrestled the boat's high freeboard into a small marina, the wind was piping over 50, and we were delighted to be inside. When the storm went by, we had fog most of the rest of the way up the bay.

In several cruises we took in June in a borrowed ketch, we developed a routine of sailing through the bulk of the day, usually with an awning over the mizzen boom to shade the cockpit, not caring how far we got as long as we were sailing. About 1530, we would then pick a target for the evening's anchorage and power to it, trying to beat the inevitable squall in. Often we would power in an hour or two as far as we had drifted under sail in the previous hours, but the Chesapeake is ideally suited to this sort of planning. There is always some place near at hand to duck into for the night. In fact, there are probably enough little gunkholes named Mill Creek all through the Chesapeake so that you could anchor in a Mill Creek almost every night.

October usually treats you better, though October '76 was an exception, producing day after day of cold, rainy, blowy weather just to prove that there are always exceptions to traditional weather. We had better luck in two other Octobers when we based *Tanagra* in the Annapolis area for a few weeks. Annapolis itself, especially in October, when the Sailboat Show is on, the Annapolis Yacht Club Fall Series is in swing, and transients are flooding through on their way south, is about as busy as any yachting center I have ever seen. It is almost impossible to find a berth in town or its satellites like Spa Creek or Back Creek (not to be confused with Back River at the other end of the bay). We were lucky to be invited to leave *Tanagra* at the private pier of Bill Stone, whose father, Herb Stone, was editor and publisher of *Yachting* magazine for almost 50 years. Bill himself was our Washington correspondent and a frequent contributor of cruising articles when I was editor.

Bill's place is on the South River at the back door to Annapolis. It forms the other side of the peninsula that Annapolis is on, with the Severn on the north. It is only a short drive from downtown Annapolis, but a long way round the peninsula by water in the typical configuration of Chesapeake tributaries. There is really only one stretch of Chesapeake shoreline, from the West River (which, by the way, is south of the South River) to the Patuxent River on the western shore, that is a straight beach. Everywhere else the shore is broken up with

Crab Creek, Annapolis

creeks and rivers, some with off-lying islands, offering an incredible number of potential gunkholes.

The South River has its own bevy of tributaries, and Bill Stone's pier is at the headwaters of one of the prettiest, Crab Creek, which itself is broken up into side creeks and coves.

The banks here are higher than the shoreline along the open bay, with tree-covered hills and bluffs providing graceful scenery, and it is a wonderfully secure place to keep a boat. On a few nights, especially in the windy fall of '76, when a northeaster was howling through the treetops high on the bluffs, the water at the pier was unruffled except for occasional skittering ripples from downdrafts.

We were spending the weekends on *Tanagra*, and each Friday when we came back to her, the foliage would have developed new and brighter hues, building on the first subtle tints of early autumn. This was a great base for weekend mini-cruises, as well as longer ones if time allowed. You could just go out for a sail on the bay, 5 miles away, and come back in to a dozen choices or more in the South River complex. Just a few miles south, the double system of the Rhode River and the West River had many more places from which to choose. The Rhode River, off to starboard, with a narrow entrance, is a favorite target for weekenders, with plenty of room to anchor beneath the high bluffs of the south shore and High Island.

Turning to port takes you to Galesville, which is totally taken up with marinas, since it is the nearest bay port to Washington. While its permanent population heads out for the weekend, a visitor can usually find an overnight berth here, and it is worth it to eat ashore and enjoy crab cakes in the local restaurants. I find I get in a rut in Chesapeake cruising and order crab cakes every time I eat ashore.

Across the bay from the South River is the real heart of Chesapeake cruising in Eastern Bay, the Miles River and the Choptank River. Sleepy little towns like St. Michaels on the Miles and Oxford on the Tred Avon, an arm of the Choptank, have become teeming yachting centers, but the waters around them make up in choice of anchorage for the crowding in them. On a balmy October morning with a pleasant southwester blowing, we set sail after threading the narrow entrance to Crab Creek, practically running up on a white beach that you have to hug just a few feet off. We reached down the South's busy channel with boats all around us, sail and power, and hardened up for the old Bloody Point Lighthouse, standing askew on Bloody Point Bar. There was just enough chop in the open bay to give *Tanagra* some motion as she surged along on a close reach, and it was then a run up the calm waters of Eastern Bay in a steady parade of boats. I remember coming through there on our first cruise on a day when the breeze followed us around as we sailed an almost complete circle from St. Michaels, down to the Choptank, and back into Oxford, so that we had a beam reach for the whole circuit—one of those rare days.

St. Michaels

Now we had to harden up to turn to starboard into the Miles toward St. Michaels. Unless you are on a north–south course in the main bay, you seldom stay on one heading for long in the Chesapeake. Nearing St. Michaels, we had the rare treat of seeing one of the Chesapeake Log Canoes out for a practice sail, with her splinter of a hull

49

supporting a cloud of sail and her crew out on hiking boards.

There was time for a side excursion up Leeds Creek, which to me has always been a symbol of Chesapeake cruising, with its channel winding between farm fields, where the corn stands gathered in ricks, and handsome houses are set back amid stands of tall trees. It does not go very far, only a couple of miles, but it is always fun to poke into it.

At St. Michaels we managed to find a berth at the marina for a visit ashore to the Chesapeake Maritime Museum, and crab cakes—what else?—for dinner. The sail back the next day was in more of a southerly, which came in after a slow start that had us powering until we were well out in Eastern Bay. Then it whistled up with some authority and we had a fast reach back to the Annapolis area. This was a Sunday, with the Fall Series racing fleet out in full force, and it was hard to see the bay for the boats. The spread of sail from a distance as we swept up from the south practically obliterated the water. By now, the breeze had piped up to over 20 knots, and we shortened down to main and jogged around watching the acrobatics of the boats rounding the race buoys and performing all sorts of gyrations and spinnaker broaches. It was a good day to be cruising.

In our few weekends, we had time for some more favorite spots, like Dun Cove on Harris Creek, Oxford itself, and the Chester River. We had the pleasure of waking up in a quiet Chesapeake Cove to the sight of formations of geese arrowing across the sky and the put-put of a crabber's skiff moving across the still waters on his trotline, brisk sails in the center of the bay, the floating boat show of the hundreds of vessels around us, and the subtly developing colorations of the foliage. Now it was time to head farther south.

The first time we did this, Jane and I left Annapolis in a flat midday calm that persisted all day and into the evening, and we decided to power on through to Norfolk, as it was a bright moonlit night. Gradually we noticed thin little veils wisping past the moon, and then, almost without warning, we were in zero fog and the night was filled with the deep boom of big ship fog horns. It was an anxious night of carefully navigating and figuring out where the ships were before we came out of the stuff at dawn at the entrance to Hampton Roads.

Another year, friends had taken *Tanagra* to Crisfield on the lower Eastern Shore. We exchanged our car for *Tanagra*, and, while our friends drove back to New Jersey, we watched a cold front come blasting through in early evening, heralding the advent of November with a wind speed and temperature that just matched: Both were 35. In the small municipal marina at Crisfield, which is mainly a commercial seafood port, we listened to the whine of the wind and wondered about the morrow. Frontal rain had gone by, and the stars were glittering coldly when we turned in.

The wind and cold, straight from Canada, were the same in the morning, and the sky was a deep, spotless blue. I was itching to be off, but a look at the marina's anemometer bouncing around in the 30s and the closely spaced whitecaps laced with wind streaks outside the marina settled things temporarily. We poked around the run-down little town for a while, and when we came back to the marina in mid-morning I convinced myself, in a three-minute lull, that it would be OK to go.

It was splashy powering out of the harbor into the wind, but we could soon turn to port for a run down Tangier Sound. The simplest thing was to break out the roller furler as all the sail she needed, and we were immediately swooping along at hull speed, with the wind at our backs and the sun bright in our faces, glittering over the whitecap dance. Windbreakers, gloves, and wool caps killed the chill, and, for our "elevensies," which is usually a cold beer on sunny days, we had soup with a generous lacing of sherry in it. The world seemed a fine place to be after the earlier hesitation. Off our starboard quarter, the low line of Smith Island, where we had had an interesting visit yarning with the watermen on one of our earlier cruises, was slipping back, and its sister island, Tangier, came up rapidly off the starboard bow, another low thin silhouette against the glitter of the water.

At noon, the wind moderated slightly, and I set the main for a reach across the bay. We were aiming for the Piankatank River, and it was a fine sleigh ride of a sail for a while until the breeze began to strengthen again, and we were carrying too much sail. I tried to sweat the jib on the furler, but the tension was too heavy, and the sail would bind so tightly that it was impossible to get it all in. It was the kind that was on its own stay, not in a grooved head stay, and it was a simple operation to free the halyard and lower it on deck, although it was a fight to get it under control on the bouncy foredeck. Under main alone, she moved just as fast as anyone would ever want to, and the wind had grown puffy and erratic when we came into the lee of the western shore and followed the Piankatank buoys to a marina at Milford Haven. It was an elaborate place with a big hotel and fancy restaurant, almost deserted at this time of year, and we had our choice of tables in the restaurant for our evening crab cakes.

In the manner of high-pressure systems, the northwester died over-night, and we were in the windless center of the high the next day for a long session of powering down to Norfolk. Coming into Hampton Roads, with its huge coal carriers, tankers, container ships, and freighters anchored in the roadstead, the mothballed liner *United States* sitting forlornly at a pier, and mammoth carriers and the full complement of naval ships at the navy base piers, made *Tanagra* seem lost and puny, and the quiet coves and farm fields, the trotlines, and the billowing sails of the Annapolis racing fleet seemed part of another world.

The Carolina Sounds

Perhaps the least known and least visited cruising area on the Atlantic coast, compared to the ones nearer the big population centers, is the complex of sounds in North Carolina, behind the barrier beach that runs south from Virginia through the Cape Hatteras area. There is an awful lot of water there, enough to drown all the land in some of the smaller northeastern states, and very little civilization. Most visitors only know it from rushing through on the way to and from Florida via the Intracoastal Waterway, and they do not realize what they are missing by not taking the time to tarry a while and poke into some of the backwaters. Although the boat population has grown tremendously since the 1960s, it is still much smaller than in other areas, and there is no problem in finding solitude and isolation when these are desired in some of the out-of-the-way anchorages. The water is a bit thin through much of the area, and navigation marks must be carefully observed. The season is a long one from March to December, and there have been winters when sailing is possible right through. Summers are hot, but there is more a likelihood of a sea breeze out by the Outer Banks, and thunderstorms are not as frequent as on the landlocked Chesapeake. We based Tanagra at Oriental on the Neuse River one winter, and it was in her, with her accommodating draft of 3 feet, 9 inches that we enjoyed cruising this area.

It seemed a bit risky to plan a cruise anywhere north of Florida in March, but there was *Tanagra*, sitting in Oriental, there was all that

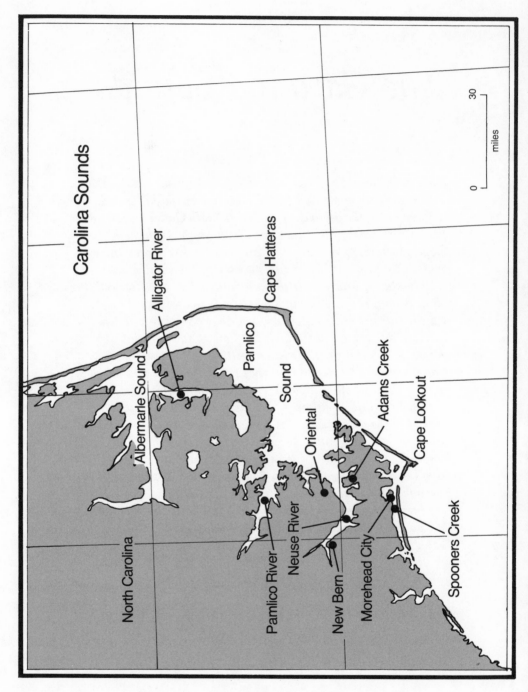

Carolina Sounds

Alligator River

Cape Hatteras

Pamlico

Sound

Albermarle Sound

Adams Creek

Oriental

Cape Lookout

North Carolina

Pamlico River

Neuse River

New Bern

Morehead City

Spooners Creek

0 30 miles

unexplored (by us and most other non-Tarheels) water, and there happened to be some free time to do it. There are good air connections into New Bern, just a few miles from Oriental, mainly because of the big U.S. Marines base at Cherry Point, so it is not hard to get to this otherwise rather isolated part of the land.

Oriental itself is well worth a visit. It is a sleepy little town between a brace of creeks that are tributaries to the broad, brown Neuse. Tall trees shade a couple of streets of attractive houses, there are a few stores, and there are also some run-down shacks on the outskirts. The countryside is pancake flat, and farm fields start right outside of town. There are also commercial shrimping and fishing on the Neuse. There is a golf course nearby, and a couple of tennis courts, but it is the kind of town where the social center, at least for the ruling clique of males, is the back room of the hardware store. This is of necessity, since North Carolina has no public bars.

Recently the even tenor of this life has been changed somewhat by the boom in sailing, and two large marinas have been built on the creeks. Over three hundred boats base here year round, and, in good years, there is year-round sailing, at least on a few special days in January and February. The owners come from great distances inland, and the local fleet is swelled each spring and fall by the flood of transients on the Intracoastal Waterway.

One of the marinas, Whittaker Creek, is run by former sailing friends from New Jersey, Ann and Dan Forman, and we had had pleasant stops there in Waterway trips in years past. When it had seemed too much of an organizing job to get *Tanagra* all the way down to Florida and the Bahamas, as we had done in previous years, we had decided to take her as far as Oriental for a winter lay-up, and she had been in a slip there since November. When we laid her up, I asked Dan about winterizing, and he laughed and said that on one ever bothered with that in Oriental.

"A lot of people sail all winter," he said. "We just let 'em sit in their slips."

That January (1977) happened to be the coldest one on record in many a year as far down as northern Florida, and *Tanagra* had been

55

frozen solid in her slip for three weeks. Fortunately, Dan and cohorts had been on the ball and had drained lines and toilets and put lights on in the engine room. There was no movement of ice in the quiet creek, so she went through it without a problem and was in full commission when we came down the last week in March, with our frequent cruising companions Helen and Ted Tracy as crew.

The weather was better than springlike when we came aboard. It was balmy and in the 70s, and it was hard to imagine that *Tanagra* had been frozen solid in her slip two months before. Another pleasant surprise was how inexpensive the storage had been compared to northern prices, and local shopping to stock the boat was markedly cheaper too. All around us there was a great stirring of activity in the 100 or so slips of the marina, and most of the boats were in full commission.

It was a cloudy but warm afternoon, with the breeze in the south when we were loaded and ready to go, and our first sail was a 5-mile reach across the muddy waters of the Neuse to Adams Creek, a tributary that is part of the Waterway route and one of the prettiest spots on it. All under sail, we eased through it, following the ranges on its dogleg, to a smaller tributary creek at its southeast end called Back Creek. We poked in half a mile from the Waterway channel and were alone in the world, surrounded by the low scrub of the shoreline, except for the occasional rumble and mutter of diesels on tugs pushing barges down the Waterway toward Morehead City. Few yachts move at night on the Waterway, but the big commercial craft keep plugging along, with the great white beam of their searchlights stabbing through the darkness as an intrusion on the peace and quiet.

In the misty calm of dawn we had our first company, a crabber working a trotline as he put-putted by us, so intent on his work that he never gave us a glance. After breakfast, we powered out to the creek entrance and turned to port to head for Morehead, down the canal. This was typical Waterway stuff, with featureless banks and a straight run until we came to more open water on the approaches to Beaufort and Morehead. I had some misgivings about the seasonal weather on this leg, since a cold wind from the sea was blowing up the canal dead on the nose. Winding through the sandy islands on the approaches to

Cape Lookout light

Morehead after leaving the canal, it looked as though a careless wash-erwoman had strewn laundry over the low bushes along the shore, but these were egrets, hundreds of them, clustered on the branches.

We kept on going past the commercial bustle of Morehead and ended up a few miles south on the Waterway in an attractive marina at a bywater called Spooner Creek.

We had stopped here before on Waterway trips and had always enjoyed the restaurant and the perfect protection, and it was a good place to be on a night of low clouds and drizzle. These still persisted in the morn-ing as we powered back to Morehead and tied up for lunch to see what the weather would bring. This was at a mammoth establishment with the rather daunting name of The Sanitary Fish Market, a no-nonsense barn of a place with row after row of plain mess-hall-type tables. Evi-dently it does a fantastic volume of business in season, and even on this March day there was a good crowd. To get in, you have to pass a large sign over the door that warns in no uncertain terms that anyone who shows signs of being drunk will not be admitted and that no liquor is to be brought in.

No matter what the attitude toward drinking was, the ability to cook fish right off the boat well and serve it in a tasty, hearty meal was certainly there. While we were enjoying it, we could look out over the harbor and see that the day was brightening, and it was a warm sunny afternoon with a mild southwest breeze when we got back on *Tanagra*.

This would be just right for heading out for the bight at Cape Lookout, on the Outer Banks, 6 miles from the Morehead jetties, and it was only a few hundred yards to pass the commercial docks, where a couple of oceangoing freighters were berthed, and sail out the inlet. Gulls wheeled and cried around us as we felt the first lift of the ocean swells and the soft saltiness of the breeze. It was March, but it could have been an August day in New England.

The Atlantic was a greenish gray, pocked by whitecaps, and we turned to port and ran along a deserted ribbon of beach toward the entrance to the bight, rolling freely in the swells under main and wung-out jenny. We swept around a long sandy spit on our starboard hand, where thousands of gulls chattered and cried on the empty beach, perched on twisted pilings, and wheeled darkly against the westering sun. Great flights of sea ducks swooped and flared over the water like wisps of smoke, fish broke all around us, and a large harbor, big enough to hold every yacht in North Carolina, and then some, opened up before us. We stood on to the far southeast corner and anchored in about 15 feet, with the tall spire of the lighthouse and its black and white harlequin pattern across the dunes to port. A few low buildings and the remains of a broken-down pier were the only breaks in the ring of golden sand on three sides of us.

I have seldom been alone in such a large anchorage, and there was a wonderful feeling of isolation and separation in the wild but benign surroundings. The summery feeling persisted through the golden haze of sunset, with a full moon rising over the dunes on the other side, but mid-evening brought a sudden change.

There were no clouds, and the moon shone more brightly than ever, when the breeze suddenly shifted from balmy southwest to northeast without a moment of hesitation and began to blow with authority. The temperature dropped rapidly with this blast from the open sea, and the wind began to play a nervous tune in the rigging, while small waves started to slap and splash along the hull. They only had a few hundred yards of fetch, so it was a secure anchorage, but the whole mood had changed, and we were well aware of how close we were to the open ocean off Hatteras.

It was a night of many small noises, but a secure feeling through it all, and this breeze was a fair one for running back to Morehead. It was strong enough to call for a reef, and, with one in, we sailed off the anchor and sped out of the bight into the short steep seas along the beach outside. The gulls who had greeted us in such numbers were there to bid us goodbye just as noisily. It was a fast sail of an hour to the inlet, where the seas steepened against the tide, making the buoys tumble and sashay wildly, but we were soon between the breakwaters and coasting into calm water.

It was only midday, and we took a detour over to Beaufort to sightsee its waterfront of fishing boats and a jumble of broken-down piers and shacks and new construction, before heading inland via the canal to Adams Creek. This time we chose a tiny gunkhole off Cedar Creek, on its eastern side, for our anchorage. The entrance was very narrow, barely wider than *Tanagra*, and the depth was supposedly 4 feet, so we made it safely and spent the quietest of nights in rural peace, with the chirping of birds and singing of insects a sharp contrast to our surroundings the night before in the sea-blown atmosphere of Lookout Bight. It was warm and summery again, and once more we had an anchorage all to ourselves.

I could not help but think of the Maine-iacs who make a fetish of getting away from it all up there, and the people who wail about how the Caribbean is becoming overcrowded, and how easily we had found peace and solitude in these very cruisable waters.

As we ran swiftly across the Neuse to Oriental the next day, it was hard to realize that summer had not arrived and that we would be going back to blustery March days in New Jersey. I suppose these waters are more crowded in summer, but they had been an exciting change of pace in this off-season cruise.

The Bay of Quinte

While I have been in the Chicago–Mackinac Race and the Interlake Yacht Association Regatta at Put-in-Bay on Lake Erie and have day-sailed the North Channel of Lake Huron and in the Green Bay and Chicago areas, the only real cruising I have managed in the Great Lakes was in Mar Claro in the Bay of Quinte, a lovely landlocked arm of Lake Ontario at its northeastern corner near the inland end of the St. Lawrence River and the Thousand Islands. We could trail her there on an overnight trip from New Jersey, and it was a delightful world apart of rural scenery, fine sailing breezes, and interesting harbors. The season is naturally a short one, and heat waves and thunderstorms can make themselves felt in the summer months, but the pluses are many. Freshwater cruising has its own special rewards, of course, of ready-made baths and hair washes over the side, no drinking water problems in most areas, and easier maintenance of the boat in a salt-free atmosphere. It was a very different feeling for us, and we enjoyed the change.

This was our first freshwater cruise, and it took a while for salt-oriented sailors to get used to the obvious advantages. Spray aboard was a cleaning agent, filling water tanks and taking baths presented no problems, and my all-girl crew in *Mar Claro* of Jane, Martha, and Alice, the girls then in their early teens, frolicked over the side on any and all occasions, swimming without a cap and lathering their hair repeatedly.

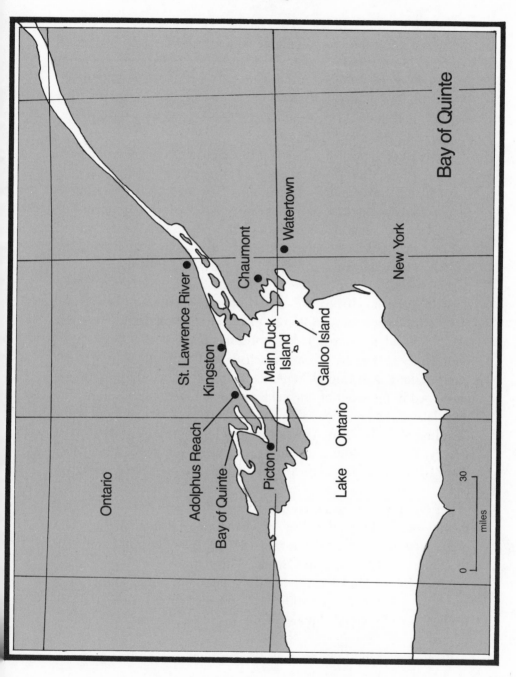

Bay of Quinte

Watertown

Chaumont

St. Lawrence River

Kingston

New York

Main Duck Island

Galloo Island

Adolphus Reach

Ontario

Bay of Quinte

Picton

Lake   Ontario

0

30

miles

There was a different feel to the sailing too. The waves were shorter and steeper, and the crests, heavier than salt water, broke less often. We figured our distances and speeds in statute miles, and the sights and sounds of the shoreline had a north country difference about them. The air smelled of meadow grass and lily pads instead of salty sand and marshes, and the farm fields along the lake buzzed with the summer sounds of a rural countryside.

Another odd aspect of it was that this radical change of scene from the Jersey shore was only nine hours away by car and trailer, less than it usually took us to go by water through New York Harbor to western Long Island Sound. Not only that, the "magic" of trailing meant that *Mar Claro* was afloat in Chaumont Harbor, New York, at the eastern end of Lake Ontario exactly two months to the day after leaving the Bahamas, with six weeks sailing in New Jersey in between.

After rigging up and provisioning in Chaumont, a busy marine center with a top-notch boatyard and a large concentration of sail and power cruising boats and one-design racers, our first sail the next morning was a fine ad for Great Lakes cruising. There was a fresh, puffy northwester to give us a beam reach down Chaumont Bay, and we smoked along over smooth water as rapidly as she could possibly go, enveloped in the scent of hay fields and pine forests, until we met the open lake at the entrance. The blue water danced and glittered to the clear line of the horizon as we felt the first lift of these short, freshwater seas. It was now a close reach out to mid-lake to our destination, Main Duck Island, and *Mar Claro* ate her way into it with a lively, confident feel.

On the way, we passed Galloo Island off to port and soon crossed the international boundary line, as Main Duck, all alone in the center of the lake, where the St. Lawrence seaway spews its traffic out from the Thousand Islands, is in Canada. This narrow, 3-mile-long island is owned by the Dulles family, and the late John Foster Dulles, who had been going there since boyhood, retreated there for rest and recreation when he could slip away from his State Department responsibilities.

It came over the horizon as isolated clumps of trees that gradually

The open lake from Main Duck

blended into one whole. We surged closer until its wave-scarred cliffs, forest areas, and Canadian lighthouse could all be seen. The only harbor is a tiny cove on the north side. The entrance is only about 50 feet wide, and it can take 4 feet of draft inside, where we rounded up to anchor 200 feet off a narrow, gravelly spit that protects it from the open lake and almost closes off the entrance. Since this was a weekend, there were a few motorboats inside. We were the only sailboat.

To protect the island from a conservationist point of view, and to preserve its privacy, landing is only permitted by invitation, which we fortunately had. The caretaker and his wife, who had to spend most of their time kicking people off the island, were delighted to have legitimate visitors, and they turned themselves inside out to make us feel at home. The man was a Canadian woodsman who took a shine to the girls and gave them the complete treatment. He showed them how to fly-cast, took them to the Dulles cabin in its cliff top setting, gave them a forestry lecture, and showed them duck ponds and a salt lick where deer congregated. They explored the beaches and the lighthouse and were even invited to spend a night camping in a cabin, and this became one of their favorite cruising stops of all time.

Because of all these special treats, we stayed over a second night after a short sail circumnavigating the island, and we had the harbor to ourselves, since it was Sunday, and the motorboats, who had been noisy neighbors on Saturday night, had all gone away. While the girls were having their camping adventure alone in the woods, Jane and I had *Mar Claro* in husband-and-wife privacy.

Before retiring to the playground-sized double bunk, we sat in the cockpit over a nightcap, wearing windbreakers against a fresh new breeze from the north. The waves hissed and rumbled on the other side of the gravel spit, and the north woods atmosphere became complete when the aurora borealis put on a show, flickering its ghostly hues to the zenith in an ever-changing display.

The sail to Main Duck had been 24 miles, and, after dragging the reluctant girls away from their woodsy retreat, we headed for the Bay of Quinte on the Canadian shore to the north. This was a 32-mile passage to Picton, a town at the head of one arm of the Bay of Quinte known as Adolphus Reach, that was one of those rare sails when the wind follows around on the beam on each successive heading of what amounted to a dogleg course across the open lake and up the gradually curving reach. It was a fast sail on the lake, heading for an open horizon at first, with no land in sight, Main Duck dropping low astern, and only lake steamers a distant smudge of smoke on the horizon, and a couple of commercial fishing boats as company.

Adolphus Reach is long and narrow, with farm fields and forests

The Canadian lighthouse

along its shores and an attractive anchorage, Prinyer's Cove, just inside the entrance. We were the only yacht on the open lake, but there was a parade of cruising boats in sail and power, outboards and water skiers. Big lake freighters shouldered by us now and then, and as the sun warmed us in early afternoon, we poked behind an island to anchor in a little cove for one of those hair-washing swims. The water, a translucent green, was warm while the girls lathered and splashed, and inshore, children played on a beach amid barking dogs—a lazy midsummer afternoon scene.

Daylight lasts long in early August, and we took our time drifting into Picton on the final gasp of that accommodating breeze, arriving just at sunset in a golden glow of slanting light that picked out the trees and flowers of the hilly, wooded shores and the Victorian gingerbread palaces, with wide porches and cupolas, spread over the hillside.

Small Ontario towns offer very little in the way of shoreside excitement, but the harbor was a pleasant place to be. A visit to customs in the post office the next morning took in most of Picton's charms in one short walk, and we were off again down Adolphus Reach—on another reach—to Kingston, a bigger city and an active sailing center 33 miles to the east.

The breeze deserted us in late afternoon, as the sky filled with high, gray clouds, and the outboard took us the last 5 miles to Kingston Yacht Club, the only real use of power on the cruise. An International 14-Dinghy regatta was underway at the club, and the boats were as still as statues trying to drift over the last few yards to the finish line.

The high clouds meant rain the next day and a total lack of wind, but Kingston was a good place in which to be stuck. Like Picton in its gray, stone-fronted respectability, but bigger, it had more to offer visitors. Old Fort Henry, a relic of colonial days, is a gigantic tourist attraction that puts on a military show of the changing of the guard, complete with band and trooping of the colors, and there was even a movie to top off the day's activities.

We had hoped to use that day to do some exploring into the Thousand Islands, a plan that had to be scrubbed, as it was now time to head back to Chaumont, and we had a fine, clear northeaster behind a front that came through during the night. Kingston's grim, gray buildings that seemed to blend with the rain the day before had a friendlier glow in the clear morning light as I made sail and headed for the open blue of the lake outside the harbor. I had made the start while everyone else was asleep (when I wait for everyone to be ready, we sometimes don't sail at all) but soon Jane had bacon and eggs on the stove, and we had breakfast while skirting Simcoe Island, where the lighthouse keeper's children were romping on the beach.

Our course took us by Allan Otty shoal and right across the main channel of the seaway and its steady parade of ships. They would loom over us with their high superstructures shining in the sun, and there would be a quick bounce or two as the wake hit us, a gust of that hot, pungent ship smell, and then a diminishing view of the stern before the next one came along. As a finale, this was as good a sail as any we had had, matching the first one in the blueness of the water and the sparkle of sun as *Mar Claro* sped along. When we moved into Chaumont Bay, the mainland stretched off into the distance on a gentle rise to hills capped in cumulus, and closer at hand the buzzing warmth of a summer noon closed over us. We had made such good time that we could stop and anchor for a last swim at lunch, and even though everyone's hair was very clean, there was a last, happy lathering.

While this cruise easily broke the record for hair washings, there were many other pleasant memories to take away from this freshwater expedition.

Part II

EUROPE

Denmark

The nautically minded country of Denmark is made up almost entirely of islands, except for the Jutland Peninsula, which forms its western half and separates its protected inland waters from the blustery North Sea. In these inland waters between Zealand, site of Copenhagen, and Jutland, there is a maze of islands that makes a fascinating cruising area. Farm fields and forests alternate along the low, rolling hills of the shoreline, with dollhouse villages out of a Hans Christian Andersen fairy tale, and almost everyone in Denmark and surrounding countries seems to be afloat there at the height of the summer season. This season is a short one, with very changeable weather because of the high latitude (56° N) and the unpredictable North Sea just across Jutland, but the good weather is very pleasant and summery and there is a lot of daylight for enjoying it in midsummer at these latitudes, roughly the same as Labrador. Our cruise there was in a locally built sloop called a Bianca 27, a fiber glass development of the folk boat type so popular in Scandinavia.

A cruise in the Fyn Archipelago in Denmark was the first time Jane and I had ventured by ourselves into a foreign country. We were alone in a Bianca 27 sloop, with no interpreter or local crew, and there was some concern over dealing with language problems, along with the usual uncertainties of weather difficulties in a strange boat in a strange area. As it turned out, there were two magic catch phrases that solved

Denmark & Sweden

Norway

Stromstad

Fjallbacka

Smögen

Sweden

Skagerrak

Goteborg

Kattegat

Denmark–Jutland

North Sea

Copenhagen

Zealand

Mullerup

Svendborg

Lohals

0   60

miles

Rudkobing

West Germany

the whole problem, while the weather solved itself by being very pleasant.

The first phrase, spoken loudly and distinctly, was "I only speak English." The second was a combination, used, when eating ashore, in the proper order. It went *"schnapps," "øl,"* and *"fiske."* This was enough to get us a predinner drink of schnapps, or *akavit*, beer (*øl* equates to the English ale), and a fish platter as we explored ashore in the pleasant islands of the archipelago, a wonderful cruising ground of protected water that attracts boats from all over northern Europe.

We had been told that almost everyone in Denmark speaks English, which is true of younger people who have been to school since World War II, but out in the islands this did not necessarily hold true, and the older people definitely had not studied English in school. However, that magic phrase enunciated loudly as we hovered off the piers of a marina always brought a scurrying about that eventually turned up someone who would shout instructions to us in English.

As it developed, we were in a marina every night, since there were no protected anchoring areas and everyone makes for the special yacht harbors for overnighting. They are called *lustbodhavns*, which you can work out phonetically in English if you equate *lust* with pleasure. In fact, many of the directions in the Danish language cruising guide could be understood if pronounced with English phonetics (but never as the Danes pronounce them).

This was European cruising as the locals do it, the equivalent at home of heading for Martha's Vineyard and Nantucket. Sailboats outnumbered powerboats by about five to one, and most of the boats were fairly modern fiber glass craft under 30 feet, developments of the basic Scandinavian family cruising boat, the folk boat. It was definitely family cruising. Almost every boat had little towheads popping above the cockpit weather cloths now and then, and diapers drying on the lifeline were a common sight.

In the *lustbodhavns* in late afternoon, when everyone was safely shoehorned into a berth in incredibly cramped quarters, the youngsters would all be put into little rubber dinghies, or Optimist sailing prams, and shoved off to fend for themselves within the confines of the marina while the parents relaxed over schnapps in the cockpit and prepared dinner.

Every harbor was equipped with a washhouse, toilets, showers, and laundry facilities, and the parade of families to them each morning was a wonderful sight. The Germans, and there were a great many German boats there, as Kiel is only a day's sail away, would march *en famille* in a virtual goose-step formation, each member with a towel draped carefully over the forearm. They would chorus *guten Tag* with great formality to everyone they passed, but that was the limit of communication. With World War II a 30-year-old memory at the time, there was still little inclination among the Scandinavians to fraternize with the Germans, and we would run into this feeling in some of our visits to shops and restaurants.

Since it was obvious we were not Danish, there would be a certain cool formality to start with, especially with Jane's marked blondness, and we came to recognize that we were thought to be German. When some English phrases dispelled this impression, there would be an instant thaw, broad smiles, and much talk about "my cousin in Bridgeport, Connect-aye-cut," or the like. Somehow it was nice not to be ugly Americans for a change.

One night at dinner at a restaurant in Svendborg, the metropolis of the Fyn Archipelago, a young couple at the next table seemed to be talking German to our untutored ears, and we could tell that they were watching us warily. When we had an exchange in English with the waitress, they suddenly leaned over and began to talk to us, and it turned out that they were Dutch. They too had thought we were German but now were eager to talk boats and cruising in their excellent English. This ended up with their coming back to the boat for a drink and a very pleasant evening of "sea stories." They had come all the way along the North Sea coast from Holland in a 22-foot sloop, practically camping out, and were headed north to the fjords of Norway, an ambitious expedition for a boat of that size.

Encounters like this were a great deal of the charm of this cruise. For the dual purpose of giving Jane a break from galley chores and the desire to explore and to see what would happen when we worked the

74

schnapps–øl–fiske routine, we ate ashore every night. We just took pot luck with what restaurants we could find in the Hans Christian Andersen atmosphere of the little island towns, and each evening was a new experience. In late July, the Scandinavian skies would retain a twilight glow until almost 11 o'clock, and we would wander around in the glowing half light until a place took our fancy. Only once did the magic formula fail to work, and somehow we ended up with rather tough chicken.

Our boat, *Inge*, was a modern fiber glass sloop, a version of the folk boat form like almost all small Scandinavian cruisers, with a deeper hull, more freeboard, and more headroom than the conventional folk boat. She had modern equipment on deck and below, a 10-horsepower Bukh Danish diesel that put-putted to life faithfully whenever we needed it, and she sailed well, with a big boat feel to her when she breezed on and a chop developed. There was no dinghy, and the anchor had never been broken out once, such is the convention of berthing in *lustbodhavns*. She had been built at Rudkøbing, one of the bigger towns in the archipelago, and we had a pleasant dinner visit with her builder, Holger Christiansen, and his wife during the cruise that ended up as a swinging evening in a Svendborg disco.

She was one of a fleet of bareboat charters based at the small yacht harbor of Mullerup on the west coast of Zealand, and we began the cruise from there. It was an adventure to stock the boat in the local market, where we did quite well in avoiding mistakes, except for not realizing that *sukerfri*, which we should have pronounced in English, meant sugarless for jellies. We shopped for breakfast and lunch materials only, and Jane became very adept at concocting her own version of Danish open sandwiches for our lunches.

The most traumatic experience was in buying liquor. It is very expensive in Scandinavia. Even schnapps and *øl* come high, and items like gin and whisky are out of sight. Indulging ourselves, we bought a couple of bottles of these plus vermouth for the obligatory martinis, while a group of locals hanging around the grocery-cum-liquor store watched in amazement. When we had our package together, to a man they leaped up to help us out the door, with all sorts of admonitions

A small boat harbor on Zealand

about being careful, and muttered comments of "much money," "very costly," and the like.

We had also received very definite advice about the need for keeping schnapps and *øl* cold, but the boat had just one small cake of ice when we took off, and that soon evaporated. From then on the great challenge of the cruise was to find ice. First we found out that *eis* means frozen water, true, but it also means ice cream, and we went on many a wild goose chase to a Danish version of a Dari-Freeze in following instructions when we asked for *eis*.

In Svendborg, we were told that the hotel, at least a mile from the *lustbodhavn*, would sell us ice cubes, and we made the pilgrimage across town with a plastic bag, eagerly anticipating the cold drinks we would soon have. The result turned out to be one trayful, and we dashed back across town as quickly as possible to make one martini before the precious cubes melted. Finally we found the solution. The only place to get ice in this country that insists that the drinks be frosty cold was at commercial fish piers, and finally, late in the cruise, we ended up well supplied.

The cruising was of the easygoing kind in protected waters, in sur-roundings that reminded us most closely of the Chesapeake. Farm fields and forests lined the low, rolling hills of the islands—the highest point in Denmark is less than 300 feet—and navigation was mostly through channels winding through flats, with occasional open stretches between the more widely separated islands. The side channels were marked by stakes topped by brushes that were either up or down to show which way to pass them. Practically the only lack on *Inge* was binoculars, and I had not brought any, and it made for some anxious moments while getting close enough to tell with the naked eye whether a brush was up or down.

We had been warned about the weather with such local jokes as, "Last summer was very nice; it was on a Friday," and the like, and we were psychologically prepared for the worst, so it was especially pleas-ant to have warm, sunny summer weather, with good breezes, for almost all of our week. A tip-off on what to expect was the fact that all boats are equipped with cockpit weather cloths, but there was no need for them while we were sailing. It was bathing suit weather most of the time.

We were surrounded by other cruising boats, and ferries, ranging from mammoth railroad ones carrying whole trains to dinky ones serv-ing the smaller islands, were ubiquitous. Fishing boats and small freighters were also very much in evidence, and these are busy waters,

The marina and boatel at Mullerup

as the islands live by seafaring. The towns on such islands as Lange-
land, Fyn, Aerø, Täsinge, and Drejø are called skipper towns, since
they have provided sailors and masters for trading ships over the centuries. They reek with tradition and atmosphere, and an interesting
maritime museum at the skipper town of Marstal gives a fine picture
of this history.

The breeze was mostly from the south. Only on the last day, when
we had just arrived safely back in Mullerup after a fast 40-mile run up
the archipelago, did a swift front sweep in from the North Sea, preceded by ominous black clouds and a 40-knot breeze spitting rain.

78

That was our longest day's run, and our total mileage was about 125 as we zigzagged through the islands, taking our time to absorb the atmosphere.

Of that there was plenty, and we felt it had been one of the most relaxed and picturesque areas we have ever cruised. Considering the price of gin, we were even getting quite addicted to schnapps and *øl*.

The Swedish Skerries

The population of Sweden is roughly 8 million, and these people own 800,000 pleasure boats, which comes to a great many boats per number of families. In midsummer, when the whole country virtually shuts down for a mass vacation, it seems as though almost everyone in Sweden is out on the water taking advantage of the long daylight hours. On the east coast, out of Stockholm, there are thousands of islands in an archipelago that stretches along the shore and across the Baltic to Finland, offering hundreds and hundreds of anchorages. This is almost matched on the west coast, where there is an "inland waterway" for virtually the whole distance from Malmo in the south to Stromstad at the Norwegian border at 59° N. Especially from Goteborg, Sweden's second city, northward, there is an intricate spread of passages, thoroughfares, rivers, coves, and small bays inside a string of rocky islands that runs along the Kattegat, which separates Sweden from Denmark, and the Skagerrak, an arm of the North Sea between Sweden and Norway. This is ideal protected-water cruising, with an occasional chance to venture out on the open, and often challenging, waters offshore when the weather seems benign. Small auxiliaries, mostly 30 feet and under, stream along in a bow-to-stern parade that looks like the traffic on an American freeway, and somehow they all manage to tuck themselves in somewhere for the night. It is a joyous, companionable operation of great goodwill and camaraderie, and I had a chance to sample it in a Comfort 34, a top-grade auxiliary built in the yard that had turned out Sverige, Sweden's entrant in the America's Cup challenge eliminations.

To port and to starboard, the Swedish skerries, contoured mounds of rocks, bare on the seaward side and dusted lightly with heather and low shrubs the farther inland they were to starboard, spread out in intricate patterns. Ahead and astern, there was a steady stream of small auxiliaries, some under sail on a reach, some powering. There were so many boats that it looked to me like a nautical version of the New Jersey Turnpike. I figured that a good percentage of the 800,000 Swedish boats must have been right there on that narrow channel between the skerries, and yet I knew that the Stockholm archipelago on the east coast of Sweden was probably twice as crowded.

In the Comfort 34 *Mover*, we were approaching Smögen, one of the most popular cruising ports on Sweden's west coast. This was a stag cruise of three American boating journalists, guests of Lars Ahren, *Mover*'s owner, on a cruise designed to show us what a wonderful boating area this was. Lars was the Public Relations Director of Volvo, very adept at that phase of the business, and he was also a dedicated sailor who had handled public relations for Sweden's first America's Cup challenge in 1977. A tall, dark, handsome bachelor, he had explained to us that *Mover*'s name was significant in that he and his boat were always on the move to where the action was.

And now he pointed ahead off the port bow to a tight cluster of houses, small, jumbled cubes on rocky hills, topped by a distinctive tower. It was white and its circular upper section flared out widely over the pillar supporting it.

"There's Smögen," Lars said. "That's where the action is, because even the water tower is shaped like a schnapps glass. Smögen is the party place, but it won't be as busy as last month, when everyone was on vacation. In August there isn't so much going on here."

This was the first week in August, and most Swedes had finished their vacation, which almost everyone takes in July, when the sun is almost perpetually in the sky and the weather tends to be the best. Actually, we had heard that July had been cold and wet, and we were enjoying a fine spell of weather, cool but sunny, with good breezes.

As we powered into the narrow entrance to the long slit of Smögen's harbor, I could not imagine how it could have been any busier. Barely

The packed harbor at Smögen

100 yards wide, it slices deeply into the rocky island, with houses tumbling over each other on the steep banks on each side. It looked as though the quays were completely taken up by boats moored fore-and-aft, but we picked a spot between two boats that were only a couple of

feet apart and managed to shoulder our way in, with complete, cheerful cooperation by everyone on both boats.

Soon we were secure and part of the scene, while boat after boat come slowly into the harbor and pulled the same stunt somewhere along the way. After the harbor had looked completely full to me, perhaps 150 more boats came in and managed to tie up. It was a gay, festive scene. Along the quay, for the full length of the harbor, was a wooden boardwalk, lined with bars, restaurants, and shops. A steady stream of people wandered by, ogling the boats, taking pictures, looking up friends, and stopping for drinks in the bars.

There were families with towheaded kids darting between adult legs; bearded sailors; fat, overdressed tourists; and a steady stream of Swedish girls, who must rank, all in all, as about the best looking anywhere, in everything from bikinis to Ohio State sweat shirts and foul weather jackets. The steady parade set up a rhythmic clatter on the boards, and the air was filled with laughter, shouts of friends finding each other, and the strains of disco music from some of the bars and restaurants. Even though Lars had predicted that there would not be much action in August compared to July, he had soon hugged and kissed a good variety of girls, who swarmed aboard for a visit. I wondered whether any of them had their mothers along for me.

Although many Swedes were back at work, the yellow and blue of the Swedish ensign was very much in evidence, along with the reds and whites of Denmark and Norway, an occasional red, white, and blue from England or Holland, and a goodly mix of the somber black, red, and gold of West Germany. Germans take their vacation *en masse* in August, and many of them cruise up this far. The sun slid on a low-angled path toward the northwest, making for a slowly developing sunset and long twilight. It cast a clear, slanting light over the vibrant scene that lingered lovingly in this far north latitude of 58°.

We had a busy night of dancing and carousing ashore with Lars and his friends, and Smögen more or less wrapped up the atmosphere of a skerries cruise, but there were still many contrasting delights before the cruise was over.

It had started with a view of OpSail 78, the biennial Tall Ships

83

Kruzenshtern at the OpSail start

Festival that had been such a hit in New York Harbor at our bicentennial. There were not as many square-riggers as in 1976, only about half a dozen, including *Christian Radich, Kruzenshtern, Dar Pormorza,* and *Gorch Fock,* but the spectator fleet, on a day of calm seas and light air, was the biggest and most impressive I have ever seen anywhere, even at the America's Cup or OpSail 76. Goteborg, a city of 350,000, produced a fleet of 15,000 spectator boats, most of them small auxiliaries, that stretched to the horizon in a 360° perspective that had my mouth agape for most of the afternoon. It was a huge, good-natured armada, circling the square-rigged behemoths at arm's length or less in a fine display of seamanship and cooperation.

The cruise itself started at Steningsund, 24 miles north of Goteborg—pronounced "yoot-a-bor" by the Swedes, but usually politely Anglicized when they talked to us; almost all Swedes we met spoke excellent English. This was where *Mover* had been built in the shed constructed for *Sverige. Sverige*'s builder, a forceful young man named Sven Enoch, had been chosen for that task because of his knowledge of aluminum welding. He had had no previous experience in boat building, but became so involved with the *Sverige* program that he decided to go into the boat business full-time and started turning out the Comfort line as well as one-off custom boats. *Mover* was a cruiser/racer model, and a full racing model was also available. She had comfortable cruising appointments, given that European lack of concern with iceboxes, was nicely finished, and was also a fine sailing performer. Lars said she had done well in club-type racing.

Steningsund is at the southern end of the skerry area, and a busy yachting center. It is far enough inland to have trees and flowers in profusion, but it is a quickly noticeable phenomenon of the area that the islands become much more barren the nearer you come to the Kattegat, the arm of the North Sea between Sweden and Denmark that lies outside the skerries. Through the thousands of skerries, from large ones of several square miles, with villages like Smögen, to lonely little rocks, it is possible to stay in inland waters all the way up to Stromstad at the Norwegian border. As in Denmark, the emphasis is on family cruising in auxiliaries 30 feet and under, and no one ever anchors overnight. The boats either jam into harbors or pick a spot among the skerries to nudge up to a rocky ledge and tie to a tree or to the many iron rings set in the rocks. These had evidently been put there by operators of commercial boats, but the yachts use them.

For a little more action it is possible to poke out into the Kattegat at almost any point for some deep water sailing, and we did some of both. For the whole time we had clear weather and fresh winds, cool enough for windbreakers, but great sailing, and *Mover* was fun to sail. When the wind was right, we put the spinnaker up, but the courses never remained the same for very long in weaving through the islands, and we had a good amount of sail drill.

Our first stop was well inland at a hamlet called Malo, where we tied to a pier in front of a country store called Flincke's, made famous in a ballad by a popular Swedish folk singer named Taub. High hills dusted with a lavender film of heather surrounded the little cove. A special smorgasbord party that night at the store's cafeteria was a strenuous exercise in keeping up with Swedish hospitality. Several Swedish journalists had driven up from Goteborg for the party, and, because of the stringent laws on drunken driving, which call for mandatory jail sentences for driving after more than one drink, one poor guy had "the duty" and had to stay sober for the drive back home while his buddies "skoaled" themselves into near-oblivion. All this made the next day's sailing a bit tentative for us, but we warmed to the sun and a brisk sail in the Kattegat before the charms of Smögen took over.

On our continued sail northward, we had a steady floating boat show in the "turnpike" traffic of the narrow waterways, and it was fun to sail by a junior sailing group in Optimist prams off one town and hear the same sort of chirping cries, giggles, and shrieks drifting down to leeward that would be heard from youngsters in sailing programs anywhere. At the next town, Fjallbacka, the harbor was not quite as crowded, but the long, lingering sunset cast such beautiful reflections, shadows, and slowly changing hues over the mirror of the harbor that we sat for hours taking it all in, not worrying about high life on shore after the previous nights.

Stromstad, where we finished, was a good-sized commercial town

A typical mooring spot in the skerries

and resort center, where we all visited the enormous, spotlessly clean, and very busy municipal baths and swimming pool. Nature's waters are a bit Maine-like here, and all swimming is done in these indoor establishments.

Across the marina from us at Stromstad, a long jetty was lined with at least 50 German boats cruising in company toward Oslo to catch the finish of OpSail. They had all dressed ship with signal flags, and there was much blowing of trumpets and firing of salutes as the long, slow panorama of sunset silhouetted them against an ever-changing spectrum of colors. They flared brilliantly at first and then gradually subsided into subtler hues as a fitting coda to a cruise that had very definitely convinced us of the delights of cruising the Swedish skerries.

Canal Barging in England and France

There is a very different form of cruising from the operations in auxiliary sailboats that make up most of these chapters, and that is to take a canal barge through the French country-side (or Holland, Belgium, and England, which have the same sort of thing). Quite a tourist trade has developed from rather casual beginnings in boats that had been converted from commerical craft. Now there are specially built "hotel barges" carrying anywhere from a dozen to two dozen passengers on regular routes through Europe's amazing network of water-ways, the most relaxed and undemanding way possible of get-ting afloat. You are a pampered passenger, eating more than too well, sampling the wines of the various regions, and sight-seeing the graceful countryside by foot, bicycle, or the barge's own motor transport while your home afloat makes its way from lock to lock at a stately pace in the passing parade of canal traffic. This can consist of hundreds of commercial barges as well as self-operated hire cruisers of modest dimensions and even a stray auxiliary, with her masts on deck and looking a bit lost as she makes her way through the rural scenery. In a double-barreled adventure, we had a week each in the Loire Valley of France and on England's Thames from Oxford to Hampton Court. Both cruises were in hotel barges and it was an interesting contrast in life-styles and atmosphere.

About the only connection between barge cruising in Europe and the rest of the chapters in this book is that they are all done in something that floats. Other than that, to be gliding at 2 or 3 land miles an hour past châteaus, ancient churches, cattle-dotted pastures, and neat rows of poplars is far removed from a trade wind reach through the Grenadines or a beat up Buzzards Bay in a smoky sou'wester. Yet there is a nautical fascination to a barge trip in addition to being one of the most relaxed ways possible to see the countryside.

There are locks to go through almost continuously, sharp turns to negotiate, often with a big commercial barge coming at you from the other direction, and decisions on mooring spots, plus the maneuvers to get into them. The life aboard has a shipboard feeling, and there is a wonderfully relaxing sense of ease in watching the scenery slip by from a deck chair. I would not give up cruising under sail for a life of barging, but we found it a thoroughly fascinating experience in our two-part adventure in France and England.

The French cruise was in a 94-foot conversion of a Dutch work barge, and it was our charter alone, with just Jane and me and our friends Gen and Al Gagnebin. The vessel was *Wirreanda II*, named for an Australian tree by her Aussie owner–partners, one of whom, Diane, was our cook and hostess. It was a highly international mix on board. The captain was German and the deckhands were two brothers from Sri Lanka (formerly Ceylon), Dilip and Preetem. Al Gagnebin was brought up in Connecticut in a French-speaking Swiss household, Jane and I are from New Jersey, and Gen is a Virginian. Al, who speaks French like a native, was our interpreter and reveled in the assignment.

Wirreanda, dating from early in the century, but newly refurbished for the hotel barge trade with comfortable cabins for six and a pleasant lounge, was powered by a ponderous three-cylinder German diesel of uncertain vintage that pushed her along at a chunk-chunking top of 4 knots. It took about 20 minutes to prime it and build up pressure to get it started, and then it acted as though it would run forever. A colorful adjunct was *Wirreanda*'s "tender," a London taxi looking very much out of place in the French countryside in its high, black auster-

A canal scape

ity. One of the Sri Lankans would drive it along the canal bank, meeting us at every lock, and it was therefore available for side expeditions at any time if we happened to spy something interesting.

The only problem was that French provincial police were highly suspicious of this exotic vehicle and its drivers. They were sure that the Sri Lankan boys, who could only be seen in the interior of the taxi when they flashed their incredibly white-toothed smiles, were Algerian terrorists up to no good, and they were always being stopped for questioning. Half the time they had forgotten their passports, which probably would only have confused the police even more, and there were several times when they had to be sprung from the local pen.

There were also bicycles aboard for the passengers to combine sightseeing and exercise, and such was the pace of progress, that it was easy to walk between locks and catch up with the boat as she was going through.

The locks were a perpetual source of interest and they seemed to come up every half mile or so, although there were some longer stretches. Each one had a very individualistic lockkeeper's cottage and garden, and most were beautifully tended. Each also had a dog that would herald our arrival with a salvo of barks and then busily supervise the transit. We had a barge dog aboard, a schkipperke, who would run up and down our deck keeping track of the dog on land and making his own contribution of barks, so lock transits tended to be noisy. Sometimes the lockkeeper would be a man in farmer's clothes and rubber boots, and sometimes a woman would bustle out of a cottage kitchen, wiping her hands on her apron, and take over the operation. Crew members and passengers were always welcome to turn the big handles that controlled the locks, and someone usually did. The locks all had names and kilometer distances.

Some of the canals and locks dated back as far as the eighteenth century, and the whole system was complete by the nineteenth. Despite the advent of the internal combustion engine, the life is still tuned to the horse-and-buggy pace of having the barges towed, but the engineering of the canals and locks, and particularly the bridges that carried the canals over natural rivers, had been beautifully thought out.

Moored in a Burgundy village

We moored at night to trees or strategically placed bollards, and once or twice along a bulkhead at a town.

We were on the Canal Latéral de la Loire, working south in the Loire Valley in southwest Burgundy. It is more farm country than vineyards, which are farther east, for which Burgundy is famous. Most of the countryside had almost a parklike look to it, with well-tended fields separated by walls and fences, rows of tall trees lining the banks, and pastures dotted with the white Charolais beef cattle. Most of the land seemed to be in use, with not many wild or undeveloped stretches, and the towns, first glimpsed as a church spire as we would rise in a

93

lock, were compact and neat. I had never heard of any of the towns we went through, except the modest-sized old city of Nevers, and it was something of a journey from nowhere to nowhere.

The start was in Marseilles-les-Aubigny, a two-hour train ride on the Midi Express from the Gare de Lyon in Paris, and a backwater there off the canal serves as a marina for U-drive cabin cruisers and several barges. It was early June, and the U-drive traffic had only just begun, hitting a peak in the midsummer months.

The early June weather was very changeable. There were days of intermittent rain and blowing mist, and some bright ones of warm sunshine. It had been a rainy spring, and the countryside, contoured in low rolling hills was wonderfully lush and green. Each day started with the great treat of fresh croissants, brought back from the nearest bakery by Dilip or Preetem, and from then on the eating was de luxe. Diane was a fine cook, and the local cheeses, breads, and vegetables were excellent. Occasionally we varied things by eating in a country inn, where farmers in their work clothes sat around rough tables drinking red wine and pontificating on life in general. Once we had an excellent lunch in the restaurant of a local railroad station, where the maître d' wore a tuxedo, and the table linen, silverware, and crystal glass were of the first order, matched by the food.

It was a dreamy life of days blended together, but eventually, after eight days, it ended at a commercial center called Monceaux-les-Mines, and three changes of trains got us back to Paris in about three hours. In those eight days we had progressed less than 100 miles, but we felt as though we had been a million miles away.

It was a strong contrast in styles to fly to England, spend two days "doing" Oxford in the miserable cold, rainy weather that marred the Queen's Jubilee, and then board *Bonjour*, a brand new hotel barge built expressly for the trade and on her maiden voyage. She was 72 feet long, had berths for seven, and was powered by a 113-horsepower Leyland Thornycroft diesel that had a lot more oomph than *Wirreanda*'s antique machine.

She was owned by an American, Stanley Kroll, who, with his wife, had become fascinated by barge travel and was starting a company

At ease on *Bonjour*'s sun deck

called Floating Through Europe that has since established operations in France and the Netherlands as well. Her captain was Norman Riddle, a retired Royal Navy officer with many years of canal barge operations behind him, with his wife Anna as cook–hostess, and they made a fine team, with a college lad as deckhand. Norman had the wonderful, bluff seaman's manner of an RN officer and was full of sea stories and anecdotes to keep the passengers amused, while Anna presided in the galley with skill equal to Diane's on *Wirreanda*. Anna specialized in English dishes like beef Wellington, salmon, Pavlova cake, chicken curry, and lamb and did much to belie the British reputation for stodgy cooking.

This was a "by-the-ticket" vessel, and there was another couple and two ladies traveling together, all Americans, to share the trip with us. Despite being strangers, compatability was no problem; one of the ladies was what might be called the executive type, and tended to be a bit difficult, but we just ignored those tendencies.

As a "tender," *Bonjour* had a van, a moped, and bicycles as well, and one of Anna's duties was to get on the moped after finishing with breakfast or lunch and retrieve the van from where it had been left. It was just as well we had shore transport, as the foul weather had raised the Thames so high that we were pinned down just outside of Oxford by a low bridge at Clifton Hampden. We moored along a cow pasture with several other similarly trapped barges and hire cruisers and had the built-in entertainment of watching the herd stampede up and down the field under the urging of the British "cowboys" tending them. Walking ashore along the towpath to the van was an exercise in tripping carefully through the normal hazards of a cow field, and there was one tense moment when part of the herd tried to come up our gangplank, but one of the cowboys steered them away just in time.

In our enforced inaction, we had van rides to Blenheim Palace, where Winston Churchill was born, and to his grave at Bladen Church, and to Stoke Poges, where the church was the subject of Gray's "Elegy." A cousin in my mother's generation had been Vicar of Stoke Poges in the twenties and thirties, and it was interesting to see his name on a plaque in the church. The verger, who had a good business selling postcards and copies of the poem—I had never realized how many familiar quotations came from it—from a small stand in the churchyard, remembered my cousin and was delighted to hear about it.

After two days, the waters subsided enough for *Bonjour* to squeeze under the bridge amid loud cheers from the passengers, and we were off downriver to Hampton Court in London. It was an interesting change from the rural atmosphere in France. There was some farmland and forests and some "stately homes," but there were towns all along the way, and, as we came nearer to London at the end of the trip, handsome suburban houses with lawns, clipped and a lush green, rolling down to the bank. There was also all sorts of river traffic, as the Thames seems to have collected every oddball vessel that ever floated. There were ancient mahogany launches, gleaming and lovingly kept, battered landing craft serving as houseboats, all sizes and shapes of power cruisers, one-design racing fleets, a few cruising sailboats, and rowboats, punts, and canoes. Jammed marinas could be seen in little backwaters, and almost every house had some sort of boat in front of it.

Norman was driven crazy by the hire cruisers, mostly because they were being badly handled. It was a difficult job to maneuver *Bonjour's* bulky hull into the many locks along the way that bypass the weirs where the water level changes, and the little hire boats would dart in front of us, spoiling our approach. I spent most of my time on the bridge swapping sea stories with Norman, and he would burst into irate tirades as boats cut him off, calling them "bloody trogs." I racked my brain for some Royal Navy slang that would identify "trog," but could not come up with any, and finally I asked Norman what a trog was.

"They're misshapen people who live in caves and behave abominably, old chap," he snorted, "troglodytes, mud-wallowing bloody trogs."

Despite these difficulties, he handled *Bonjour* well on the winding course of the river and through the locks. These were a distinct contrast to France. There were no dogs, and the lockkeepers were all formally decked out in brass-buttoned uniforms. The houses were government issue from the same mold, but some of them did have gardens, and they were all neatly kept.

The river route was so winding that we covered about 100 miles in six days in what amounts to a direct auto drive of two hours. After our imprisonment behind the bridge ended, we did most of our sight-seeing from the barge, and history was with us at every turn. We saw Eton, Windsor Castle, which came at us from every angle as the serpentine course of the river wound past its extensive grounds, Runnymede, Henley, the church of the Vicar of Bray, and Cliveden, including the Profumo scandal cottage. Occasionally we had good meals ashore at places with names like The Boat House, The Barley Mow, and The

Little Angel, all very atmospheric, and there were a few more side trips in the van. Swans glided over the water with new families on parade and fishermen lined the banks in profusion, though we saw very few making catches, and I half expected to see the mole and the water rat from "The Wind in the Willows" sliding into the water.

As we approached Hampton Court, civilization closed in more and more, until we were surrounded by city scenes and the great red brick sprawl of Hampton Court stood before us as the last monument of our winding passage through a lot of history. Salty we were not, but it had been a different kind of rewarding adventure.

Sardinia–Corsica

The Mediterranean holds a fascination for cruising sailors because of its interesting geography and the ever-present sense of history in this cradle of Western civilization. It is also the warmest part of Europe, with a longer season than in northern waters, but it is a sometimes tantalizing mistress to those who seek out its delights. Weather is the reason for this, as it is a sea of contrasting moods and quickly changing conditions, surrounded as it is by land masses that generate their own special winds with names like mistral, bora, meltemi, levanter, bise, and sirocco. It is notorious for alternating flat calms with the sudden blasts from one of these localized winds, and a cruising sailor has to thread his way carefully through these ever-changing challenges. From the Aegean to the Straits of Gibraltar, the Mediterranean world offers great variety, from the ruined reminders of the ancient world to medieval pageantry, from the isolation of some of the more remote islands to the glittery crush of the Riviera. I have had several cruises in the Med basin, and an area that presented steadier conditions than in other parts of it was the island world of Sardinia and Corsica, where an American designed Ranger 29, a modern fiber glass cruiser/racer, provided a bareboat charter out of Sardinia's Costa Smeralda, 125 miles from the Italian mainland (and the same latitude, 41° N, as New York).

This was jet set country. Here we were at Porto Cervo, nerve center of the 30-mile stretch of coastline at the northeast tip of Sardinia called

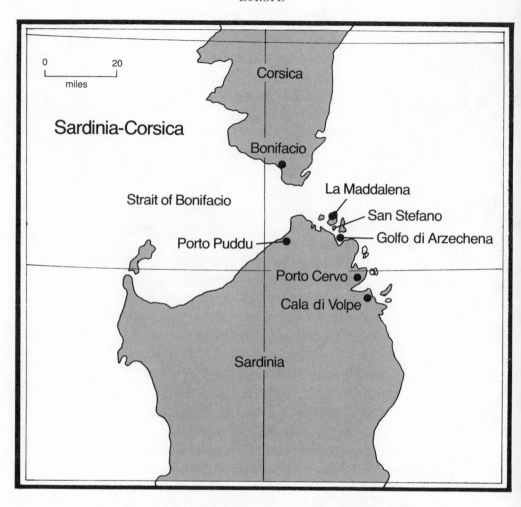

the Costa Smeralda. Owned by the Aga Khan and developed under his personal supervision, it is a carefully planned resort complex of hotels, marinas, golf and yacht clubs, and private villas. Fresh off the plane, we were shedding jet lag at the Cervo Hotel, a white building of many levels sprawled over the hills above the harbor.

Across the way, the concrete piers of the new Cervo Marina, solid as submarine pens, all but filled the western cove, and a large yacht club rose above the marina at the outer end. All the buildings were in the carefully controlled style of Costa Smeralda, a Moorish Mediterranean effect of whites and pale pastels, featuring arches; each one had been especially designed for its location to blend in with the overall effect of the whole area. The Ranger 29 sloop we would be taking out the next day was at the marina while we were being wined, dined, and, in the process, briefed on the cruising by the Aga Khan's people and the charter operators.

Although it was early June and the season had not started, there was a steady flow of people on the Cervo's terrace high above the harbor, and a few big yachts were in slips at the largely empty marina. A cool breeze pushing low, puffy clouds through patches of sun drifted in from the Med, a blue line beyond the harbor entrance, which was a narrow cut between stark, sheer rock cliffs of pinkish brown.

This was 1977, and we had not been there since 1971, when the resort was just beginning to take shape. The marina, the yacht club, and many of the buildings were new since '71, as was the bareboat charter service. In 1971, I had been invited by the Aga Khan's organization to survey the area for its possibilities as a yachting center, and it had seemed a fine one, both as a base for ocean racing and as a cruising center. The waters north of it are filled with islands tumbled together in the Strait of Bonifacio, which separates Corsica and Sardinia. As we sped through the islands at 50 knots in the Aga Khan's sport cruiser amid the magnificent scenery of Sardinia's high central mountains soaring in jagged lines far in the interior and the craggy hills along the shore weirdly sculpted at their base by wave action, I remarked to him that this would be a great cruising area. Now, six years later, we could solidify the impressions from that fleeting passage.

Certainly the marina was evidence of confidence in the area's yachting potential. Everything was solid concrete and built to last, with a mammoth service area, where even the biggest yachts could be moved about by lifts. In addition to the elaborate club, there was a chandlery and a supermarket, and, wonder of wonders, an ice machine—first one in the Med. Progress had been made.

Our Ranger 29, *Grecale* (Greek wind), was a Gary Mull design, built in Italy under license to avoid the enormous import duty. Although she had room for seven to sleep in a double-bunk forward, convertible dinette, double-quarter berth, and single-settee berth, she would be better suited for a maximum of four, and Jane and I found her very comfortable and easy to handle. We were familiar with the 10-horsepower Bukh diesel from our Danish cruise, and it proved reliable as ever. She was a fast, lively sailboat, more fun to sail than some of the larger, heavier charter boats we were used to.

Briefed and stocked, we were ready to take off by noon after our restful night at the hotel, and there was an easterly, gentle under a soft blue sky, to give us a reach down the coast to the southernmost harbor of the Costa Smeralda, Cala di Volpe. The number one luxury hotel of the complex is here, along with the golf course. We had stayed here in '71, when it had just opened and the golf course was only a gleam in the eye of Robert Trent Jones. Even then, its low, orange-buff buildings had been so carefully planned that they looked as though they had been there for centuries, and now, with construction complete, the total effect was one of long-established opulence.

This was augmented by several glossy yachts at anchor, and we spent a quiet night among them, settling in and getting to know the boat. Although hard liquor, as in all of Europe, was expensive, we had splurged enough for the obligatory martinis, and we found that the white Sardinian wine was quite pleasant. The water is not reliable for drinking, and we used bottled water for that and coffee and tea.

The wind was still in the east as we headed north the next day toward the islands in the Strait of Bonifacio. There had been a drought for three months, and we had the luck to have it break, with low rain clouds scudding over us, but we had a good sail up the coast and in toward the big island of La Maddalena. The charter operators had given us enough recommended anchorages to last for more than twice our week's time, but many of them were open to the east and had to be passed up in these conditions.

The winds are more normally from the west, and, from all reports, are more reliable, with fewer periods of flat calm, than in most of the Med. The main threat is the dreaded mistral, an Alpine norther that blasts down across the Gulf of Lyon with legendary force, but it has usually spent much of its fury by the time it reaches the Strait of Bonifacio—not always, though, as we have heard of wild seas when a particularly virulent mistral makes it through there.

Moving along well in a slop of sea, we were off La Maddalena and its neighbor, San Stefano, by noon, too early to stop, so we took a swing by the busy waterfront and headed on westward. The Sardinian coast here is continually cut by bays and coves, with long mountainous points sticking out on the sea. White clusters of houses could be glimpsed in villages at the head of coves now and then, and large, modern resort hotels, great fortresses of tier upon tier of cubic balconies, topped some of the points. This was no longer the Costa Smeralda, with its carefully placed and contoured buildings.

We were heading for a spot with protection from the east called Porto Puddu, which was a long way in around a barren island, avoiding rocks on a bar, to an anchorage we had snugly to ourselves. Inshore, the coastal foothills rose gradually to the 4,500-foot blue mystery of the inland peaks. In late afternoon, the sun broke through to spotlight isolated areas with shafts of gold, but it was back to rain and low visibility for our crossing of the strait the next morning. It was about 15 miles from Porto Puddu to the harbor of Bonifacio at the southern end of Corsica, and the visibility was low enough so that we were out of sight of both Sardinia and Corsica for a while, with only the small islands scattered across the strait in view.

It was a fast, damp sail, with freighters and tankers crossing our course in a parade, as this is a busy commercial route, and finally, through the mists, we began to make out ghostly shapes up ahead. The visibility improved enough to reveal them as the deeply eroded white cliffs at the south tip of Corsica, Cape Pertusato, rising sheerly from the crash of surf at their base, and soon we could glimpse the bulk of great mountains looming faintly in the interior.

Bonifacio is one of the most unusual harbors I have ever been in, and its entrance is especially dramatic. The cliffs extending northward from Pertusato are forbiddingly steep, gashed by caves and eaten away in odd formations by eons of wave action. Five miles north of the cape, a collection of buildings can be seen hanging over the cliff edge as though ready to tumble to the sea, yet they must have been there for centuries, since Bonifacio is an old city. There is no sign of a harbor entrance in the rugged face of the cliffs until several deep caves appear to starboard, and just beyond them a cut, barely a hundred yards wide, can finally be seen. Not until it is entered, with the walls leaning in far above on both sides, does an opening into the inner harbor appear.

The cut widens, and the overhanging rocks give way to gentler hills covered in yellow flowers. Then it can be seen that the town is on a narrow peninsula paralleling the coast and enclosing a 2-mile-long ribbon of harbor. The flowery fields give way to more steep escarpments and the packed buildings of the town, a symphony in gray and buff relieved by brightly colored shutters and the gay umbrellas of cafés along the quay. The French and Italians sensibly don't bother with customs and immigration in this area, so we could enter without formalities.

Even this early in the season, buses were disgorging hordes of tourists who spread through the cafés, browsed in the shops, climbed the rocky path to the heights above town, or boarded excursion boats for a tour of *les falaises* and *les grottes* (the cliffs and caves). The harbor was full of yachts and fishing boats, and I could imagine what it would be like in full season. The thing to do, it seemed, was to moor fore-and-aft to the quay at the inner end of the harbor, but we managed to find a spot alongside on the southern quay, just short of the corner. It was right at the row of cafés and shops, and we were as public as monkeys in a zoo. Tourists, other yachtsmen, and several large, friendly, sali-

The harbor at Bonifacio

The entrance to Bonifacio

vating dogs were ever at our rail, but things calmed down later at night when we wanted to sleep.

Astern of us was a red barge with a live well for lobsters, and a man from the café opposite it occasionally came out to tend them or bring a couple into the kitchen. Called the Hotel des Voyageurs, it was more a restaurant than a café, with real tablecloths, and, on the strength of the lobster barge, we decided to try it for dinner. Having made this decision, we failed to check the menu posted outside in accordance with French law. We had a modest dinner of soup, half a lobster apiece, and a bottle of wine, all pleasant but served in a decidedly offhand manner. When time came for *l'addition*, we had our introduction to Corsican banditry. The prices were steep, but in addition, they would not take a credit card and, since we had arrived after the banks had closed, we only had U.S. American Express checks. The official exchange was five francs to the dollar, but the restaurant would only give us three, and our dinner cost us $70, which in 1971 was a bit out of sight. The waiter, a husky, bluff man who had spoken some English when we were ordering, refused to understand a word of English as I protested, and my French collapsed completely under stress.

Ah, well. Other than that, Bonifacio was a delight, and we explored along the colorful waterfront and up the path to the top of the cliffs the next morning as the weather began to brighten.

The sunny day gave us another fast reach back toward Sardinia, and this time the mountains of Corsica could be seen in more detail, rising monstrously behind Bonifacio's startling array of houses. Sardinia was misty in the distance but took shape while our wake curled merrily off toward Corsica's cliffs, where they gleam whitely in the sun.

Once again we ranged through the harbor at La Maddalena, eyeing the naval vessels, fishing boats, ferries (one was named *Jolly Ferry*), board sailers, and a collection of yachts at the town quay all ashine in the sparkling sun. Heading out past San Stefano, we rounded a point and were faced with a large U.S. Navy sub tender at a pier, with several subs alongside, a surprising sight so far from home.

In late afternoon, we swept south into the Golfo di Arzechena, a deep indentation on Sardinia, and found an enormous, deserted concrete pier at a place called Cala Bitta, with a huge hotel under construction on the land. It was deserted, but I saw no reason not to tie up. Soon another sailboat came in and we were hailed in Italian. I shrugged my shoulders and called back that I only spoke English.

"Oh, jolly good," came a very British voice. "We just wanted to know what this place was."

They decided not to stay and we had the whole vast affair to ourselves as we explored ashore in what would eventually be quite a large resort. It was just as well we had selected a well-protected spot, because the wind started to howl during the night, and in the morning the gulf was a welter of whitecaps. It would be straight to windward for about 4 miles on the way out, and the boat was due back at Porto Cervo that afternoon, so I pondered the alternatives. Powering would be messy and slow, and I decided to put it up to *Grecale's* sailing ability. Up till now she had been fine on all points.

The wind was at least 30, and the best bet seemed to be a reefed main, trying it without headsails so that I could stay off the foredeck. The minute we poked our bow out of the lee of the pier, it was a plunging, spray-shot elevator ride. Med water is cold in June, but the spray was not solid, and I let *Grecale* jog as easily as possible a few degrees off of close-hauled. This was not a mistral, just a plain, hard norther, and the seas grew bigger as we slowly fought our way out of the gulf into the open Med. Here we could head off a bit on a reach, however, and it was not long before we had made it around the northeast tip and were roller-coasting on big blue seas on a run toward Porto Cervo. The charter people were surprised to see us when we rode the surf through the entrance, but by now we felt confident in a good little boat, and it was a smashing climax to the cruise.

The Dalmatian Coast

A very special corner of the Mediterranean world is the long, narrow finger of the Adriatic Sea, separating Italy's boot from the Yugoslavian mainland, and, in its own way, embodying as much of the ebb and flow of history as the Aegean. There is no organized chartering in this communist but very tourist-oriented country, and cruising there has to be done in a private boat or in a charter originating in Italy or Greece. Despite this, there is a great deal of pleasure boat traffic in the season, and the rewards of making it to this stretch of coast are well worth the effort. For its entire length from Italy in the north to to lonely, forbidden Albania in the south, which separates Yugoslavia from Greece, there is a continuing feast of cruising delights. Off-lying islands sleep in the atmosphere of distant centuries, with peasant life seemingly undisturbed from that time, while the mountainous, constantly scenic mainland coast swarms with modern hotels, beach resorts, and old cities, like Zadar, Split, and Dubrovnik, that have kept their atmosphere despite the pressures of tourism. My introduction to cruising there was on a family cruise in my son Robby's 25-foot Westerly Tiger sloop, Shere Khan, *which he operated in the Mediterranean for several summers, taking advantage of a teacher's vacation time.*

The allure of the Dalmatian Coast had been a part of my "someday" world for many years. Members of the family had gone there on a

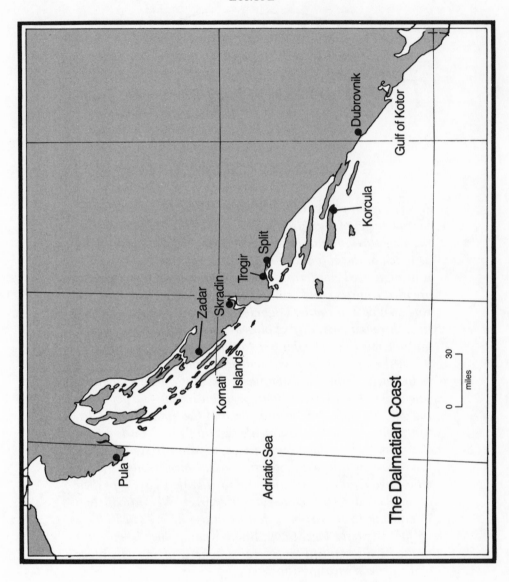

Dubrovnik

Gulf of Kotor

Korcula

Split

Trogir

Zadar

Skradin

Kornati
Islands

Pula

Adriatic Sea

0   30

miles

The Dalmatian Coast

cruise ship in the thirties, returning with tales of romantic isles and walled cities, and just a look at the chart and the lay of the land, with its necklace of closely spaced islands, added fuel.

Jane and I had flown into Dubrovnik as tourists for two days in May 1973 and were taken by its ancient charm, lovely views, warm spring weather, and particularly a steamer excursion to the Gulf of Kotor 40 miles to the south. This is a fjord cutting deeply into the mountains of Montenegro, which ring it with splendid peaks, forming some of the grandest scenery we have seen anywhere.

A year later, I had the chance to do some sailing there when Robby and his wife Carol invited me to join them for a short week. It was my first cruise as a grandfather, with Elizabeth aged 3 and Willie a "basket case" of 6 months, and it was a tight squeeze on the 25-footer. The Tiger is remarkably roomy for her length, however, and we managed quite well. I had extra luggage while flying over, like a full duffle bag of Pampers, and I had to again get used to the fact that frequent tears are really not that serious at those ages. I must say that it was something of a contrast to go directly from *Shere Khan* and the nursery-oriented life aboard, to sail in the 103-foot replica schooner *America* the following week in OpSail 74 in the Baltic.

I joined *Shere Khan* in Zadar, a bustling resort city in the northern stretch of the coast. To get there, I had flown to Frankfurt and then to Ljubljana (*j* in Yugoslavian is pronounced as a *y* and is a vowel, which makes the pronounciation of place names a lot easier) to change planes. Ljubljana, once the capital of the Kingdom of Illyria, is in Slovenia, and I had a chance, while sitting on the airport terrace over a drink as I waited for my plane, to get something of the feel of the lush countryside with afternoon sun shining on the green of the surrounding hills.

Zadar, where *Shere Khan* was in a crowded marina that could be reached only by a short ferry ride, did not seem half as romantic as the old capital of Illyria, but it was a fascinating port, with all sorts of traffic. There were quite a few yachts, with Austrian and German ensigns predominating and a steady parade of work boats, small freighters, and small, lopsided passenger ferries that looked as though they had been

Dubrovnik

The marina at Zadar; rowboat ferry at work

there since shortly after Robert Fulton. Later we often saw them plying the offshore islands.

There are locally owned small boats, despite Yugoslavia's communism, but most of the yachts were visiting, and the only way to get there on charter is to originate in Greece or Italy, as there is no local charter activity. Most of the motorboats were small outboards trailed in from all over Europe, and inflatable sport boats, loaded with camping gear, were particularly noticeable. Yugoslavia may be communist, but it is wide open to tourism and one of the most heavily visited areas in Europe. Tourism is an important part of its economy, and the people who deal with tourists are matter-of-fact and efficient without being overly solicitous or friendly. These are generalities, and there were always exceptions on both sides. Robby had found port officials very brusque and unpleasant on some occasions, but people in the shops and markets were usually quite helpful and friendly, given the language barrier.

Shere Khan was operated European style without ice, since this is totally unavailable in that part of the world, so Carol would start each day by going off to market for milk and fresh food. Shopping by gesture could have its problems, but she seemed to manage remarkably well. Sometimes she went by herself, sometimes she went to the butcher while Robby went to the fruit and vegetable market and I baby-sat, and sometimes we all went. You had to get used to warm drinks, but otherwise the system worked well.

Robby said that the weather had been mild and calm most of the time, and that was the way it remained for my whole cruise. While we had some sailing every day, we did have to power quite often under the little Volvo 10-horsepower diesel, and we had no heavy air except for the edge of a squall or two for a few minutes. In their previous year's cruise up the Adriatic, Robby and Carol had found a preponderance of light northerlies, with one or two strong southerlies to vary things, some calms, and a few thundersqualls along the coast. A particularly vicious one caught them at the base of a mountain in the Gulf of Kotor, and the downdrafts hit them with tornado-like fury. In general, the scenery and the atmosphere ended up to be more important than the sailing experience.

Out of Zadar, we were soon in the Kornati archipelago, and it was an amazing contrast in a very short time. From the rich greens of the mainland, the busy cities, and the enormous tourist hotels, usually standing boldly on hillsides over the water, with stepped tiers of boxlike balconies rising to six or more stories, we were in another world. The Kornats are almost totally devoid of rain, and therefore are the most barren, bleakest kinds of rocks, spectacular in shape, but without vegetation. Here and there, a low valley would have a few trees, and unbelievably, some of the hillsides were terraced for agriculture. How anyone managed to grow anything, I would not know. The sailing was inconsistent: We would have a breeze for a while, go between two islands in a narrow channel—or *kanal,* as they are called on the chart—

and find none on the other side, so there was sail drill and lots of on and off with the engine. The sky was a soft, milky blue and the sun was warm. Incidentally, this was the same latitude, 44°, as the Maine Coast, and there was a nice long evening twilight in July.

The choice of anchorages is unlimited throughout the Dalmatian Coast, the charts are good, and the eyeballing is fairly easy. The main concern is in avoiding restricted military zones. We tried an empty, private cove the first night and an island village called Zlarin the next. Only a few miles from Zadar, it was centuries away in its cluster of stone cottages along the cobbled quay, where women in shawls carried buckets, bundles of twigs, and baskets on their head, or sat around in groups gossiping while the men mended nets or worked on their boats nearby. Carol managed to market here, and we had a good dinner ashore of local fish in a plain little restaurant, where we were reminded that it actually was the twentieth century by men in sleeveless under-shirts gathered in front of a TV screen in the barroom drinking beer or wine and smoking their pipes.

A fascinating expedition took us back to the mainland, through a wide bay, and 12 miles up a winding river to a hamlet called Skradin, which is at the head of navigation. Here several yachts were moored to the town quay, including a big Hatteras, one of the few motor yachts we had seen. We had heard there was a big waterfall upriver, and the way to get there was to hire a local lad in an outboard. He took us through an ever-narrowing channel along pastures and under over-hanging trees until we arrived at a parklike clearing, where boats were pulled up on the bank. As we got out of our small boat, we could hear a rushing, roaring noise coming from beyond the trees, and, making our way through them, we found ourselves suddenly bursting out to a bank at the edge of a vast hillside that was all waterfall. It was not a steeply falling cataract but, rather, a sprawl of white water, split here and there by outcroppings of rocks and trees as it tumbled down into pools spaced over a wide area. The noise was overpowering and the visual effect was of a great lacy kaleidoscope of froth and spray.

This was no hidden retreat. A goodly proportion of the tourists in Yugoslavia seemed to be gamboling around the area. They splashed in

The waterfall near Skradin

the pools, climbed over the rocks that glistened in spray, or just stood along the banks in open-mouthed appreciation. It was a carnival atmosphere, with vendors selling ice cream and balloons, and pony rides for the kids in the woodsy clearing. Eventually everyone had dunked in the clear, cool pools, Elizabeth had had a pony ride, and it was time to take the outboard ride back to Skradin. It had been a magical interlude, far removed from the salty breezes of the Adriatic and the gaunt rocks of the Kornati.

By late afternoon we had made our way back down to an anchorage at the mouth of the river, where a neighboring yacht proved to be a Canadian couple Robby and Carol had met in previous summers in other parts of the Med, and we had one of those catching-up reunions over happy hour that sailors the world over enjoy.

Yet another contrast was our next stop after a motoring session the following day: the walled town of Trogir. This was a perfectly preserved medieval town on the mainland, separated from an offshore island by a narrow cut with a drawbridge. The town breathed the essence of the days when the city states along the Adriatic were of vital importance to the trade between Venice and the Middle and Far East, and yet the island just off it was all industry, with a big ship building yard covering the banks across from Trogir's crenellated walls. The gaunt skeletons of half-built tankers towered over the ugly mix of cranes, warehouses, and machine shops.

Trogir was a trip back five centuries in its well-preserved buildings, courtyards, and churches, with the thick walls of a fortress enclosing everything, and we wandered through it with crowds of tourists.

This should have prepared us for the scene at Split, just a few miles further south, where I was to "split." This ancient city, dominated by the gargantuan ruins of Emperor Diocletian's palace, seems to be the focal point of midsummer tourism in Yugoslavia. There was some sort of jazz festival going on when we crept into a marina at the outer rim of the harbor, and the entire area was crawling with visitors, mostly teenagers in T-shirts celebrating such American universities as Ohio State and UCLA—these were the most popular. In town, and even out on the fringes by the marina, there was a restless surge of bodies crowded together and ever on the move in a seemingly undirected search for something they were not sure of in the fading twilight of a hot summer night. It was almost frightening in sheer numbers, and in the rather vacant-eyed lack of direction as the hordes continued to shove along. There was no overt violence or unpleasantness—just a strange sense of aimless urgency.

As I packed and got ready to fly to Denmark to join *America,* I could not help but be amazed at the contrast between Split's feverish activity and the lonely isolation of the Kornati. I guess both of them were perfectly typical of life along this coast of thoroughly dramatic contrasts.

The Aegean

Nowhere else in the world is there a more glamorous setting for cruising than in the Greek Islands of the Aegean Sea. The combination of starkly beautiful scenery, brilliant blue seas, soft Grecian skies, and the dramatic evidence of centuries of history reaching back to ancient times on almost every point and island hillside is not matched anywhere else. And the sailing is good, though often presenting a special challenge in quick changes of weather and the midsummer prevalance of the meltemi. This is the local "trade wind," a strong norther that blasts down the central Aegean during the hot weeks of July and August, one of nature's most awesome thermals. It blows out of azure sky, usually cloudless, under warm, golden sunlight, with a heft that has to be felt to be believed, often gusting between 40 and 50 knots at its most authoritative in late afternoon. For this reason, spring and fall, as in the Chesapeake, are the preferred cruising times, but my intro-duction to this fabled world was on a July cruise in the sturdy 46-foot British-built cutter Toxotis, *with her Greek owner and crew as hosts. We had our share of windblown meltemi days, but it was still one of the experiences of a lifetime to mix exhilarating sails with visits to the storied relics of ancient civilization.*

"Why are we reefing?"

My question to John Sikiarides, owner of *Toxotis*, seemed a logical one. We were powering over a flat calm Aegean, bright blue in the

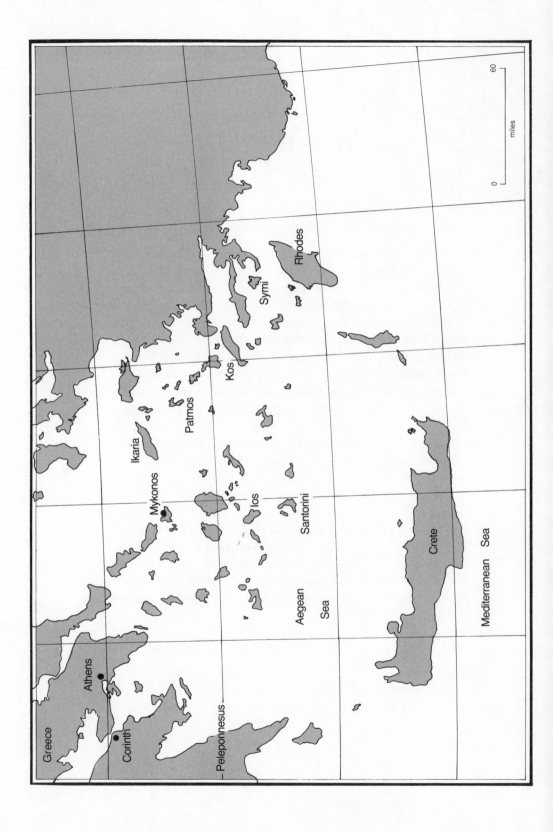

sunlight, not the "wine dark" of Homer's beaten-to-death description. To starboard, the 3000-foot bulk of the island of Ikaria created a lee accounting for the calm. It was a cloudless, warm day, and we were on our way from Patmos to finish up our Greek Islands cruise at Mykonos, where we would catch a steamer to Piraeus.

Markos, the husky professional captain of *Toxotis*, a fine seaman from the isolated little island of Orthonoi, northernmost outpost of Greece in the Adriatic, was busily tying a reef in the main and getting the smallest staysail ready, obviously expecting heavy going.

"Markos thinks it may be blowing when we pass that cape up ahead," John explained. John, a Harvard Business School graduate with his own textile company, spoke English perfectly, but communication with Markos was limited to a few Greek sailing terms I had learned, like *panni* for mainsail, *flocca* for jib, *baloni* for spinnaker, *lasca* for let out, and *ferma* for haul in, plus sign language, gestures, and smiles. Actually, the sailing terms, spelled phonetically from memory here, are more or less a nautical *lingua franca* of the Mediterranean, used by sailors of most of the nations there.

The cape John was referring to was a small spit of land sticking out southward from the east–west axis of Ikaria. It was still a couple of miles ahead in mid-morning, and a long wisp of white, the only blot on the blue of the sky, was stringing southward above it.

Markos was so right. When we had the cape abeam and headed past it into the open, central Aegean, it was as though we had suddenly entered a wind tunnel. From flat calm, we went, in a matter of a couple of hundred feet, to a 40-knot breeze slashing the surface into whitecaps decked with wind streaks. The sky was still clear, the sun was warm, but the white streamer of mist had been a signal to Markos, and all of a sudden it was "hold onto your hair."

Markos had set just the right rig and had the sails up and ready when the wind came. The motor was turned off, and *Toxotis* buried her rail and charged off on a spray-flinging reach. The windward rail aft of the cockpit was the driest place on the boat, and we perched up there between wheel tricks and enjoyed the great feeling of a sailboat powerfully handling rugged conditions.

Since this was midsummer, this was the storied meltemi, the trade wind of the Aegean that Greeks laughingly blame on the Russians. This giant thermal sweeps down from the lands to the north, where Russia is, through the central Aegean, on most summer days. It fans out to the southeast and southwest as the Aegean broadens, but it is a straight norther where we were. Early morning and early evening are the best times to find it in a gentler mood, but we were in it at the height of its midday power, and it was some sail.

The wind was too far forward to weather Mykonos and approach it from the north, so we bore off on a close reach to pass the island to the south. It was an exhilirating 30 miles, made more so by the fact that the Aegean is a lot colder than the air, and the spray that occasionally found us was bracing, to say the least.

Mykonos loomed ahead against the sun glitter on the water, a misty bulk growing better defined as we crashed toward it. It was late afternoon when we came under its lee, and this calmed the seas a bit, but Mykonos, whose hills are only about 1,000 feet, was not high enough to block the meltemi as Ikaria had. Instead, the breeze accelerated down the leeward slopes and was now up to about 50 as it screamed across the water, blowing the tops off of the closely spaced whitecaps and leaving a frothy tracery of wind streaks patterning the dark blue of late afternoon sea. *Toxotis* took it well, with an occasional wallow when an extra gust put us more than rail down, but the last mile into the harbor of Mykonos was dead to windward in the narrow strait between Mykonos and Delos, and it took us almost an hour to plug our way under power into the steep chop and blasting gusts. Once inside the harbor, we moored stern-to a long stone jetty on the northern side, secure in smooth water, while the meltemi howled overhead, waves crashed against the other side of the jetty, and boats on the far side of the harbor bobbled in the chop kicked up in that short distance.

The white buildings of the town gleamed in the late light under the hills, starkly brown in the background, while the hundreds of Mykonos windmills stood as its symbols against the darkening sky. Mykonos, highly overdeveloped in boutiques, souvenir shops, restaurants, and honky-tonks, is the supreme tourist trap of the Aegean, in sharp con-

The stark hills of Ios as a backdrop to an ocean racer

trast to some of the islands we had been seeing, but, in the sunset light and after the stimulation of our fast reach through the meltemi, it was a picturesque coda to our cruise.

This had been our first Aegean adventure in 1966, and therefore the most memorable. It had started when I crewed in *Toxotis* in the Aegean Rally, Greece's premier ocean racing event. We had King Constantine's Olympic Gold Medal (in Dragons at Naples in 1960) crew with us, Odysseas Etzigzoglou and Georges Zaimis. We won the two-part race from Piraeus to Rhodes via Ios, and the celebrations at Rhodes had been monumental. With all the prize award banquets, folklore dancing, fireworks, cocktail parties, and pub crawling at Rhodes finished and the racing crew departed, Jane had switched over from the VIP Tall Ship that had accompanied the race down, and we had taken off on a return cruise with John, Markos, and another American friend of John's.

Aside from all the obvious charms of an Aegean cruise, there was a real attraction for Jane in that she has always been an archeology buff. She had majored in Greek at Smith and had become particularly interested in the archeological side of Greek history. She has read countless books with titles like *The Greek Stones Speak* and accounts of the exploits of Heinrich Schliemann and Sir Arthur Evans in digs at Mycenae, Troy, and Crete, and it was a great plus for her in cruising to come in from a fine sail and, for example, be able to visit the ruins of the Aesculapion on Kos, the world's first hospital. Even without her background, I have to admit that this side of Greek cruising is a great added attraction.

In the *Toxotis* cruise, we naturally could not touch all the high spots of the Aegean, and we have since been back on later cruises to take in Crete, Santorini, Hydra, Aegina, and Paros, to name some we missed on the first visit, but *Toxotis* gave us an introduction we will never forget. Ios, where the race laid over on the way to Rhodes, was about as typical an Aegean island as could be imagined. Homer is supposedly buried there on a remote hillside, and participants in the race were all given medallions to commemorate this.

In its bare, brown hills, dotted with little white chapels, with its waterfront village at the harbor and its main village lying atop the highest hill like some improbable snowdrift, Ios is the epitome of Aegean scenery. Here and there a gnarled olive tree or cedar would be bent to the wind as a lonely break in the brownness, and the incredibly steep slopes would be terraced off here and there for some sort of cultivation, usually grapes.

Jane and I spent the night in a little hotel at the harbor in the cleanest, barest room I have ever been in, with the hardest bed and pillows. When we went to bed, the waterfront plaza below us was still alive with crowds greeting the racers as they arrived. Bouzouki music drifted from the *tavernas* while the islanders cheered the boat crews, and it was quite some time before the revelry tapered off. In the morning everyone was having coffee at the open-air tables, and the racing fleet made an interesting contrast mixed in at the quay with the brightly painted local caïques.

To start our cruise back from Rhodes, we were greeted by the remnant of a meltemi blowing in from the northwest hard enough for Markos to decide on a reef. Our eagerness was tempered by the morning-after effects of the last night of celebrating *Toxotis'* victory, but it was time to be sailing. Markos settled all hesitations by flashing his widest grin and using up a good part of his English vocabulary by saying, "Is okay," and we were off.

A stiff chop greeted us at the entrance to Mandraki Harbor, where deer on pedestals on each jetty mark, in myth only and not fact, the spot where the feet of the Colossus of Rhodes supposedly stood. Across the whitecapped indigo of the strait, the mountains of Turkey were brown against a clear sky as we started to beat westward. The row of Miami-modern hotels on Rhodes beaches dropped slowly astern, giving way to dusty olive groves, spirelike cypresses, and dozens of slowly turning windmills, and the wind began to ease with the rising sun, contrary to the usual behavior of a meltemi. The reef was rolled out, and by noontime we were sliding over a gentle sea approaching the Greek island of Symi, 20 miles from Rhodes. Symi's jagged peaks are enclosed by a pincer of Turkish capes in the Gulf of Doris, and it is one of the least-visited and less-known and lightly populated of the

Aegean islands. In noonday sun we came in from the heave of the sea via a rock-lined dogleg channel to Paneiro Harbor, landlocked and calm. Along the far shore, a long, white building with a red roof and ornate bell tower in the center stood out against the pale blue of the harbor water and dun hills.

Markos backed us into a stern-to mooring at a little pier off the building. From somewhere inside it, accordion music could be heard, while women were hanging wash out the windows and children played in the shade of the pale green tamarisk trees lining the quay and splashed in the shallows. This was Panormiti Monastery, and these unmonastic evidences came from the fact that only an abbot and two monks were left in a dwindling order, and they were making ends meet by renting out the cubicles formerly housing hundreds of monks as low-cost vacation rooms.

Markos found that a fish had been freshly caught that day and arranged for dinner in the little *taverna* outside the monastery. He took tomatoes, lettuce, and cucumbers ashore from the boat, and we gathered, after a siesta, under the feathery tamarisks to start with ouzo as an aperitif. Greeks always eat when they drink, and a small tray of olives, octopus, and feta cheese comes on the table with the drinks. Ouzo, an aromatic liqueur that turns milky when ice or water is added, is one of those native drinks that seems fine in local surroundings but never travels very well when you try to capture the excitement of strange lands while back home in the States. It is also powerful enough so that an ouzo hangover is to be devoutly avoided.

We had beer with the fish and vegetables, though the Greeks do have some pleasant wines and that very special Greek wine *retsina*. Permeated by a strong taste of resin, it is often described as an acquired taste that is very hard to acquire, but none was available for this meal.

Afterward the abbot invited us on a tour of the monastery. A short, dark man with a beard, he led us through his chapel, with its highly intricate carvings, hanging censers, and gold and silver offerings left by worshippers. He was particularly happy to show us, since we were sailors, a small museum of ship models, and he said that some of them had miraculously sailed into the harbor on their own. To wind up, he served us wine and candy in a special sitting room that was mainly used for the twice-yearly visits of the Bishop of Rhodes. Glimpses like this behind the scenes of local life always add to the charm of a cruise.

It was back to sight-seeing more normally the next day, and we had a good sail along the Turkish coast for 30 miles to Kos. At one point, we were close under a lighthouse high on the cliffs, and the flag outside it was dipped in salute, which we returned with our British ensign. In those days, very few yachts were under Greek registry because of high taxes, a situation that has since been changed.

John laughed and said, "If they knew we were Greek, they would probably shoot at us instead," referring to the centuries-old animosity between Greeks and Turks.

The aspect of the islands changed constantly as we weaved through them and took in the rugged hills, the terraced vineyards, the white dots of chapels in improbably isolated spots, and the hilltop villages and monasteries. Over the centuries, the Greeks, who have been invaded and conquered time and again, have learned to defend their villages by building them in the most inconvenient mountaintop locations.

The Aesculapion, where it is possible to see how well it was laid out for ventilation and drainage, was impressive in its hilltop setting, and we then took a drive to the far end of Kos to Astypolea and the ruins of the ancient capital, where we had a swim on a deserted beach below the ruins of a Byzantine church. On a tiny island off the beach, a miniature one-room chapel stood on its highest crag, brilliantly white in the afternoon sun against the deep blue water. It had been built years ago by a seaman as an offering to St. Nicholas for having survived a bad storm at sea. Once a year, priests rowed out to light candles on its altar.

From Kos to Patmos, we were in waters where British and Italian warships staged World War II night battles at high speed in the incredibly narrow waters, and at Leros we made a luncheon stop in a large harbor that was the main Italian naval base in the Dodecanese when Italy held them between the two world wars. Enormous deserted warehouses lined the shore as a reminder of the Italian presence.

In late afternoon we came into well-protected Scala Harbor at Pat-

Patmos, with the town of Chora and monastery on top of the hill

mos, where we anchored stern-to the quay with other yachts returning from the rally. One of them was the 92-foot ketch *Aries* of John Theodorakopoulos, which was originally built for R. J. Reynolds. We were handsomely entertained aboard by John, who later sold her and bought the 12-Meter *Nefertiti*.

At sunset, after all the town's taxis were finished with taking passengers from a cruise ship on tours, we were able to get one to take us to the mountaintop monastery of St. Christodoulos, which dates from

Tavernas on the Piraeus waterfront

1088 A.D. It soars into the sky in a dramatic show of battlements, with the village of Chora forming a snowy white skirt around it. John Sikiarides knew the abbot, and we were welcomed by him as we crossed a moat and passed through a huge, heavy gate. Leading us through a maze of corridors and courtyards, he showed us the chapel's incense-filled Byzantine chambers, where every inch was crammed with jeweled crosses, icons, censers, candles and jeweled presentation pieces, some from the Russian royal family, in almost suffocating profusion.

The relic of St. Christodoulos was on a special silver shrine.

As the last light settled over the harbor far below, we were taken to the battlements. The sunset still glowed in the west, but the sea below us was dark, perhaps that "wine dark" it is supposed to be, and a soft gold light covered the landscape stretching away below the monastery walls. The white cubes of Chora's houses reflected the sun's colors before night took over, and we walked back down to the harbor through the windswept night.

Again we ate in a waterfront *taverna*, with the rigging of the boats at the pier outlined by lights. It was a night when the men would get up from their dinners of lamb, fish, and eggplant and dreamily dance solo to a xylophone and scrappy fiddle, gradually joining handkerchiefs and whirling faster and kicking higher as the tempo increased.

When a visit like this was followed by our meltemi-swept sail to Mykonos, we felt we had wrapped up Greek island cruising about as well as we possibly could.

Part III

THE PACIFIC

Puget Sound

In contrast to the East Coast, with its many indentations and Intracoastal Waterway, the Pacific Coast is a comparative desert for the cruising yachtsman. Southern Californians have only Catalina and the Ensenada area of Mexico as nearby targets, or else they have to take the long journey to the Gulf of California in Mexico. North to San Francisco, the coast has few harbors and no inland waters, and San Franciscans are confined to their bay and the Sacramento Delta for limited cruising. It is not until the very far northwest that there is inland cruising, and Puget Sound makes up for other lacks in its profusion of harbors and islands and its spectacular scenery. In itself, it is a fine cruising area, and it gives on interesting ones to the north, reaching all the way to Alaska.

As a price, Northwest yachtsmen have to put up with a general lack of wind in the summer months, plus more rain than most areas produce, but they have the benefit of mild winters and a consequently longer season that can almost be stretched to 12 months by hardy enthusiasts.

This, if you will excuse the expression, was a powerboat cruise, our only one except for canal boats. If there had to be a powerboat cruise, this was a good time and place for it, and it worked out well. It did not, however, go so far as to make me act like the yachtsman in the famous cartoon by Darrell McClure published years ago in *Yachting* in which the man, surrounded by pictures of sailboats in his room at

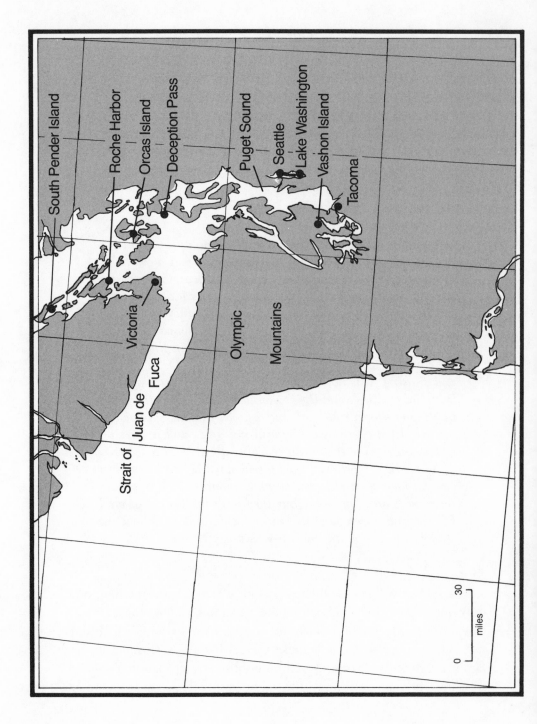

South Pender Island

Roche Harbor
Orcas Island
Deception Pass

Puget Sound
Seattle
Lake Washington
Vashon Island

Tacoma

Victoria

Olympic
Mountains

Strait of
Juan de
Fuca

0   30
miles

home, is down on his knees, saying, "Dear Lord, forgive me. I went on a motorboat, and I LIKED it!"

Though not converted, under the circumstances we "liked" it enough to be grateful for the chance to see so much of a fabulous cruising area in the short span of a week. I had covered the start of the Transpac Race, San Pedro to Honolulu, on July 4th, and this northwest cruise was a way of filling in the interval while the race boats were on their 2,300-mile course, before we headed for Hawaii to catch them at the finish. This was the 1963 race, and, like so many other cruises of that era when our daughters were in their teens, Jane and the girls came with me. Meanwhile Robby was in the transatlantic race Newport, Rhode Island, to England, halfway around the world.

Our boat was a 32-foot Fairliner cruiser, loaned out of Tacoma by the manufacturer. She was a wooden planing boat capable of 40 miles per hour with her twin 250-horsepower Crusader engines, and a very popular local type. Although she had that maximum speed, she cruised "on top" easily at about 22 knots. All of this was very new to us, indoctrinated as we were to *Mar Claro's* 24 feet, six-horse outboard, and absolute top speed of about 7 knots, technically more than she was capable of, and we had a few lessons to learn.

It was hard to adjust to the new type of scheduling, in which we could cover in an hour or so the distance that would take us a whole day in a cruising auxiliary. Instead of arriving at midafternoon, we would find ourselves at a destination before noon, and we had to work up things to do once we had arrived. We also found that the atmosphere aboard was entirely different. Instead of lolling at the tiller, I had to sit tensely at the controls, ever watchful for driftwood, which abounds in Puget Sound, and for the navigation marks that flashed by. If we went any slower than a planing speed of more than 20 knots, which allowed us good visibility ahead, the boat settled back with her bow up at an angle, and it was impossible to see over it.

So we hung on at this dizzying speed, but the girls were not happy, as it was too noisy to listen to the radio or even talk, and there was nothing I could assign to them in the running of the vessel, no sheets to tend or wheel tricks to take. Getting there, therefore, was not half the fun, in fact it was much less. Then, when we got there, we found there was a social drawback. Normally we would fraternize with people on other sailboats, comparing notes and talking the same language. Since we were on a powerboat, however, we found we were nonpersons in the eyes of the cruising sailboat people in the marinas, and we felt ostracized. To overcome this, I would sidle up alongside a cruising auxiliary and strike up a sailboat-type conversation with those aboard, establishing our true credentials before eventually admitting that we were "temporarily" on a stinkpot.

This was just a matter of personal adjustment, and, actually, with a week at our disposal, we were able to visit a lot more of this marvelous cruising area than a sailboat would have allowed us to see in our allotted time. Early July is not the best time for sailing anyway, as the breezes are very light and fitful, and much of our passaging in an auxiliary would have been under power during the time we were there. We saw very few real sailing breezes, and the tidal currents are something to be reckoned with.

We did see a great variety of weather, most of it wet. The Pacific Northwest is famous for its rain and fogs, and we had a goodly share of them. Even in the "sunny San Juans," the group of islands between the mainland, where the U.S.–Canadian border lies, and Vancouver Island at the seaward side of the Sound, we saw clouds and rainy days. The San Juans are supposed to have their own separate weather in a special pocket where the boisterous wet breezes coming in through the Strait of Juan de Fuca from the Pacific separate and leave an area of mild, generally sunny conditions.

Rain and clouds or not, the scenery that backdrops Puget Sound cruising is as awesome as any in the civilized world. In the Tacoma area, Mount Rainier hovers over the scene like a great white father. Northward from Seattle, Mount Baker's snowcap and lesser satellite peaks have a distant grandeur far inland, and the Olympic Range is in dramatic profile on the south side of Juan de Fuca. To an Easterner used to the sand dunes of Southern New England being the tallest things visible from a cruising boat, it is a matter of constant shock and wonderment to look up from the immediate surroundings of water,

136

buoys, and boats and catch a breathtaking glimpse of a distant snow peak.

The foreground scenery would seem familiar to a Maine-iac or someone used to the Georgian Bay area of the Great Lakes. Pine-clad rocks and myriad coves, channels, and passes through a maze of islands have the same aspect as these areas, with a wonderful, heady feeling in the air. All in all, considering the lack of wind and the number of places there were to see, we were probably lucky that we had a swift powerboat to take us on our cruise.

On the first day, it took us wetly from Tacoma 30 miles north to Seattle. The evening before, flying in from Southern California just at sunset, which remained perpetual as the jet followed it north, Rainier had been a stirring spectacle as we banked around it into Sea-Tac airport, with the snowcap catching the last rays of the sun in glowing fire. Now it was lost in gloom and murk as we made our way through half-mile visibility and driving rain into Seattle's fantastic Shilshole Bay marina. At that time it was the biggest marina I had ever seen, a 1,200-boat facility with control tower, large administration building, uniformed attendants, and acres of concrete.

We were in freeway-type traffic as we closed the entrance and were directed to a transient berth at the end of one of the long floating piers. With a 10- to 12-foot tide range, floats are a necessity here. There was everything ashore a cruising yachtsman might need, except a handy liquor store. Washington had one of those state-controlled package store systems that kept the shops hidden in strange locations and open only at odd hours.

Once we found a package store that was open, we were off on a bright clear morning that followed the rain, running north inside Whidbey Island and headed for Deception Pass. The names of passing landmarks had an exotic ring, like Utsaladdy, Possession Point, Strawberry Point, and Swinomish Channel, the Olympics were a blue loom far off to port, and Mount Baker and friends were playing hide-and-seek in a tumble of cumuli on the eastern horizon. Deception Pass was an eye-opener and another good reason to be in a powerboat. It made Hell Gate and Woods Hole look like millponds, with its eddies,

Orcas Island

whirlpools with depressed centers, overfalls, and swirling patches of foam racing by at over 5 knots. It also marked another aspect of Puget Sound cruising. As we approached it we were in breezy sunshine, but a few hundred yards beyond the high arched bridge that spans it between Whidbey and Fidalgo Islands, we were on a flat, windless sea with low overcast; ahead the San Juans' peaks were shrouded in mist.

This was our first target, with a stop at the summer home of friends at West Sound on Orcas Island, largest of the San Juans at 57 square

138

miles, capped by 2,400-foot Mount Constitution. The peak was lost in mist as we made our landing, as was most of the surrounding area of handsome camps and summer homes, with yachts and private planes moored in front. Despite the drippy skies, a clambake was in progress on the rocks above the cove, with evening twilight lasting until almost 2200, and our girls perked up at the sight of waterskiing equipment on the shore front floats. Their faces fell a bit when they saw that the youngsters skiing were all in wet suits, a must with the water temperature in the low 50s.

From here it was onward internationally, with a fog-shrouded run to South Pender Island to enter Canadian customs as part of a parade of boats. The formalities were over in minutes, and we were on our way again to Victoria on Vancouver Island. More odd-sounding names popped up as we moved along, such as Coal Island, Canoe Cove, and what seemed to be the aptly named Useless Bay. Victoria is tuned to tourism and is a colorful, hospitable stop for visiting boats, with free dockage at floats in the heart of town amid formal gardens and velvety green of lawns. The city reeks of atmosphere allied with its name and plays it up with London-style double-decker buses, a wax museum, and bagpipers to meet the ferries from the States. A special feature on display in a waterfront park is *Tilikum*, the odd, three-masted converted Indian canoe that Captain Voss used to circumnavigate the globe early in the century in an attempt to outdo the renown that had come to Joshua Slocum after his voyage in *Spray*.

Voss' book, *The Venturesome Voyages of Captain Voss*, is a classic of small-boat voyaging, and I have always chuckled at a couple of the incidents. He had signed on a newspaperman to come with him and do the necessary writing to get Voss the publicity he wanted, but the first storm they met sent the writer scrambling up the foremast like a terrified cat. Despite all Voss' pleadings, and the very real danger to the vessel of this lofty weight, he refused to come down, and Voss had a rugged time trying to keep *Tilikum* from capsizing. Needless to say, the writer disappeared at the next port, and Voss wrote his own book.

Later on, in Sydney, Australia, he exhibited *Tilikum* in a park a mile from the water, charging a shilling to those who wanted to have a look at the vessel. As crowds came and went, one stout lady remained plunked in the cockpit. Voss finally asked her how long she intended to stay, the woman informed him that she was not budging until she got the sailboat ride she had paid a shilling for.

Tilikum is a strange sight in today's world of fiber glass and synthetics.

Added local color in Victoria includes the nineteenth century parliament building right on the harbor, which is outlined in lights at night, and another relic of that century, the Empress Hotel, a true bastion of Victorian atmosphere with its dark stone battlements. We took the girls to dinner there, telling them that they would not see many places like this elsewhere in their lifetime. It was a step back 75 years in its high-ceiling rooms, flowered carpets, dark paneling, and heavy napery, with a string quartet playing behind potted palms, and waitresses dressed like characters in "Upstairs, Downstairs." As a reminder of how we had gotten there, a seagull sat on the windowsill outside our table and regarded us with a beady eye all through dinner.

This was our outermost point, and we headed back east in a fresh sea breeze that blew in through Juan de Fuca replacing the foggy calm of the last few days. We could have used a sailboat now, but the Fairliner took it well on her quarter while we crossed Haro Strait to Roche Harbor on San Juan Island. We came in through a narrow entrance called Mosquito Pass, and the atmosphere changed from salt sea breeze to north woods as we tied up at the 200-boat marina and entered U.S. customs.

As an odd reminder that we were back in the U.S. of A., the uniformed customs officer staged a sunset ceremony, flanked by three dock attendants in T-shirts and khakis, executing evening colors on the roof of the customs house with snappy military precision while a loudspeaker blared the "Colonel Bogey March."

For the first time since we had seen Mount Rainier reflecting the evening light, we had a sunset here, a spectacular display of colors playing behind the dark silhouette of the evergreens, followed by a gradually fading glow that pearled the sky until well after 2200.

Our homeward push was straight down the middle of the Sound to

Mt. Rainier looming over Commencement Bay, Tacoma

Port Townsend, with a patch of clear weather off to port showing why the San Juans have earned the tag "sunny." Port Townsend was a drab, neglected looking commercial town, with a softball game in a field near the marina the big excitement, but I understand that it has since been developed along "quaint" lines and has enjoyed some prosperity as a result.

At Seattle we poked through the canal to Lakes Union and Washington, sight-seeing the marinas, boatyards, and waterfront homes in a bright sun that was the best weather of the week, and it held for a morning run down the west side of Vashon Island, a long skinny affair of wooded hills that almost fills the Sound in this area. In the narrow channel, we were close enough under the shore so that there were no distant views, and as we rounded the southern end of Vashon and came into Commencement Bay off Tacoma, a fleet of racing sailboats under spinnaker spread before us in a light breeze. Then, as a sudden shock to the sensibilities, there was Rainier towering behind them in sunlit splendor, breathtaking in the startling new dimension of grandeur it lent to the scene. It was a fitting last reminder, we thought, of just how special the cruising scenery can be in Puget Sound.

Fiji

The Fiji archipelago, in the middle of the South Pacific, just across the date line is a large complex of islands and inland waters that would be one of the world's prime cruising areas if it were a little more handy. Its 300-plus islands range from tiny rocks to massive Viti Levu, 100 miles long, with mountains close to 4,000 feet in its interior. The islands and their fringing reefs enclose a body of water called the Koro Sea that is 100 miles wide, and it is possible to be in the middle of it, inside the Fiji group, and be out of sight of land.

Fijians are a handsome, physically powerful people who have only recently, in historic sense, come to civilized ways, as cannibalism was prevalent there until late in the nineteenth century. They have been joined by a large population of Indians (from India, not the American variety) who handle much of the commercial life as storekeepers and businessmen.

Long a British colony, which it was while I was there, Fiji is now an independent nation.

Wartime subchaser duty had taken me to many places in the Gulf of Mexico, Caribbean, and South Pacific that I never wanted to see or hear of again, but there were others which remained in the memory differently. They had something that made me want to go back, and at the top of the list was Fiji, the mid-Pacific archipelago 2,800 miles southwest of Hawaii and 1,700 miles east of Australia.

One of the strongest impressions I carried away from the dragged out three-month convoy that took us across the Pacific from Panama

143

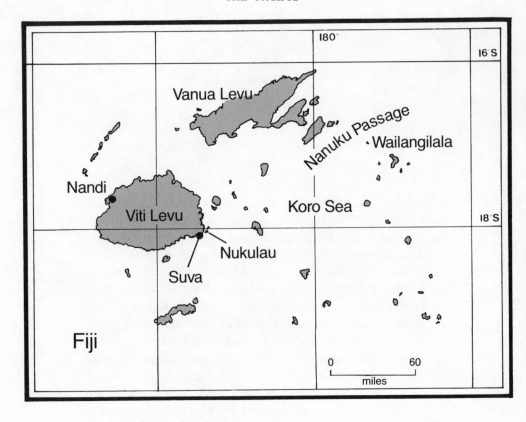

Fiji

to Australia via Bora-Bora, Samoa, Fiji, and New Caledonia was a
day-long passage across the Koro Sea, a 100-mile-wide body of water
completely ringed by Fiji's islands and reefs. We entered it in early
morning through Nanuku Passage at its northeast corner, with an island
called Wailangilala marking the pass in the mauve light of dawn.

All day long we steamed southwestward with our slow convoy of
LSTs as a southeast trade fresh in the warm sunlight, built the blue of
the sea into marching whitecaps. At first we were out of sight of all but
a few low-lying islets, but gradually the blue loom of mountain peaks
appeared in the west in the approach to Viti Levu. This is the main
island, 3,700 feet high and over 100 miles across, site of Suva, the
capital. In those days it was a British colony, but it has since achieved
independence.

That day of what would have been ideal sailing weather, with islands
and reefs to explore all along the horizon, stayed with me as a vague
dream of the distant waters I would someday like to cruise, and it
remained just that, a vague dream, for many years. Then came the
chance to implement it. On the way home from a trip to Australia on
which I covered their 1962 America's Cup preparations, I could, by
taking advantage of the day gained at the international date line, spend
a three-day weekend in Fiji. By writing to the Fiji Visitors Bureau,
where a yachtsman answered my letter, I was able to arrange the charter
of the queen of the fleet at the Royal Suva Yacht Club; this was the
Arthur Robb-designed pre-war 8-meter sloop *Tamatea*, owned by Heath
Hemphill, who was secretary of the yacht club.

The main airport of Fiji is at Nandi on the northwest coast of Viti
Levu, and it is a 130-mile flight across the mountains and jungle to a
small airport at Suva. In checking into the hotel at Nandi after an
evening arrival from Sydney, I gave my luggage to a barefoot bellboy
gotten up in a white jacket and a lavalava skirt. He had the massive
bush of hair that is usual for Fijians, and I plunked my fedora hat on
top of the bush as he disappeared down the hall, while I was still
checking at the desk. It was not until I got back to civilization in San
Francisco several days later that I realized I had never seen the hat
again. I am sure he was the hit of Nandi in it.

The Fijian crew

Fijians are famous for their magnificent physique as well as their hairdos, and they have a slow, crinkling smile that is the essence of friendliness. Their greeting is a booming "Boolah!" In the modern-day surroundings of its airport, hotels, the bustle of Suva, and the yachts and freighters in the harbor, it was interesting to contemplate that there is a monument near Suva on the spot where the last white man was killed by cannibals. At the time of my visit, that was only 85 years previously.

The Royal Suva Y.C., where I joined *Tamatea* after a morning flight from Nandi (fedora-less), is a rambling building with wide porches overlooking a lawn at harbor's edge, and it could be any one of a number of familiar clubs in the States, except for the exotic blooms of its garden. Its display of burgees from other clubs tacked up on the walls contained many familiar U.S. ones. I was amused that that of the Corinthians, taken there by one of my fellow members, Hank Strauss, a couple of years previously, was right over the men's room.

Hemphill had fortified himself with companionship in case, I assumed, the visiting Yank proved difficult. His friend, Rick, a fellow New Zealander (Kiwi) like Hemphill, had been recruited to come along, and two Fijians were also aboard as crew. They were beautifully coordinated and swift in moving about the deck, with typical slow, friendly Fijian smiles, and they hardly talked at all, even to each other, in the three days aboard. Rick seemed a very suave and cosmopolitan man of the world for someone who had just finished 15 years on a banana plantation deep in the heart of Viti Levu. He said there were areas up there where it rained almost constantly in both wet and dry seasons. Hemphill was a rangy, freckled man with a booming voice, outgoing, and at home in dealing with all sorts of people. As it turned out, we made a highly compatible crew, at least from my point of view.

Tamatea, a dignified old lady, had been kept in fine shape for tropical use. She had few frills or brightwork, but everything was freshly painted and functional. As a meter boat, she was naturally cramped for her 50 feet of overall length, with sitting headroom only in her narrow cabin, four transom bunks (the natives slept on deck), a bottled-gas stove, and a chemical head. Her only auxiliary was a Seagull outboard on the dinghy. Her sails were cotton and very carefully tended and in good shape.

After a welcoming session in the club bar, we took off at about noon as a sea breeze riffled in from the southeast, tacking past the piers. Freighters were being worked by dusty stevedores, whose shouts carried across the water. Home ports of the ships were a worldwide geography lesson. Sailing a meter boat is always an exercise in lively action, as they are so close winded, accelerate so beautifuly, and set up their own breeze so well in carrying through lulls. Relaxed as we were, it was still practically like starting a race to make our way out of the harbor.

Tamatea at Nukulau

Once outside, the breeze took on new authority, and we headed off to the eastward on a fast, close reach, heeled well over. It has to be a virtual flat calm for one of these narrow boats to stay on an even keel, and their sailing lines are figured at an angle of heel. We were headed to a round dollar of an islet called Nukulau inside a pass through the barrier reef at the edge of the Koro Sea, and we slid along gracefully over a smooth surface, with the sun bright on the clear, green water, and the surf on the barrier reef a creamy fringe off to starboard.

As we neared Nukulau, the weather lost some of its brilliance. The sky was filling rapidly with high clouds and the breeze hardened. The higher peaks of Viti Levu had already disappeared behind drifting rain clouds when we dropped anchor off a little concrete pier on Nukulau and took a stern line over to the pier in the dink. This was the leeward side of the island in normal conditions, but we were in the tag end of the rainy season in March, when the weather often does abnormal things. We had hardly settled down before the wind veered into the west and began to blow harder. We could see a frontal line of froth headed for us under a low-flying swirl of clouds, dark and menacing, and Heath decided to get out of the now-exposed spot before it hit us. The boys worked rapidly in getting the anchor up and the staysail set, and we reached out to the protection of the pass, only a few hundred yards away, heeling rail down before the first gusts of the squall. Bursts of rain lashed us and swirled on by, making a great splashy fuss on the water.

In the pass, with reefs on two sides, there was no sea, and *Tamatea*, with the easy maneuverability of a meter boat, reached back and forth in the protected water, making easy going of it, until the last dash of rain sped on by and the wind dropped off to a wet whisper. Back at the anchorage, Heath decided not to moor fore-and-aft but, rather, to swing at anchor, because of the uncertainty of the weather, which Radio Suva predicted would last for another day.

At sunset, there was a temporary clearing period revealing a dramatic play of clouds suffused in color over Viti Levu, amid vast perspectives back into the mountains of peaks misting in the twilight, and more great tiers of clouds. The night settled in black and quiet, with night sounds drifting out from Nukulau and vagrant splashes and plunks in the water alongside.

Heath cooked a fine dinner of native vegetables and fish, and we spent the evening over pink gins reminiscing about wartime New Guinea, where it turned out all of us had done duty. We won the war easily many times over that night.

Radio Suva had been right about the next day, which happened to be Saint Patrick's Day. There was not a breath of wind and the rain continued, varying only in its intensity, from heavy to very heavy. If I had not been reminded of New Guinea with all our stories the night before, this very New Guinea-like day would have brought back its atmosphere forcibly. And if I had hoped for atmospheric South Sea Islands music on the radio, I would have had to settle for "Danny Boy," which was played over and over again all day on Radio Suva.

The rain was so warm that it was comfortable to be out in it in a bathing suit, and we explored the reef in the dink and beachcombed ashore on a complete circuit of Nukulau—about a mile. The beach was covered with shells, especially on the side toward the pass in the reef, with many strange varieties I had never seen before.

Another session of pink gins and sea stories got us through the evening, after another sunset panorama that allowed us glimpses through avenues of clouds to the blue-black storms pouring their watery freight on Viti Levu. The morning was better, however. A disturbance south of the islands had moved on, leaving a bright sun to steam over the saturated scene, and the trade came back from the southeast, blowing briskly across the reef.

After her day's inactivity, *Tamatea* came alive enthusiastically for another fine reach inside the reef to Suva. Inland, the cloud castles still formed fantastic shapes over the mountains, but we were in a fresh salty breeze from the open sea. I had not experienced the whitecapped excitement of the Koro Sea I had hoped to recapture, so the Fiji archipelago still stands as one of those places of future challenge, but this had been a colorful interlude.

Les Iles sous le Vent

Since the days of Captain Cook, Captain Bligh, Herman Melville, and Nantucket whalers, the islands of which Tahiti is the anchor have been a universal symbol for tropical glamor. Les Iles sous le Vent, or the Leewards, if you will, in English, are a French colony in the South Pacific at 17° S and 150° W, some 4,800 miles from Panama, and the name comes from the fact that the other islands, Moorea, Huahine, Raiatea, Tahaa, and Bora-Bora, are all downwind from Tahiti in the prevailing easterly trades. Tahiti has long attracted world voyagers, and its waterfront hosts many of them today, but the sailing we did was in the outer group, 100 miles northwest of Tahiti. Here Raiatea and Tahaa share one big fringing reef, with Bora-Bora 25 miles to the west and Huahine the same distance the other way. It is a delightful, compact area that has recently opened up to bareboating. The climate is a steady one year round, with hurricanes much less of a threat, on percentage, than in the Caribbean or in the Western Pacific. Pleasant trade winds blow as steadily as winds blow anywhere.

In June 1943, at the end of a 23-day convoy from Panama, the distinctive double peak of Bora-Bora loomed over the horizon as our first landfall and my first sight of a South Pacific island. From the bridge of a navy subchaser it was a thrilling sight, never to be forgotten, and I had often wondered whether I would ever see it again.

Now, almost 40 years later, it was there once more. This time the

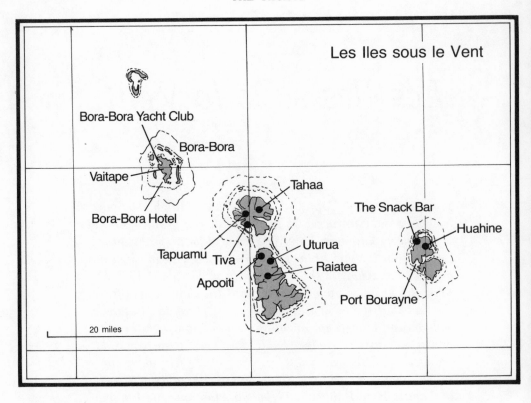

Les Iles sous le Vent

Bora-Bora Yacht Club

Bora-Bora

Vaitape

Bora-Bora Hotel

Tahaa

The Snack Bar

Huahine

Tapuamu   Tiva

Uturua

Raiatea

Apooiti

Port Bourayne

20 miles

auspices were much more pleasant. The vessel was the Peterson 44 *Essouffle* run by South Pacific Yacht Charters, and the view at sunrise was from a harbor called Tapuamu on Tahaa. We had just spent our first night aboard, a deep sleep of conquering jet lag after the flight from the East Coast via Los Angeles, and the first rays of the rising sun, which had not yet cleared the mountains of Tahaa and penetrated our anchorage, were turning Bora-Bora's bold profile a misty greenish gold. In a short while, as soon as our anchor chain was recovered from the 80-foot depths of Tapuamu's harbor, we would be off on the 25-mile westward sail across the open Pacific to Bora-Bora and a long-awaited fulfillment of a dream.

In the days before bareboat chartering was established in this area, the fulfillment of the dream would have meant a 4,800-mile passage from Panama or a 4,000-mile one from the Pacific Coast, and an amazing number of people have taken the time out of their lives to do just that. All too often, disillusionment set in before the magic landfall appeared, and many a boat sitting forlornly stern-to the quay in Papeete, Tahiti, tells the story of broken dreams, disrupted crews, and abandoned plans.

For us, it was a lot easier. We had taken over *Essouffle* at South Pacific Yacht Charters' headquarters in a new government marina at Apooiti in Raiatea, hard by the airport where our connecting plane from Tahiti had deposited us after the 100-mile flight.

After deplaning, we had had a thorough briefing from South Pacific Yacht Charters' local manager Dave Baglow, who had previously sent us off on charters in the British Virgins and Tonga over the years. He had written a very complete guide to the more than 80 possible anchoring spots in the four islands, and had marked up the French charts as well. We were to have a helping hand aboard, Larry Nufer, a young Californian who had given up a plumbing career in Santa Barbara to deliver a Peterson 44 to Raiatea and decided to stay on, but it was still good to get the word from Dave. His main advice was to get into the passes in the reefs before 1530 to have good light. This is a sensible precaution, but we found the passes very easy to identify and negotiate. It might be different in a low-visibility rain squall or with a late afternoon sun

Part of the fleet at the quay in Papeete

in your eyes. When I heard that the most shallow overnight anchorage we would find would be at least 80 feet, I was doubly glad to have strong-backed young Larry along. There was a windlass, but it was still quite a job to get the all-chain anchor rode up. As far as I am concerned, this is the only drawback to a wonderful and very exciting cruising area.

The briefing over in late morning, we had taken off on a fast reach in the trades northward to Tahaa, slipping along in the smooth water inside the reef. Alone in Tapuamu, we barely made it through the dramatic rise of a nearly full moon over Tahaa's peaks before we collapsed in jet-lagged torpor and slept the night through. The sight of Bora-Bora glowing on the horizon was enough to wake us up quickly, and after Larry had sweated up the anchor out of the depths, we were off down the coast of Tahaa past the village of Tiva and its typical, dominant, red-roofed church to a pass in the reef.

The passes are a distinctive feature of Les Iles sous le Vent. There are only a few on each island: Bora-Bora only has one, and there is a feeling of excitement and expectancy when the surge of the open sea meets the calm lagoon waters. On the reefs on each side of the pass, which is usually a couple of hundred yards across, fishermen stand as lonely splinters in the watery waste, casting lines or nets, with a small boat anchored somewhere nearby as transport. The never-ceasing surge of long swells from the open sea forms a necklace of white as the combers selfdestruct on the reef; and on the leeward side, as this was, the spray blowing backward from the last great curl of a wave is a lovely, lacy counterpoint to the thrust of the surge.

Out of the wind cone of Tahaa when we cleared the pass, we picked up the fresh trade and had an exhilirating reach across the deep blue of the Pacific, with Bora-Bora looming closer as *Essouffle* swept toward it. Flying fish skittered away from us in frantic showers, and booby birds swooped low around us while we rose and fell in an easy rhythm over the open-ocean swells, sailing at its hull-speed best.

When we rounded the southwest tip of the reef, the seas quieted and the wind became puffy and erratic in the lee of Bora-Bora's steep double peak, as distinctive a landfall as there is anywhere. We powered through the pass over a diminishing surge, entered at the village of Viatape, which was unrecognizable from the sleepy collection of shacks I remembered from 1943, and then went eastward in the lagoon to anchor off the Bora-Bora Hotel. This is on a point at the east end of the main island, one of those combinations of simplicity and luxury that is the epitome of an out-island-type resort.

We watched the now-full moon rise above the point countering a multihued sunset at the other end of the lagoon, and then went ashore to the hotel for a fine seafood dinner and a floor show of native dancing and song that was professionally done but simple and pleasant. The famous drums of Bora-Bora were a part of it, and their insistent rhythm throbbed in our subconscious long afterward. Once again we were in 85 feet of water, but the next day we went into the "shallows" between a small island and the outer reef and found a 35-foot spot for a midday anchorage while we explored ashore. The pastels of the water here, in gradations out to the exposed reef, and the deep cobalt beyond match any I have seen in clarity and variety of hues, especially on a day of bright sun.

In late afternoon we moved westward in the lagoon to the Bora-Bora Yacht Club, actually a commercial restaurant that is a gathering place for long voyagers passing through. There were perhaps 10 boats anchored off it (again in about 90 feet), including *Havaiiki*, an Alden ketch with a New Zealand family aboard with whom we had exchanged charts in Antigua two years previously while cruising in our own boat. It was a happy reunion, and they told us that we had hit the right night, since the yacht club was staging a pig roast luau for the boats in the anchorage and all were welcome (for a fee, of course).

It was one of those nights when sailors from many lands and many backgrounds mingle freely and easily, swapping sea stories, tossing off rum, dancing, singing, and having a fine time. The music was loud and enthusiastic in that insistent South Sea Islands beat, and we found ourselves dancing happily with a variety of strangers. I even thought I could speak French fluently before the evening was over.

Larry said that many charterers just go to Bora-Bora and enjoy themselves there, but we wanted to see the other islands too, so we headed back to Raiatea in the morning. The trade was enough in the northeast so that we made the pass off Apooiti in one tack from the tip of Bora-Bora—another fine sail. We tucked into a cove inside the pass as the only boat there, surrounded by hills on which rows of trees had been planted in an exact pattern, a quiet night in contrast to the revelry of the previous one.

Huahine now lay 25 miles to windward, and we headed for it by

Essouffle in Port Bourayne, Huahine

powering around the north end of Raiatea, doubling back past its capital city, Uturoa, a bustling commercial center of about 10,000 people. As we went by, a fleet of little Optimist prams, with red and green striped sails, was maneuvering off the piers, where two freighters were berthed, one bright red and one a glistening white. The little boats were manned by schoolchildren in orange life jackets, followed by an instructor in a Boston Whaler, and they were having short races. Sailing instruction is a part of French schooling in these maritime areas. We had seen the same sort of thing in St. Bart in the Caribbean. They were going at it seriously, with great concentration, an unexpectedly colorful scene with the town and freighters as a backdrop.

The wind had been lightening, and when we cleared the pass and set sail for Huahine's blue bulk, it went even fainter, so we ended up motorsailing most of the way across, over an uneven, lumpy sea, restless in the absence of the trade. We might have made it under sail, as the Peterson is an able performer, but it would not have been by the 1530 deadline for making the pass. There was no problem in negotiating it, and we anchored in about 70 feet off the sleepy little town.

Huahine has never had the publicity and glamor buildup of Bora-Bora or Moores, although there is a Bali Hai hotel there, a sister to ones on Moorea and Raiatea. They are another example of simple luxury that retains the atmosphere of the area while providing all the modern comforts.

We were glad we had chosen to come, because the town and the island are an unspoiled example of local life. The village main street, sleepy under tall trees, is lined with stores, mostly run by Chinese, catering to the native trade and crammed with every conceivable kind of goods in a picturesque jumble. A haven for visiting yachtsmen, of which there were quite a few on the half dozen or so boats at anchor, is a snack bar aptly named The Snack Bar, run by an American, whose elderly schooner is anchored off, and his Polynesian wife. There was nothing formal going on, as at the Bora-Bora Yacht Club, but there was an easy camaraderie around the tables and enough local color to go a long way. We had a snack-type dinner there while watching the "floor show."

The highlight of Huahine, though, was a wonderful landlocked lagoon a few miles to the south inside the reef called Port Bourayne. The entrance is narrow but easy to follow, and it then widens out into an "inland lake" several miles long and almost as wide, with perfect protection from any direction. An untouched shoreline is backed by graceful peaks, not as dramatic as Bora-Bora, Tahaa, or Raiatea, but pleasantly contoured and decorated in trade wind clouds. I went off in the dinghy

Native village, Tahaa

for some photography, and *Essouffle* made a brave sight as she swept across the lake-smooth waters of deep blue, backed by the hills and clouds.

Bourayne was a wonderful anchorage, though even deeper than the others—almost 100 feet—and we spent a quiet moonlit night there, savoring a setting that would be hard to match for peace and isolation. Its special aura stayed with us long after our last sail back to a final night's anchorage in Tahaa before turning the boat in at Apooiti.

Tonga

Tonga, the only independent kingdom in the Pacific, consists of three main groups of islands on a 200-mile northeast–southwest axis, at 18° S and 174° W. It is 2,600 miles southwest of Hawaii and 300 miles from Samoa, and the international date line runs on a diagonal between them, so they are on different days. The island groups of Tonga are Vava'u in the north, where the bareboat operation is based, Ha'apai in the center, and Tongatapu, the capital, in the south. The royal family has ruled since long before the advent of white explorers, and it is famous for the stature and weight of its members. Queen Salote, a statuesque woman well over 6 feet, made a tremendous impression at the coronation of Queen Elizabeth II, and her son and successor after her death in 1965, King Taufa'ahua Tupou IV, is 6 foot 2 and 325 pounds, give or take a royal feast or two.

Tonga is in the trade wind belt and had not had a hurricane in many years until a devastating one in 1982. In general, there is good sailing all year in a completely protected area inside the fringing reefs.

At the end of our Tongan cruise, a taxi took us through neat groves of palm trees and vanilla bushes, with their aromatic beans drying in the sun on rough tables, to the tiny airport for the STOL plane connection to Samoa and the civilized world beyond. In the little thatch-roofed waiting room, a Tongan family, from grandmothers to babes in arms, was seeing a woman off en masse, and, in typical Polynesian

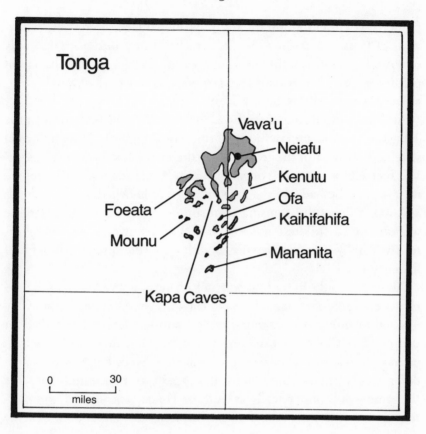

fashion, where emotions are always at the surface, there were paroxysms of tears and wailing. So pleasant had our cruise been that only our Anglo-Saxon upbringing kept us from joining in the display of parting sorrow. It was hard to leave perhaps the most "away-from-it-all" cruise we had ever had.

And this outpouring of grief was the only time we had not seen the Tongans laughing and in merry spirits, which seems to be their normal state and was one of the reasons why the cruise had been so pleasant. We had had a stalwart Tongan, Safeliti Taufa, as our guide aboard with us, and he had added a great deal to our knowledge of the islands and was a delightful cruising companion. Stocky and muscular, he was one of 12 children and now had 9 of his own, and meeting his relatives and visiting native villages with him were special highlights of the experience.

About the only thing that was not exotic was the boat, a CSY 44 center cockpit cutter named *Omoo*. Having cruised in three other CSY 44s and owning a 37, we found her reassuringly familiar and ideal for the purpose. Her name came from Herman Melville's book, in which *omoo* is the Tahitian word for happy wanderer. Since Polynesian tongues differ widely through the islands, it was perhaps a bit unfortunate that the same word, phonetically at least, in Tongan means a pit for roasting pig, which amused the Tongan maintenance staff at South Pacific Yacht Charters tremendously. In any event, she suited us well.

Even though Safeliti would be aboard, we had a thorough briefing on the Vava'u group from the South Pacific Yacht Charters staff, going over the special chart and guidebook they had put together, which showed a choice of 42 anchorages within the compact group. Though the area could be compared to the cruising scope of the British Virgins, with which we were thoroughly familiar, the islands are even closer together, and the reefs circling the group give perfect protection from the long Pacific swells. There is the same feeling of new perspectives and vistas opening up constantly while sailing between the islands, the major difference is in the absence of other boats. On most of the days we did not see any, and when we did, it was usually one of the two other CSYs that were out on charter at the same time.

We had become quite familiar with their occupants in an 0530 scene at the Pago Pago airport in Samoa on our way down, where we found four happy-go-lucky stags from California, already halfway through a bottle of scotch, and a large German family from Hamburg who had just flown in over the North Pole, all waiting for the one little Otter plane to Vava'u. It seems that the Germans, whose voluminous luggage included a folding sail board, were oversold, and they had to wait over for a day.

There was a reunion, under happier circumstances, on our second day out. Our first day, with an afternoon start from South Pacific Yacht Charters' base in Neiafu, the only town of any size in Vava'u, had taken us out the long, fjordlike outer harbor on a brisk reach in the easterly trade to a nearby cove. The next day was the occasion for a native feast, put on once a week for South Pacific Yacht Charters' boats and any long voyagers that happened to be in the area. The entire population of a small village, from toddlers to senior citizens, stages the affair at $5 per head, with everybody pitching in on the cooking and serving, and music and dancing. In late afternoon, Safeliti conned us into a lovely round harbor on the eastern side of the archipelago. Close-in reefs formed its major protection, and far beyond them the surf could be seen breaking on the outer fringing reef. Picture-book palm trees lined the beach, where there was a long open-sided *fale* (building) with palm frond roofing on a level grassy area. The three CSYs and two other yachts, passing long voyagers, provided the customers.

Guests sit cross-legged on the ground, with the food spread on a matting of banana leaves. Among the identifiables were roast pork, clams, octopus, fried fish, raw fish (marinated in lime juice), papayas, bananas, and heavy, grainy yams. The beverage was coconut milk, to which the happy California stags added a black rum. There were other items that will forever be anonymous to us, and all of it was finger-licking good—of necessity, since there were no utensils.

While we were destroying the symmetry of the beautifully laid out food with our forays, the villagers danced for us to the music of a local "combo," and it was all done in a free and easy spirit of fun. Some of

Beachcombing on Foeata

the dancers were comely maidens with all the proper hip moves, while others were grandmothers, including Mrs. Taufa, and tiny kids. The costumes were casually authentic, with none of the tinsel associated with Hawaiian-type floor shows stateside. Guests were lured up to enter in, demonstrating various degrees of competence and clumsiness, and when I was cajoled up by one of the grass-skirted maidens, the band switched from native tunes to "The Beer Barrel Polka." I took it personally.

This was the gregarious highlight of the week, as we split off on our own after that for a succession of lazy, blended-together days. There would be some easy sailing over smooth water, a lunch stop for swimming and beachcombing, and then another afternoon sail with the breeze perhaps a bit stronger to an overnight anchorage in some protected cove. The stops had names with a wonderful South Pacific ring to them, like Foeata, Ofa, Mounu, Kenutu, Kaihifahifa, and Mananita, but we usually worked by the numbers of the cruising chart in referring to them. Shelling was rewarding on all the beaches, especially those on the eastward side of cays near the windward fringing reef, and a glass-bottomed dink made for relaxed "sissy snorkeling." Opportunities for snorkeling or scuba diving were everywhere and excellent.

At Kenutu, a break in the fringing reef allowed a surge from the open Pacific to sweep in against the next island, where the waves would break against the cliffs in showers of spray. While we beachcombed casually next to flat water, this wild scene of crashing seas and spray clouds just a few hundred feet away was backlighted by the afternoon sun in glittering motion.

In contrast, Safeliti took us to a native village on Ofa, where human activity was everywhere. Neat little houses lined a long, white beach under rows of palms, and along the shore men worked at nets and small open boats while women stood waist deep in the water stripping reeds for making grass skirts. There were several churches in the village and next to one a lively co-ed volley ball game was in progress with much shouting and laughing. Children were everywhere, chasing each other in circles, squealing, and giggling, and pigs, goats, horses, chickens, and dogs roamed freely. Most noticeable was the scrupulous neatness of everything. Gardens were trimly bordered by rows of beer bottles pushed neck downward into the dirt, the houses were in good repair, the grass was cropped to a parklike smoothness, and there was none of the rusty clutter of debris and litter one becomes so used to in the Caribbean.

Children, their dark eyes round with curiosity, surrounded us and followed us everywhere, not begging or asking for anything. Safeliti visited with relatives and caught up with the local news while we wandered beneath the palms with our train of shyly giggling kids.

When we would anchor for the night, Safeliti pitched in with the cooking, especially with native fish, at which he was very good, and the native lobster (60¢ a pound). He would get the news on the Tongan radio station and translate anything that might be of interest to us, and after dinner he would help with cleaning up, though it was not part of his job. He avidly read several of the books we had brought with us, and was very informative about everything to do with Tonga that we wanted to ask. As far as I could see, his only gap in knowledge was that he did not know the Southern Cross constellation and was delighted when I showed it to him. He said he could now show it to other charterers when they asked about it.

He did not drink except for an occasional beer, but he was a heavy smoker. We twitted him about it, and he grinned sheepishly and said he knew it was a bad habit, but he liked it. From what we could see, heavy cigarette smoking is a common South Pacific practice. One day after a luncheon stop, he suggested we go to an anchorage for the night that was about as far away as we could go in the area. I was curious why he had chosen it, since we got in just at dark, but it was all explained by the fact that he was out of cigarettes and this was the nearest place with a store that sold them.

Most of the sailing was in moderate trades. We had one day of rail-down conditions, half a day of rain squalls, and one day of near calm. Since it was June, the days were quite short, which was not a bother with all the anchorages there were to choose from, except when Safeliti was out of cigarettes. The temperatures were surprisingly cool, in the mid-70s, and a light jacket or sweater felt good after dark.

On the day of rain squalls there were unusual rainbows glowing goldenly just above the horizon in stark contrast to the blue-black clouds. The calm day, as we drifted slowly back from one of the little motus on the outer reef, saw an eerie effect in the way the long rollers from the open sea lifted and crashed on the distant reef line. The swells would loom up in eerie, disembodied fashion over the misted horizon and seem to hang there in the void for a moment. The rumble of their demise was a distant thunder in the stillness.

Cave of the Swallows

On an island called Kapa, not far from Neiafu, the Cave of the Swallows was a special stop, a world apart from the beaches and palms of the motu. While Safeliti hovered outside with *Omoo*, we rowed the dinghy through the arched entrance of the cave into a ghostly, blue-tinted interior. The light from outside was reflected up through the

167

depths below us, where schools of fish darted about in clouds that glinted and shone as they made their turns in a seemingly bottomless void. The rocks and ledges of the perimeter made weird shapes as they receded into the blue depths. The Blue Grotto in Capri had nothing on this.

Nearby a cave with an underwater entrance is a challenge and reward for experienced scuba divers.

Each stop had something special about it, and at the end it was pleasant to come ashore at Neiafu and have dinner in the simple but civilized surroundings of the Port of Refuge Hotel. The town was a perfect example of modern-day, untouristed South Pacific life, with several big churches and some nondescript wooden buildings along a dusty street, and one pier for the occasional freighter. The harbor is big enough to hold the QE2, when she stops there on her round-the-world cruises, and protected enough to be a hurricane hole, though a bad hurricane in 1982 did damage the South Pacific Yacht Charters fleet. January and February are the most likely hurricane months, but the incidence of them is rare. The churches are obvious evidence of the importance of religion in Tongan life, where most of the population of 80,000 is Christian, with Catholics (you might have guessed Safeliti was one), Methodists, and Mormons the three major sects. Sunday is strictly observed, with no fishing, swimming, or playing of games allowed—this does not apply to visitors.

Out of all the richness and novelty of Tongan cruising, easily the most unspoiled and remote area I have ever cruised in (not counting navy duty in New Guinea in World War II), one spot stands out as best symbolizing the whole experience. This was a midday stop at a tiny motu called Mananita, the farthest out "number" on the cruising chart, all by itself on the eastern fringing reef. It was about 12 miles of sailing from our overnight anchorage to reach down there in a moderate trade and brilliant sun. To our port, the necklace of reefs stretching out to the open Pacific beyond the outer barrier was a multihued patchwork, and tiny motus dotted the waters to starboard, gradually petering out as we neared the last one, Mananita.

Changes in the water color showed where reefs cluttered the approach to it, and a restless surge broke over some of them. Safeliti manned the bow pulpit and eyeballed us in, threading the reefs expertly, until we were in a little hole of brilliantly clear turquoise, surrounded by the fuss and froth of surge over the shallower heads. Jane and I rowed ashore to one of those talcum powder beaches the copywriters for travel agencies rave about, over water so clear it was hard to tell where it stopped and the sand began. The island was covered by a stand of trees that go by the not-so-euphonious name of *puko*, great tall monsters with enormous leaves standing so close to each other that the overhead canopy is continuous. Here and there, an isolated shaft of sunlight penetrated the cool, green dimness like light through a stained-glass window. Under these stately trees, the ground was clear of underbrush, and we walked through the great vaulted arch of vegetation in a strange, hushed atmosphere. The sounds of surf and trade wind were muted to a soft hum until we neared the windward side.

As we stepped out of the shadow into clear sunlight again, the murmur of a gentle surge, reduced by the intervening reefs, rustled over the fringe of coral, and we could look across the maze of multicolored reefs to the far line of breakers ending their westward journey on the barrier. No one had left beer bottles or plastic bags on Mananita, the only evidence of visits by others was an occasional footprint above the high waterline, the vaulted grove of *pukos* stood majestically behind us, and everything combined to concentrate the whole experience in one idyllic spot.

It was the memory of Mananita, and all it represented, that could have had us wailing in the sorrows of farewell at the Vava'u airport along with the emotionally extroverted Polynesian family. We may not have wailed aloud, but we would miss it very much.

Australia's Great Barrier Reef

Stretching for 1,200 miles along the northeast coast of Australia, from the subtropics to the fully tropical climate just south of New Guinea, this is by far the largest reef system in the world. It lies from up to 40 miles offshore to just a mile or two at the northern end, enclosing a sizable inland sea that is dotted with hundreds of islands and smaller reefs. One of the major island areas is the Whitsunday group, halfway up the reef at 20° S, made up of small rocks and islets and good-sized islands of several square miles, such as mountainous Whitsunday Island itself. The whole area has been declared a national park by the Australian government and is beautifully preserved in a natural state. The only construction consists of a few resorts.

 The Whitsundays were named by Captain James Cook, who discovered them on that Anglican religious holiday, June 4, 1770, during his first Pacific voyage, in which he ranged inside the whole length of the reef in Endeavour. *Cook and his crew were the first white men to see the area, and he claimed the geologically oldest but most recently discovered continent for England in the process.*

How far do you have to go to get "out of this world?"
Our Tongan cruise had certainly been the most "away-from-it-all"

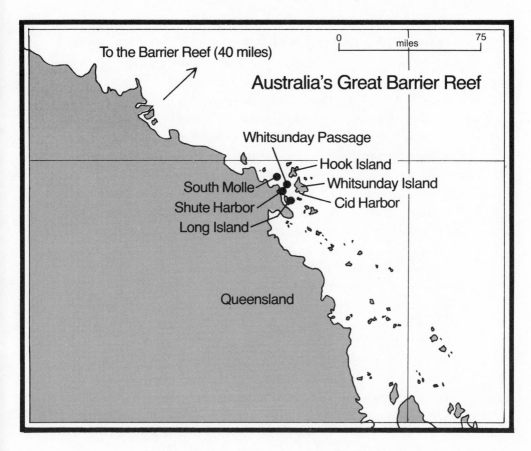

To the Barrier Reef (40 miles)

0   miles   75

Australia's Great Barrier Reef

Whitsunday Passage

Hook Island

South Molle

Whitsunday Island

Shute Harbor

Cid Harbor

Long Island

Queensland

cruise we had ever been on, taken in its entirety, but I do not think I have ever felt more of a sense of isolation and of really being on the edge of the world than in standing at low tide on the Great Barrier Reef 40 miles off the Queensland Coast of Australia. Here we were out of sight of land, not long after sunrise on a morning of absolute mirror calm, with the lumps and bumps of the reef stretching away for miles around us, and beyond them the great, flat sheen of the Coral Sea. Except for our little group and the two small seaplanes we had arrived in, we were in a great, empty, gleaming void.

This was the climax of a cruise that in itself was unusual enough. I had been invited by the Australian Tourist Office to come Down Under to investigate the local sailing, specifically charter opportunities for Americans. Other boating journalists had received the same invitation, but we all came at different times, not in a group, which made for a more personal experience.

I might almost be called "an old Australian hand," as I had been there several times in the war as part of subchaser duty in the Southwest Pacific, and I had also gone down there in 1962 and 1967 to do advance stories on their America's Cup preparations. Before going north for the Barrier Reef cruise, we had several very pleasant days in Sydney renewing old friendships, visiting the fabulous opera house, and spending a few days sailing a 28-foot cruising auxiliary around the magnificent harbor to sample the type of charter cruising that is done there. We had one day of harbor sight-seeing with a party of sailors including America's Cup skipper Jim Hardy, an old friend, a delightful day of exploring Pitt Water, a cruising area north of Sydney, and some great fun watching the crazy 18-foot dinghies racing. These are the commercially sponsored light-displacement boats that are sailed for cash prizes, carrying advertising logos on their sails and followed by ferryboats jammed with bettors. They put on a wild, spray-flinging show of planing when the breeze is up, as it was that day, in a harbor bursting with every kind of sailboat imaginable on Saturdays and Sundays.

The main thrust of our visit, though, was to sample the Whitsunday Island chain inside the Barrier Reef, where a thriving bareboat industry had recently been developed. (This was September 1979.) In 1943 I

A Mottle 33 sloop in the Whitsundays

had taken my subchaser from Brisbane north inside the Barrier Reef on the way to Townsville and New Guinea, and there was a vivid memory of passing through the Whitsunday area. At the time, I thought it looked like a wonderful cruising area, and that impression had been in the back of my mind ever since.

From Sydney and the other population centers of southern Australia, it is like a New Yorker going to Miami or the Bahamas to go to

173

this area of Queensland, a 1,000-mile flight in a jet and a short connection in a STOL plane to the little airport at Shute Harbor on the
Queensland mainland. This tiny settlement is the base for the charter
fleets, and the first thing we realized was that, because of a tide range
of 16 feet, there are no marinas in the area. From the shore, we looked
out over a fleet of boats at moorings in a big protected bay behind
several islands. The colors of the water, sand, and sky had the same
tropical look found anywhere in the world, though perhaps a bit brighter
than some, but, as we were to realize as we cruised, there is a very
different look to the Australian landscape from close up.

We were to split our eight days of cruising between two charter
operators, and our first boat was an aft-cabin model called a Mottle
33. She was practically indistinguishable from an American stock boat
in construction, rig, and equipment, and proved a lively, comfortable
sailer. The aft cabin was big, but awkwardly reached by an aptly named
"stoop way," and the only other objections I had were that the stove
and galley sink were reversed, meaning a warmly awkward reach across
the stove to the sink in preparing dinner and bartending, and the engine
instruments were located below for some reason.

Our briefing was thorough, with a marked chart and specially prepared guide provided. We were told of the good anchorages and warned
about the tidal range and the tidal currents, which could reach up to
5 knots in some of the narrow cuts between islands. Provisioning was
based on a suggested menu and was very thorough and good.

September is early spring, and the weather was absolutely delightful.
It was much more bracing than northern hemisphere spots in the cor-
responding latitude (like Cuba and Haiti), and the breezes were perfect
for sailing, mostly a steady trade wind from the southeast, which seemed
familiar enough. Evidently the midsummer months of January and
February become quite muggy and unsettled, with cyclones (hurricanes in the northern hemisphere) to be considered, but the weather
cooperated perfectly for our whole stay.

The only lack in provisioning was that perpetual problem Americans have when cruising in foreign climes: ice. We had very little
aboard when we started out, and, since the Whitsundays are a national

park, with five out-island-type resorts and one marine lab but no settlements, the prospects for getting more looked slim. There was a suggestion that the nearest resort on a long island that happened to be
named Long Island just outside Shute Harbor might have some, so we
headed there on our first afternoon. The charter service has a practice
of sending a check-out man with the boats on their first day; thus we
had a guide into the anchorage, who was then picked up by a chase
boat, leaving us to our own devices.

There was a white beach in front of the resort. In the evening it had
been quite narrow, but at low tide it looked like a great stretch of desert
when I ventured ashore in the morning. A barmaid was idly wiping
the counter when I pulled the forelock and asked for ice, and she acted
as though I had propositioned her obscenely. A man came out of the
kitchen to find out what was going on, and, after a long consultation I
was able to carry off a bag of cubes.

As I said, the islands had looked very much like similar tropical
groups, such as the Virgins, from afar, but as we sailed through them,
we now had a close-up of the landscape so very peculiar to Australia.
There were hardly any palm trees. The predominant tree was the towering eucalyptus, with spindly leaves and rounded tops. Hoop pines,
sturdy trees with oddly spaced clumps of dark-green needles set far
apart on the branches, were mixed in and also were clinging to
improbable spots on cliff faces and rocky slopes. The undergrowth was
a varied mix of ferns and spiky, long-leafed pandanuses, and the pre-
dominance of these few varieties had a certain monotony.

The most visible form of life was the white cockatoo, found only in
Australia. Flocks perched in trees at the top of the hills and cliffs,
circling off in flight and filling the air with their peculiar screech.
Occasionally the wild laugh of a kookaburra could be heard, though
these are more common further south. On the water we were con-
voyed by playful porpoises, smaller than those in northern waters, and
dark heads would occasionally pop up looking very much like emerg-
ing scuba divers in places scuba divers should not be; these were large
sea turtles. While in the Whitsundays, we saw no sign of the supposedly large shark population of Australian waters, and other charterers

were swimming off the boats, but we did not feel so inclined.

It was great sailing every day across the pale green waters of Whitsunday Passage, the 5-mile strait that separates the islands from the mainland, and we found a variety of pleasant harbors. They were never crowded, although there was always another boat or two in the vicinity. Cid Harbor on the south side of triple-peaked Whitsunday Island, largest in the group, is deep enough to take an occasional cruise ship and has several arms that provide good anchorages. There is nothing ashore on the harbors that do not have resorts, except some nature trails and discreetly placed barbecue pits and litter barrels.

Because of coral heads in all the harbors, all the boats are equipped with all-chain anchor rodes. Combined with the scope needed in a 16-foot range, this meant quite an exercise on the anchor detail, but there was a secure feeling when the hook was properly set.

After four days of pleasant sailing, we came back to Shute to trade the Mottle 33 for a Compass 29 from the other charter firm. She was equally well equipped, although she also had her engine instruments below, and, also like the Mottle, had reel winches for halyards, which I actively dislike. I find them a menace and treat them with great care. She too was a capable sailor, and, while amply supplied with bunks for a family of six, was very comfortable for two. We managed to start with more ice this time.

Everything went well on the cruise until the menu for the night called for steaks to be grilled on the hibachi. Jane informed me of this a bit timidly, knowing my aversion to this form of cooking, and I flatly refused. When I had been lined up for the trip by Australian officials, I had made a mild suggestion that perhaps my "camera assistant" might also be invited, and I was informed that "nobody else's wife was invited." I did not fancy a stag trip to Australia and a solo cruise, so I "invited" Jane, who almost always is with me on cruises, to the tune of about $2,000 for her ticket.

My answer to her suggestion that I was supposed to preside at the hibachi was a cold "I didn't pay $2,000 to bring you out here and have *me* cook."

We had a very quiet meal of pan-fried steaks.

Instead of either of us cooking, we had a couple of meals ashore at the resorts, where yachtsmen were welcomed with the usual brand of openhanded Aussie hospitality. One place was at an island called South Molle. It looked fairly simple from the harbor, but it turned out to be a rather extensive establishment with tennis courts, a small golf course, and all forms of water sports. Instead of being discreetly segregated at a table for two, we were placed at a large table with several couples who were staying at the resort, and it was a pleasant evening of exchanging experiences. They were amazingly up on American politics and interested in all sorts of aspects of American life, and we almost felt like travel guides under their questioning.

The highlight of the evening was a toad-hopping contest. A brash mistress of ceremonies in Harlequin glasses and a broad Strine accent cajoled everyone to place bets on a group of cane toads. These large, ugly, venomous beasts are a plague in Queensland sugarcane fields, so tough they intimidate dogs and so poisonous that their venom is used as an anesthetic. No one worries about their being an endangered species, as their cured skins are sent to the United States to make shoes, belts, and handbags. Here, with numbers on their backs, they were dumped out of a bag into the middle of a large circle, and the first one to clear the circle was the winner. Jane bet $1 on a toad tabbed Raquel Squelch, and it won the contest with one giant leap that cleared the circle before any of the other toads had even stopped blinking.

The climax of the cruise was, of course, the visit to the reef. This had to be arranged by radio with the plane operators. The VHF had been kept busy in frequent checks with home base, and I had become used to this enough to understand the Strine accents. We were anchored on the backside of Whitsunday Island off a mile-long stretch of powdery beach, and we were told that the plane would pick us up there at 0630 the next day. Visits to the reef had to be timed to low tide, and it was an early morning one at the moment.

As we were finishing an early breakfast, the plane circled us, wiggling its wings, and swooped in for a landing off our stern. We were instructed to drop off in the dinghy to the plane as it taxied near us, and the transfer was smoothly made. It was a short flight of about 30

Exploring the reef at early morning low tide

miles north to a lagoon in Hardy's Reef, where we could see the browns and greens of the reef poking through the pale blue of the sea. We landed on a sheet of glass, where a companion plane was already moored to a stake, and a glass-bottomed boat, which remained in the lagoon at all times, came alongside to take us to the reef. One other couple was with us in our plane, and two more had come in the other one, and the two pilots acted expertly as naturalist guides.

We had been told to bring "sandshoes" (sneakers) for walking on the reef, and we were handed tubes with glass at one end for water viewing. The reef can only be walked on at dead low tide, when it is just at the surface. At high tide, it is 6 feet under. The pilots warned us against such dangers as brown and white mollusks with poison darts, tan fire coral that burns the skin, and stonefish which camouflage in sand patches and have a lethal sting. We were asked not to tread on brightly colored live coral, as every effort was being made to keep from damaging the delicate ecology of the reef.

Underfoot there was a whole catalog of life forms in each square yard. Tiny polyps could be seen pulsating in search of food, while tridacnas, clams that can grow to giant size but which were no bigger than a foot at most here, showed "lips" of weirdly bright greens, blues, oranges, reds, and golds. Coral abounded in every shape and color, sea cucumbers *(bêches de mer)* sat in pools, and tiny fish of rainbow colors skittered about in pools left by the tide.

Soon the tide was on the make, and it was time to shift to the glass-bottomed boat for a look at the underwater face of the reef. Walking on it, we had had an awesome sense of space in the bright sheen of sun over the calm, wide sea, but now our focus was on the fish of every description swarming beneath us. The water was so still and clear that we had no need for the glass viewer as we gawked at yellow fingerlings, big fat groupers, rays, parrot fish in their brilliant colors gnawing at the reef, and red and white clown fish playing in the shadows. The "forest" they darted through was made up of stag coral with spreading antlers, huge brain corals, anemones, sea fans in delicate purple, and all sorts of shapes and colors of live coral, a multihued fairyland. A big turtle, mottled in yellow and green and perhaps 4 feet across, moved slowly out from under the boat's shadow, but then another shadow moved ominously in from the deeper blue—the first shark we had seen in these waters. It flicked its tail and was gone in a flash, but somehow the magic spell had been broken, the tide was rising and it was time to take to the planes.

I wondered about the plane's ability to break from the glassy surface, but it rose from it easily, and, as we banked to turn toward the Whitsundays, we could see the tide pouring through openings like a river torrent inundating the reef. The brief interlude had ended, but an interlude that will forever stay with us as a truly "out-of-this-world" experience.

Part IV

SOUTHWARD

The Intracoastal Waterway

Technically, the Intracoastal Waterway runs from Maine to Texas, but the heart of it, the section that gives it its real character and is what most boating people mean when they refer to the Waterway is the 1,090-statute-mile section between Norfolk, Virginia, and Miami. It is on this stretch (and also on Florida's West Coast) that the ICW has special markers and a special way of life. The markers are high-visibility orange-red triangles to starboard and bright green squares to port when headed south. The triangles are even numbered, the squares odd. The ICW also has its bible, the annually issued "Waterway Guide," a must to have aboard when making the trip. It carries a good mix of updated facility reports, navigation information, and background local color and history. Sometimes even it, with its annual update, can become outdated by changes, but it is generally accurate and helpful.

Some people, especially the paid crews of boats being delivered north or south, pay no attention to the ICW's charms and merely dash through at maximum speeds as though driving on the I-95. There are stretches between high banks with not much to look at that are boring, but in reality it is much more than the "Big Ditch" often given to it as a nickname. I have not done the whole route in one trip, though I have been on the Waterway in almost every section of it, but *Tanagra* took us between Norfolk and Charleston both ways several

*times, and to me this is a fascinating cruising area as well as
a means of getting somewhere else.*

Cruising the Waterway is perhaps America's closest approximation
to European canal cruising. The Trent–Severn Waterway in Ontario
might also qualify, but the Erie Canal and the Mississippi River system
are mainly for transportation. Few people seek them out as a special
target for recreational cruising. On the ICW there is the same feeling
of oneness with the countryside, of anticipation of what lies around
the next bend, of complete separation from the rest of the world, and,
if you are so inclined, a very relaxing pace.

This last is the hardest to achieve, as so many ICW users are trying
to "get there" in a hurry and fail to enjoy what is all around them. I
have to admit that we are usually pushing through on schedule when
we take it, but this has never prevented us from appreciating the passages as an experience. Especially in the Norfolk–Charleston section,
there are very few stretches of sheer monotony, of characterless banks
hemming you in while you plug along to the hum of the engine. One
26-mile canal back of Myrtle Beach, South Carolina, has this feel,
broken only in a few places by side creeks or marinas. In fact, the chief
entertainment here is to watch the little aerial tramway cars that carry
golfers from one side of the canal to the other on high overhead wires.
The canal splits several courses, but I do not think it is a water hazard
on any of them. I have never seen a golf ball whizzing by the mast.

Other than that, there is considerable variety along the way. The
other major canals, Virginia Cut and the Alligator–Pungo, go through
interesting wilderness, and there is a succession of sounds and rivers,
some quite broad, to change the scenery and even provide good sailing
on occasion.

One of the real charms of a Waterway passage is the "brotherhood
of the road" feeling with other boats. Especially for low-speed auxiliaries, the same boats cover about the same distance each day. Someone who was a total stranger yesterday is your long-lost friend today
and tomorrow when you come into the same marinas after a day's run.

Passing traffic on the ICW

Then "happy hour" is a time for visiting in cockpits, comparing notes, and catching up on experiences; even the powerboat people (most of them) display happy camaraderie by slowing down as they pass, waving cheerily. Only a tiny percentage cowboy on by without a backward glance as you wallow in their wake, which then crashes into the banks, undermining the growth.

185

There are pronounced and obvious differences between the autumnal trips southbound and the northbound ones in the spring. The most obvious is the disparity in running time, with up to four more hours of daylight in the spring. This allows longer runs for those trying for distance, and of course the foliage, the quality of the sunlight, and the very feel in the air are in sharp contrast. To me there is a special charm in heading south in the fall, gradually exchanging the russet and gold of the foliage for Spanish moss and palmettos, with the sun warming more each day, but still the reminder of conditions left behind from the occasional cold fronts that sweep in on blustery northwesters. We have had some good sailing in places like Albemarle Sound when this happens.

Even though one is technically in the ICW in coming down Chesapeake Bay, as we did in *Tanagra*, there is a specific moment of transition in heading from Hampton Roads into the Elizabeth River along Norfolk's commercial waterfront to port. Just before the Elizabeth River splits into eastern and southern branches, there is a huge building, the Portsmouth Naval Hospital, to starboard, and a red flasher buoy off it marks Mile Zero of the Norfolk–Miami section of the ICW. It is from here that all mileages (statute) are figured on the frequently placed markers, but the river buoyage is still the conventional "red-right-returning" stuff for a few more miles.

Just beyond Mile Zero there is a big marina right off the channel, perfectly located to grab a big share of passing traffic and a handy spot for gathering forces, fuel, supplies, and information. The management has been thoughtful enough to separate its fuel dock into powerboat and sailboat sections, so that auxiliaries with their 20-gallon-type purchases are not shunted aside for the big powerboats gulping the stuff in by the ton.

There is a sense of anticipation here, of boats and people on the move, and of adventure ahead when southbound, and a feeling of accomplishment and new horizons ahead when coming the other way. A restaurant one flight up at the fuel dock gives a fine overview of the whole scene (and a last chance for Chesapeake crab cakes), and it is a good place for sailors to chat with others bound the same way.

When we took off from here on a morning of low overcast, there was a dull tone to everything, as the Portsmouth Navy Yard is on the starboard hand. The ships and most of the buildings are gray, and it made us feel especially small to gawk at the unbelievably vast bulk of the carrier *Nimitz* undergoing overhaul. It seemed hardly possible that something that unwieldy looking could maneuver and move and might even pitch or roll in the open sea.

After about 7 miles, the commercial waterfront gives way to open countryside, and the ICW markers start. There is a choice here of taking the Dismal Swamp Canal or the Virginia Cut to get to the Carolina Sounds, but the Dismal Swamp was never open when we went by. First excitement on the Virginia Cut is the lock at Great Bridge, the only lock on the whole ICW. It is not a dramatic one, since the rise is only about 3 feet. Until a green light signals that the lock is open, boats must hang onto pilings; when the signal comes, there is a mass movement, as the lock can take a large number of yachts. Commercial traffic takes precedence, but there was none, and we tied up to the stone lock wall to await the lifting waters. It would have been a much more pleasant experience if the big cruiser in front of us had not been suffering from indigestion and blown great billows of black smoke at us. Evidently they did not dare stop the engine, because they never turned it off while the water was seeping in.

Just beyond the lock is a marina and yacht basin that are another gathering place for boats on the move. On another passage, we got to talking to a couple from Texas on a 35-foot ketch. They were on their first ICW trip and asked for recommendations on places to stop. One I mentioned was Whittaker Creek in Oriental, North Carolina. Several months later I got a letter from the Texans enclosing a picture of *Tanagra* underway in Virginia Cut and informing me that they liked Whittaker Creek Marina so much that they had bought into it as partners. Such is the "brotherhood" of the Waterway.

This time it was still early morning when we disgorged from the lock and headed into Virginia Cut, and we were glad to see the bilious cruiser speed on ahead, leaving a black miasma behind her over the still waters of the canal. Gradually the traffic thinned out according to the speed of the boats, and we were left in a stretched-out row of 6-knot auxiliaries. From then on, it was possible to gauge the lock openings, as every so often a new armada of power cruisers would move up from astern and breeze on by.

The Virginia Cut goes through thick forests, painted with subdued autumn colors in late October, straight as an arrow for 8 miles before winding into the headwaters of the North Landing River. The woodsy atmosphere gives way to more open country, with swamps and side creeks alternating with stands of pines and a few farms and small settlements with names like Pungo Ferry. The winding river eventually opens into Currituck Sound, and you are in North Carolina.

Currituck is very shallow, and the ICW channel is a narrow path down its center. For us, the northwest breeze that had gradually blown away the morning overcast meant that we could sail for a few miles. We had made good time and could afford to, but we were soon back under power and following channel bends through Coinjock Bay to North Carolina Cut. In glowing twilight we made it to Coinjock Esso Marina, a long bulkhead along the bank to port, and found an open spot big enough for *Tanagra*'s 36 feet. A dock attendant was right on hand to handle lines and give us a cheery, drawling Carolina welcome. It had been a 50-mile day.

Somehow, this marina has always symbolized the ICW for us. Perhaps the management has changed, but in 1975 it was efficient and courteous—two retired naval officers and their wives—and there was a delightful little restaurant across the street from the marina office. North Carolina is "brown-bagging" country, since liquor is not sold by the drink anywhere, so yachtsmen would walk across with their own wine or booze to be greeted by a waitress who had a wonderful set speech.

We got it as we sat down, and it was fascinating to hear her give it verbatim to each arriving party. It went something like this in a distinctive Carolina drawl.

"All of our seafood is fresh. None of it is frozen. You can start with your oysters or your clams, then you can have your hush puppies, and then you have a choice of your crab cakes, your broiled bass, your fried shrimp or your fried oysters. Then you have your salad and your

dessert, and you have your ice cream, your apple pie, or your choco-
late cake."

It was said all in one breath, finishing with a triumphant upbeat,
and we always anticipated it whenever we stopped here. Once, on a
northbound spring trip, a different waitress just poked a menu in front
of us. We asked about the speechmaker and were told that her husband
was in the hospital and she was taking time off, and the restaurant had
become just another place to eat, though the food was still good.

Several boats we had seen at the marina in Portsmouth were here,
and we greeted each other like old friends, getting together for a drink
afterward for post mortems on the day.

On most stretches of the Waterway it is possible to plan runs from
marina to marina if you prefer them to anchoring out, but the area
south of Coinjock as far as Belhaven is devoid of civilization for 86
miles. I once made Belhaven to Coinjock on a dawn-to-dusk run when
time was important, but this would require night running in the fall.
This section crosses shallow Albemarle Sound for an open-water passage of 12 miles and then runs down the broad Alligator River. It is
famous for a nasty chop, and powerboat skippers dread it with some
reason, but for us it meant a day of sailing in the still fresh northwester.
There was a whitecapped chop on the brownish waters, but *Tanagra*
took it well and it was a fine day of sailing fast on a broad reach until
we rounded a bend where the Alligator River turned westward, and
powered in sunset glow to an anchorage just outside the entrance to
the Alligator–Pungo Canal with half a dozen other boats. The low
shore was thickly wooded and devoid of any sign of life, and sunset
brought the end of the breeze for a night of star-filled stillness. On
another trip we had awakened to zero fog here, and it had been hard
to grope our way to the canal entrance a couple of hundred yards away;
but this time the dawn was clear and still and the main entertainment
was in watching an IOR-type ocean racer headed for the SORC with
a delivery crew cut the corner too soon heading for the canal and run
aground. She managed to kedge off fairly soon.

The canal has open country around much of its banks, with glimpses
of farms and grazing cattle, and the cattle would sometimes come down

The moon setting at dawn in Belhaven

to the water and stand in it, staring stupidly at the boats when the wakes washed around their legs. Belhaven is a quaint, attractive town, very much off by itself, with stately old southern mansions under tall trees and a small business district. It is a busy place during goose-hunting season as a base for shooting at nearby Lake Mattamuskeet.

Although we found it a pleasant stop and enjoyed the highly promoted buffet at the marina restaurant, we also found, after being stuck there for a week with engine trouble on one trip, that its (and the buffet's) charms faded somewhat. We also found that the marina was completely unprotected in a southerly blow. Immobilized there with engine trouble, *Tanagra* practically rolled her keel out in the heavy chop surging up the Pungo River. Since then we have used the better-protected marina further up the harbor.

Pushing on toward Charleston, we had some good sailing in the Neuse River, and we liked that area and the Adams Creek section so much that we eventually based *Tanagra* there for one winter and did some side cruising. Below Morehead City, there is very little open water and a lot more ditch crawling, but there is always a bird watch, a handsome forest grove, or a funny-looking tree to see, and a lot more in the way of intermittent civilization than in the North Carolina Sounds. Perhaps the nicest stretch is the Waccamaw River in South Carolina. By now the trees are moss covered, and on that day the sun was warming back to summerlike temperatures. The river winds through dense stands of evergreens on a graceful, curving path, and we decided to celebrate the lovely atmosphere with some caviar for "nooner" hors d'oeuvres. Jane had shanghaied some sour cream from a baked potato serving at a restaurant in Spooner Creek the night before, and we had the whole bit, with chopped egg and onion. In the bright southern sunshine, life seemed very much all right. Most of the trip was, but we learned one other aspect of Waterway life on our last night out of Charleston.

With a pleasant breeze blowing, we pulled out of the main channel and anchored in a side creek of the Santee River. It was a lovely evening as we watched the sunset over cocktails and turned in early for the morning start. At 0300, we came wide awake to the hum of a thousand mosquitos filling the cabin. The breeze had quit, and they had suddenly come out in force. I had not thought, in the evening breeze, to put in our screens.

Certainly the ICW is very special kind of cruising in many ways.

Florida's West Coast

The west coast of Florida has it all over the state's other side as a cruising area. The Intracoastal Waterway runs along it for much of its length, there are frequent passes (Florida West Coast for inlet) out to the Gulf of Mexico, and inland bays like Tampa and Sarasota Bays and Charlotte Harbor provide some good protected water sailing and gunkholing. The Gulf itself is always there for open-water passaging when the wind and weather are right.

Even though it is a very civilized area, with marinas abounding and high rises lining the shores in many spots, there are some isolated spots, like the Anclote Keys north of Clearwater. These little sandbars just offshore have a genuine South Sea Islands atmosphere. They mark the northern end of the cruising area, which extends down to the Ten Thousand Islands and Florida Bay.

The climate is semitropical, which has its drawbacks and its advantages. When the weather is settled in the winter and through spring and fall, it can be delightful, but there is exposure to winter northers, and they can whoop through with heavy rain and winds and temperatures in the 30s. Holing up in a marina is the best answer to these assaults. Fog is a sometime thing in winter, and hurricanes are the usual menace in late summer and early fall. Summer is marred by a lack of wind, high temperatures, and the high frequency of thundersqualls, but again, when the breeze blows, the nice days can be nice.

We have cruised there half a dozen times from November

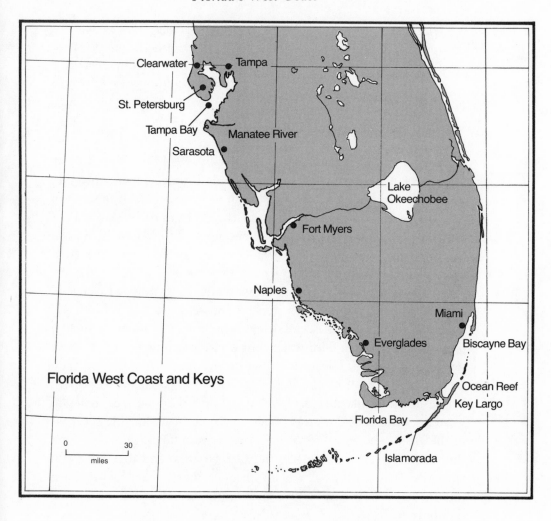

Clearwater

Tampa

St. Petersburg

Tampa Bay

Manatee River

Sarasota

Lake Okeechobee

Fort Myers

Naples

Miami

Everglades

Biscayne Bay

Florida West Coast and Keys

Ocean Reef

Key Largo

Florida Bay

0   30
miles

Islamorada

*through April with generally good weather luck, though the
day we commissioned* Brunelle *in St. Petersburg (January 2,
1979) the wind was 45 knots, with heavy rain, and the temperature was 34°. Dodging around these conditions, we have
had some very pleasant cruises.*

Tanagra's maiden southern cruise over the 1974 New Year holiday
saw a week of almost perfect weather, while *Brunelle's* first cruising in
Tampa Bay and on down the coast to the Keys was beset by a series of
cold fronts. A week's cruise in the first CSY 44 in early March 1977
saw three fronts, but five days in a Sandpiper 32 in March 1978 fit in
nicely between two fronts. A November cruise in *Tanagra* was in generally pleasant weather, and so it goes.

On *Tanagra's* New Year's cruise, with Hugh and Winkie Livengood
as crew with us, we were all stocked and ready to take off by early
afternoon of New Year's Eve. There was no time to move on to another
port from our base in Clearwater, but we were itching for a sail, so we
headed out through Clearwater Pass and its drawbridge into the open
Gulf, where a fresh southerly was kicking up a parade of whitecaps.
The Gulf looks like the ocean, but it has a different feel. In calm
weather, there is seldom the restless surge of an underlying swell, as
in the open sea. In a breeze, the waves are different too. They are
shorter and steeper, more like the Great Lakes, and they pack real
authority. The Gulf's color is an opaque green when looking down
into it, and it only smiles blue in distant vistas when there is a clear
sky above it.

Tanagra charged offshore with her rail down, and it was a stimulating few hours before we were back at the drawbridge and powering into
the waterway and Clearwater Harbor.

In the harbor, which is really a tidal flat between a barrier beach
and the mainland, there is a series of spoil banks between the waterway
channel and the barrier beach, built up into little islets by the frequent
maintenance dredging of the channel.

The chart showed 6 feet between two of the larger banks, so we

Cormorants on an ICW marker near Clearwater

pulled off to starboard from the channel and dropped the hook. Although the high rises of Clearwater Beach were a jagged backdrop to the north, with neon lights beginning to flash in the twilight and the world's biggest wooden building, the Bellaire Belleview Hotel, sprawled endlessly along the low hills of the mainland shore, there was a sense of aloneness here, as the only boat at anchor, while the clouds in the west put on a typical Gulf Coast sunset show. The high, open sky above the clouds showed through them as a pale, apple green, while much stronger colors played through the cumuli in reds and golds, shooting upward from where the sun had disappeared in the sheen of the Gulf.

While this was providing a fine show for happy hour, the ever-present pelicans gave us a good one closer by. Lines of them arrowed in, barely over the water, alternately gliding and giving short bursts with their wings in unison while their long beaks dowsed toward the water. In purposeful flight, they aimed for the islets, where gulls and cormorants were already packed in a chattering gaggle. The pelicans are forever silent, but the cries of their friends filled the twilight as the sunset show flared and faded. This was Gulf Coast atmosphere at its best, and nature's show seemed a far cry from the festivities that were by now abuilding in the neon towers a mile away.

Although it was New Year's Eve, none of us made it till midnight. I was the last one, trying to stay awake to listen to the Notre Dame–Alabama game in the Sugar Bowl, but when that came to its nail-biting climax, I was already three-quarters asleep in the cockpit and barely managed to stumble below before sleep took over completely.

It was a surprise in putting my head out the hatch for a first look at 1974 the next morning to find that it was invisible. Zero fog enveloped us, and the only identification of where we were was a soft nattering from the birds on the sandbars to port and starboard. I could barely see the bow, much less the islets a few hundred feet away. After a leisurely breakfast, we could feel the sun's warmth begin to penetrate the gray stuff, and gradually the circle of visibility spread and the gray turned whiter.

By mid-morning we could see the channel markers, and we got

The St. Petersburg waterfront

underway, heading southward in the waterway for the Tampa Bay area. The sun broke through at noon, and at Johns Pass, the only one between Clearwater and the Tampa Bay area, we headed out through the draw, eager to have a sail. The hazy sun made it warm enough for shirt-sleeves or bathing suits as we made sail in the lightest of easterlies and began to drift southward over the pale-green mirror of the Gulf. From inshore, the cries of children playing on the beach and the hum of outboards towing water-skiers drifted out to us. Other sails dotted the Gulf in all directions.

Our lazy slide ended at Pass-a-Grille, the inlet at St. Petersburg Beach, and we powered into its wide channel and the winding turns to take us to Port of Call Marina. This is at the inner end of a large man-made lagoon on an island that is connected to the mainland by a drawbridge. There is perfect protection and a good spot to eat ashore. The good weather stayed with us as we continued south the next day, starting with a fresh easterly that took us across Tampa Bay inside Egmont Key, an island athwart its entrance. There was heavy ship traffic in Egmont Channel heading in and out of Tampa Bay. Inshore of us the Sunshine Skyway's tracery spanned the bay. It was intact then, but the western span was later knocked down by a ship.

Past Egmont Key, we headed offshore through Passage Key Inlet, hoping for more sailing, but the easterly faded in the noon lull, and it was never replaced by an afternoon sea breeze, which often happens in fair weather here. Instead, we did another ghosting job, drifting along in the warm sun and taking most of the afternoon to get to Big Pass at Sarasota. It looked as though a mammoth dredge had the channel blocked, but there was a buoyed passage around it, and we went through the draw to Sarasota Bay. In here, there was a nice southeaster, in contrast to the windless Gulf, and we turned to port out of the channel to Sarasota's downtown piers and anchored half a mile from shore in 8 feet.

Again, civilization teemed along the shores, and yet we had a pleasant feeling of being off by ourselves. If a norther should come in, we were in an exposed spot, but none was forecast, and we spent a quiet evening after watching another spectacular Gulf sunset flare across the sky over Longboat Key.

It would have been pleasant to poke further south, and in later years we had pleasant stops at the Venice Yacht Club, Plantation Key, and Naples Yacht Club, but this was turnaround point for the time allotted to this cruise. We had relatives on Siesta Key, which makes the southern shore of Big Pass, and we could anchor right off the house and paddle ashore for a morning visit. Later we lunched at Bird Key Yacht Club with other relatives, weaving our way through a maze of islands and keys to find it, and afternoon saw us heading up Sarasota Bay to a marina called The Buccaneer on Longboat Key. We had been there before and thought it one of the best-kept and best-managed marinas we had seen anywhere. There is a side channel into it from the water-way, and in making the turn I misread a marker; we nosed up onto the flats, solidly aground.

I was trying to power us off, when a little boy in an aluminum dinghy with a three-horse outboard came along and said, "Wish I had a bigger motor. I'd pull you off."

I told him he could still help, and gave him the spare Danforth to carry out to mid-channel as a kedge. It took hold well, and a little sweat with the anchor line on the genny winch had us sliding off into deep water as the boy beamed at us.

He said, "That's my first rescue. I just got the boat for Christmas," and dashed off down the channel with a great grin on his face. As we came along toward the marina, we could see him talking to his father at a small pier, pointing to us with great pride. We saluted him and waved to his father, and there were smiles all around.

Dinner at the Buccaneer was pleasant, with some visiting around the marina on other boats, and a good southerly the next morning allowed us to sail northward under main in the winding channel of Sarasota Pass, out into Tampa Bay. To keep sailing, we reached out through Passage Key Inlet for a swift jaunt offshore before turning around for an equally fast sail into the Manatee River. We followed it inland to Bradenton for some maritime sight-seeing while the ever-present Tampa Bay porpoises frollicked around us, leaping alongside and cut-ting across the bow. Overhead we spied a flight of the rather rare white pelicans, which we have only seen in Tampa Bay, and they were a graceful picture as their turns and swoops caught the sun on their wings.

The Manatee was alive with jumping fish and skittering bird life when we reached up to the bridge at Bradenton and then turned around to sail out to the entrance. It is lined with handsome houses, with the west shore more heavily populated, and at the entrance there is a semi-circular cove inside DeSoto Point that we have used often as an anchorage. The point, which legend has as the site of DeSoto's landing, is a park and is nicely wooded and lined with beaches. The other side of the cove is straight Florida-style suburbia, with large houses and well-tended lawns, but the undeveloped point lends a deceptively wild aspect to the anchorage. Why DeSoto would have picked it as a landing spot, since he did not have the Sunshine Skyway to take him inland, is hard to fathom, but it makes a nice story.

Again we were treated to a sunset show, with a couple of other cruising boats for company on the quiet waters, and it was a peaceful anchorage for the night, in contrast to another visit when a southerly preceding a cold front had whipped up a good chop in the short open water span across the Manatee. Sailing across the bay the next day to the Sheraton Bel Air Marina hard by the causeway in St. Pete brought us back to a busy, civilized aura. The marina, packed with glossy cruisers, bustled with the activities of the Annapolis Sailing School.

Although this seemed more like the Florida we knew and expected, we had had a surprising amount of fast sailing and good anchorages in a rewarding cruise that ended with a final power run up the waterway to Clearwater. There were porpoises convoying us even in the narrow channels, an incongruous sight against a background of road signs, motels, condos, and fast food eateries, and the long, purposeful lines of pelicans were still skimming low across Clearwater Harbor to welcome us back.

The Florida Keys

The Florida Keys have a barrier reef of their own, not as long as Australia's by any means, but one of the major ones in the world, fringing this closely spaced group of low-lying islands on their Gulf Stream side as they string south and then west from Biscayne Bay to Key West. The Straits of Florida are on the south, and the Gulf of Mexico is at the back door on the other side. Key West is the southernmost point of the forty-eight United States, at 24°30! (Hawaii took over the honor for the whole country when it became a state.) It is not quite tropical, but the warm water on both sides gives the Keys the mildest climate, and winter northers, which can occasionally blast through, tend to lose some of their bite by the time they make it to the Keys.

A railroad connecting Key West with the mainland early in the century changed the life there considerably, and it has changed even more since the railroad causeway was converted to a highway after a hurricane in the thirties wiped out sections of the railroad. Hurricanes have been a dominant factor of life in the Keys, causing death and destruction over the years, but there is a year-round boating season here, with special emphasis on the excellent sport fishing.

The Florida Keys are not ideal for sailboat cruising, and I ordinarily would not choose them. The water is thin, the channels are narrow and winding, so it is hard to negotiate them under sail, and northers can be encountered in the winter. Natural harbors are few and you are dependent on anchoring in a lee or in marinas, which are normally dominated by fishing boats. There are almost no beaches, and evidence of heavy tourism has taken over what used to be quaint little towns.

Still it was a perfect area for us for a Christmas vacation cruise in 1958, when Robby was 15, Martha 13, and Alice 10, and the boat was *Mar Claro*, which I had trailed down from New Jersey to Miami while the others flew down when school let out. It was the only time all five of us cruised in her for more than long weekends. Although she was extremely roomy for 24 feet, the whole family all at once put quite a burden on her. On the other hand, her shallow draft and ease of handling made her a fine boat for poking around the Keys.

Despite the drawbacks cited above, the Keys had many features of benefit to this kind of family cruise. There were marina hotels and motels where we could get a room to take some of the pressure off the conditions on board, which we did on several nights. There were all sorts of new things for the children to see and experience: birds, fish, exotic vegetation, and gorgeous clear water.

There was also civilization in the way of movies and ice-cream parlors, necessary items for a teenage cruise.

In fact, the movies and Seaquarium in Miami plus a visit from Santa Claus in a cabin cruiser to Coral Reef Yacht Club, where we were basing, made it hard to convince the kids that we should take off for the Keys at all, but we finally managed to on a day of perfect sailing conditions. The wind was moderate from the east, riffling the pale green of Biscayne Bay with a light chop under warm, cloudless skies, as we dropped Miami's white towers astern and headed for the cut through Featherbed Bank that lies across the bay at midpoint. Once we were through its narrow channel, with the powdery white bank stretching away on both sides, little blobs and lumps up ahead gradually blended into a line of mangroves, the first of the Keys. Porpoises playing around us made up for leaving the Seaquarium behind.

After 30 miles of great sailing, we rounded into Angelfish Creek under power to head for its seaward side and the marina at the Ocean Reef Club. Today Ocean Reef is an enormous marina and real estate

We based out of Coral Reef Yacht Club, Miami, to cruise the Keys

complex and a private preserve, but then it was just getting started, with one small bulkheaded lagoon as a marina, a modest-sized hotel, and a few cottages, and was open to the public. Angelfish Creek wound eastward for a mile, with a few outboards lazing around us and a big white diesel yacht's superstructure looming over the mangroves up ahead as she came in from sea. Then we were in open water, with Hawk Channel between us and the outer reef and the indigo of the Gulf Stream on the far horizon beyond the spindly tower of Carysfort Reef Light.

The narrow entrance to Ocean Reef was a mile to starboard, and sunset flared brilliantly over the bow while we came in the marked channel and were greeted by a dockmaster on a motor scooter, who escorted us to a berth alongside the bulkhead next to the hotel with all the ceremony due a 100-foot motor yacht. Next came a maître d' in tuxedo, handing down jumbo-sized menus for ordering dinner from the hotel dining room. Before I could check the prices, the kids were so overwhelmed that they had put in their order, so we lived it up for one night and did the rest of our eating ashore at the lunch counter for paid hands.

This was our Christmas base. Jane and I took a room in the hotel, which was shower room and bathhouse for everybody, since the kids were constantly in and out of the pool. There was a sizable juvenile contingent among the hotel guests, with all sorts of games and programs for them, and our group was soon absorbed into it. Robby fell in love and was seldom to be found, while Jane and I relaxed and visited around the boats in the marina. The only other sailboat belonged to a family whose name we caught as Sparks, and we had a fine time comparing notes. Next day I found out that Sparks was actually Dr. Spock, and we laughed at the thought of what impression our children might have made. Years later we ended up in the slip next to Dr. Spock in our permanent base in the British Virgins, and both of us remembered our Ocean Reef visit.

I have always enjoyed a traditional Christmas at home despite the 3 A.M. problems of inserting "axle holder A into slot B" and the end result of piles of dishes, baskets full of wrapping paper, tinsel crushed into the rug, and scattered toys, but this one, our first away from the "old-fashioned" Christmas, was a joyful contrast. After a carol sing service at the hotel Christmas Eve, we were all in bed early and slept late. The drill was one present apiece from each to each—Robby dashed off and bought his sisters packs of gum at the last minute—and the Yule feast was then prepared on the Sterno stove. It consisted of corned beef hash, string beans, champagne, and Jane's previously home-made plum pudding, complete with burning brandy and hard sauce.

After it, we took a sail out to the Gulf Stream and back in a balmy south wind, with everyone gawking over the side at the sight of the bottom slipping by 40 feet below in the clear water. Out in the Stream itself, on the bottomless deep blue, there were the lavender sails of Portuguese men-of-war, sea turtles, and frantically skipping flying fish to watch, and the feel of open water seas under the hull.

On each of the three days we spent at Ocean Reef, we took a sail offshore, and the children would have been content to spend the whole vacation at Ocean Reef with their new-found friends, but it was time to explore some more, and the weather also changed. From days of balmy sun and light southerlies, it switched to a gusty, cloudy north-easter, with low-flying clouds and a few spits of rain, and this helped to break the spell of Ocean Reef. It also helped us to a fine, fast sail down the lee side of the Keys, once we had worked our way back through Angelfish. Even though the wind was on the nose leaving the Ocean Reef channel where we made sail, the chop had been held down by the reefs, and once in the lee, there was no sea at all.

Over waters blackened by the overcast, we sped on a broad reach through Card, Barnes, Blackwater, and Buttonwood sounds and Tarpon Basin, only using the outboard for the Route 1 drawbridge over Jewfish Creek and one or two spots where connecting channels between the sounds headed briefly to windward. We covered the 30 miles to Tavernier in less than 5 hours and hardened up in the increasing breeze for a close fetch into the pier of Key Haven Motel, careful to pick out the private markers of the channel amid the profusion of stakes and mangrove clumps on the surrounding flats. This is bird-watching country, with an Audubon Society Station and frequent conducted birding cruises out into Florida Bay and the neighboring keys.

After dark, the clouds disappeared and a bright moon rose. The girls decided to try sleeping bags on the pier instead of triple-bunking with Jane in the platform bunk forward in *Mar Claro*, but a sudden deluge sent them scurrying below. Ten minutes later, the moon was out again, silvering the big black cloud as it moved to leeward, but more clouds were sweeping in from the Gulf Stream, and it was a night of frequent brief but hard showers. On the same day, Fort Lauderdale, 70 miles to the north, had a record downpour of 14 inches.

The aftermath was two hot, windless days that meant a power trip to Islamorada, 8 miles further on across the pastel green of Florida Bay. At Islamorada Yacht Basin, it was the younger generation's turn to sleep ashore. They took advantage of it, with showers on the half hour, and had the room looking as though it had been lived in for months within a few minutes of checking in. Jane had been after them constantly to pick up their things in the confines of *Mar Claro's* cabins, where each one had their own net hammock for stowage, so objects quickly flew to the four winds in the comparative freedom of a motel room.

Islamorada was good for more of the shoreside entertainment that made the Keys a fitting teen-group cruising ground. There was a pet monkey at the marina, and there was also a movie in town. It was also our turnaround point, as it was time to wend our way northward to Miami and the end of the vacation period.

The calm persisted the next day, and we retraced the route of our glorious sail down entirely under power. It was a day of a championship pro football game, and Robby and I wanted to listen to it. The only way the portable radio would work when we we were under power was to take it all the way up to the foredeck, far enough away from the outboard to escape its interference. We sat up there following the game while the girls steered, and I checked back frequently to signal course changes in the winding channel.

At one point the game got very tense, and we were oblivious to all else while the situation developed. Suddenly, however, I looked up and found us headed straight for a large clump of mangroves. I yelled back at Jane at the tiller, waving a course change, and we veered off just in time. When I complained later, I got the usual wife-versus-football reaction: "You wouldn't talk to me or tell me anything." It happens fairly often at home, but this was the only time on a boat. I cannot remember now who was playing in the game, but I am sure I would never forget it if we had plowed into the mangroves at full speed.

When we came back into Ocean Reef, it was like a college reunion as the kids greeted their long-lost friends of four days ago and got right back into the swing of things. One of the special entertainments here had been a round-faced, smiling Bahamian paid hand on one of the big powerboats. His name was Byron Bowleg, and he had an endless repertoire of calypso songs, both traditional and original compositions. Accompanying himself on the guitar, he could go on for hours, much to everyone's delight. One of his own compositions was a song about going through a drawbridge, using a conch shell horn for signalling, called "De Bridge Obey de Song of de Tropical Conch Horn." We eventually acquired a conch shell horn for *Mar Claro*, which the kids would fight over each time we came to a bridge, and someone would always sing Byron's ditty while the lucky winner of the fight was blowing the bridge signal.

On our way from Ocean Reef to Miami, we went via Hawk Channel outside the Keys to Caesar's Creek, 6 miles to the north, instead of using Angelfish. Caesar's Creek is named for the pirate Black Caesar, who supposedly hid his ships here by careening them to a mooring ring on a big rock in the middle of the creek. The breeze had come back from the east, and we had a swift sail to the entrance of the narrow, twisting channel into the creek, privately marked by stakes. The water colors of Hawk Channel are brilliant and ever changing over the differing depths.

Once inside, we stopped to give the kids a chance to explore ashore and locate Black Caesar's rock, but they were back in a hurry, reporting an excess of spiders in the area. The breeze held to give us a last fast reach up Biscayne Bay, out of Caesar's Creek, and through a small cut at the eastern end of Featherbed Bank known as the Safety Valve.

An area that had its drawbacks had performed nobly in providing special attractions for a family cruise, and the children had something to report in Show-and-Tell when they were back in school besides what their grandmother gave them for Christmas.

The Abacos

The Abacos are a separate world in the larger one of the vast Bahama chain, cut off as they are from the rest of the islands by the deep-water areas of Northwest and Northeast Providence channels. Being the furthest north, they have a slightly different climate, with more effect from northers in the winter. In January 1977 it actually snowed on Grand Bahama and Abaco Island, a phenomenon unheard of in recorded time, but that was an extreme that probably will not happen again.

The Abaco Cays, and the best cruising waters, lie along the eastern side of the Little Bahama Bank, which is little only in comparison with the Great Bahama Bank on the south side of the Providence channels. In good weather, they have the same winds from the easterly quadrant that blow in the rest of the Bahamas, and the body of water between the outer cays and the larger island of Abaco is a fine, protected one for cruising, with room to sail and a good choice of harbors. Our boat for an Abacos cruise in 1965, before the start of much of the development in marina facilities and resorts that can be found today, was a borrowed Soverel 28 stock sloop, Drifter II, which was comfortable and well set up for two of us and which could handle up to four more people who knew each other well.

Starting an Abacos cruise at West End on Grand Bahama, where we picked up *Drifter II*, usually means a beat to windward across the Little Bahama Bank in the prevailing easterlies, but we had a southwester

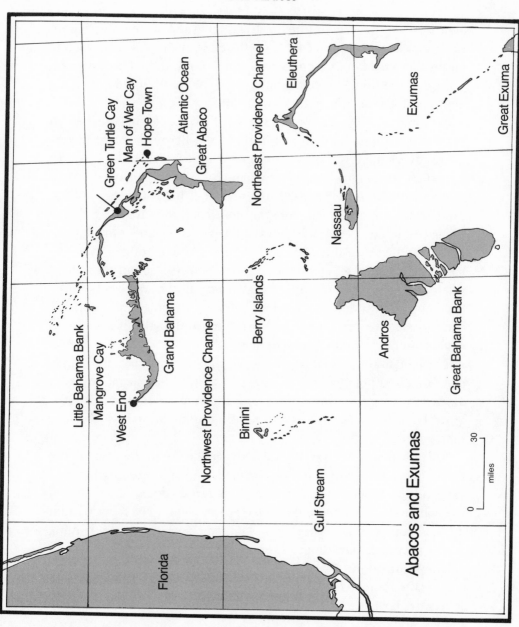

Abacos and Exumas

blowing when we were finished with shopping and stowing, so we were eager to take advantage of it. A southwester in the Bahamas usually means that a cold front is on its way, with a northwester likely after the passage of the front. Since this was April, the front should not be too severe, as they sometimes are in midwinter.

Crossing the Little Bank is a lot easier than the 90-mile pull across the Great Bahama Bank from Bimini to the Berry Islands further to the south, as there is some sort of protection every 20 miles or so. In the center is Mangrove Cay, aptly named, with nothing on it but an abandoned light tower, and 20 miles beyond that is Great Sale Cay. From a late-morning departure we hoped to make the 22 miles to Mangrove in good light, and it was a pleasant slide under main as we got acquainted with the boat. She sailed well, easily driven with a 3-foot draft, board up. The only problem seemed to be in the galley, where a large expanse of very slick formica all the way across under the companionway made it hard for Jane to keep things under control. There was also a tendency to put your foot in the salad if not careful while coming down the companionway.

The light tower popped over the horizon like a toothpick, and, since its bearing did not change, and a few little lumps appeared next to it as we drew closer, it was obviously not a boat mast. Typical of a mangrove landfall, the lumps were not visible until we were within less than 5 miles.

A large power cruiser was already anchored in the lee of the southwester, and we went further inshore from her a couple of hundred yards off the tower in about 5 feet. Birds twittered and flitted around the mangroves while the sun lowered across them, to be replaced after a placid sunset by a bright moon. The radio spoke of a front coming in the morning, but the gentle southwester was still wafting over us when we turned in.

It was morning when the front arrived, but just barely, at 0130. A jolt as the boat swung around to the first blast of a northwester woke me up, and, as I popped out of the hatch, I was just in time to see a buoyant cushion take off from the cockpit on the fresh breeze. It was still a bright, moonlit night, with no rain or clouds in our area, though reports in the morning indicated that there was some heavy rain in Northwest Providence Channel, across Grand Bahama to the south of us.

As the anchorage became increasingly uneasy in the new breeze, perhaps 20 knots, I dozed in the cockpit to keep an eye on things, and finally decided at 0400 that there was little profit in bouncing around here when there was a fair wind for where we were headed and no dangers to leeward. While Jane slept, I hoisted the main, weighed anchor, and took off to the east.

Soon after gathering way, I saw something gleaming whitely in the water, reflecting the moon, and it turned out to be the errant cushion, drifting back against the wind on a tide change, directly on our course. It was an easy "man overboard drill" to pick it up.

The breeze eased and kept swinging north. By daylight it was in the northeast, and, with Jane up and about, we set the genny and began to make knots. For the next nine days, in one of those wonderfully settled weather patterns that are often a feature of spring conditions in the Bahamas, it stayed somewhere between northeast and southeast and blew mostly in the 14- to 16-knot range, never more than 20 or less than 10.

It was 45 miles to Allens-Pensacola, a single cay that used to be two before a hurricane realigned things enough for them to be joined. It was too early to stop at Great Sale, where there were quite a few white milky patches in the bottle green water, enough to frighten a new-comer not used to the fact that these are usually caused by schools of fish feeding. There is understandable hesitation about going through one the first time, but after a while they become routine.

Allens-Pensacola was a quiet haven, with nothing on shore but a tracking station on the far side of the cay, but after that we began to experience more of the civilization of the area. It was a 23-mile beat in a fresh southeaster down to Green Turtle Cay, one of those sails with the boat well balanced and enjoying herself in the light chop, while we tacked on and off the Abaco shore. Although it looks like narrow water on the chart, there is from 2 to 5 miles of sailing room between the main island and the off-lying cays. The cays are prettier and more interesting than the low, featureless shore of Abaco, with glimpses between the cays to the deep-water waves breaking on the offshore reef.

Bluff House at Green Turtle provided a good place to eat ashore in a pleasant setting, looking down from the 80-foot bluff across the harbor to the picturesque huddle of New Plymouth's doll-like houses. We had another good dinner ashore at our next stop, Guana Harbour, 18 more miles to the southeast. The Guana Harbour Club is a small club-type resort, where we sat with the hotel guests in a big group at cocktails and then ate with them family style. The climax to a beautifully done, menuless meal came when the Belgian chef, complete with white hat, made a dramatic entrance behind the dessert soufflé, carried on high by the maître d' (who was evidently the chef's very good friend, from what the guests said). The chef then served the soufflé with great flourishes and exaggerated gestures amid rounds of applause from the diners.

One of the guests was a retired navy admiral, Jesse B. Oldendorf, who had commanded the U.S. battleships in the Battle of Surigao Strait in the Philippines, the historic occasion of the last "crossing of the T" in naval warfare. When I recognized his name and brought up the subject, he beamed in delight, and we had a fine time swapping navy sea stories, even though my command, a 110-foot subchaser, had not quite matched his.

Beyond Guana to the southeast, the neighboring cays of Hope Town and Man of War are the heart of the Abacos and loaded with local color. The settlements, with little New England-style cottages, are predominantly white, as the inhabitants are descended from Loyalists who came here during the American Revolution. Sizable colonies of winter residents have moved in here as well.

Hope Town, with its much-photographed candy-striped lighthouse, was alive with activity, since The Cruising Club of America winter cruise was in port, jamming the harbor with handsome yachts. Dinghy racing, rafting parties, and festivities on shore livened the already busy scene.

We had damaged *Drifter's* rub rail during a nightime wind shift at

Hopetown Harbour and its familiar lighthouse

the Guana Harbour pier, and I wanted to get it fixed before turning the spotless new boat back in at West End. Everyone advised a visit to the Edwin Albury Yard in Man of War, just across the way. Everything in Man of War is run by Alburys. Edwin was laying out frame stations for a stock motor sailer the yard builds, working from a carved model on a big sheet of plywood under the trees when we tied up at his bulkhead, but he interrupted his work long enough to find a suitable piece of scrap teak and put his brother to work on the repair. The job took 5 hours, and the bill was $12.25. (Oh, for 1965 prices!) While the work was being done, we explored Man of War, bought some groceries at Mrs. Albury's store, had some conch chowder at Albury's Snack Bar at Albury's Marina, took a look at the William Albury Yard, where a miniature replica of a Spanish caravel was building, and visited Albury's sail loft.

It was time to turn westward from here, and Bluff House at Green Turtle had been so pleasant that we stopped there for another dinner. At dawn the next morning, with the wind nicely in the east, we took off, hoping to make Great Sale for the night, a good long sail of 50 miles. We wung the genny out on the spinnaker pole and slid along nicely in the smooth water, ticking off colorfully named landmarks such as Crab Cay, Center of the World Rock, Hawksbill Cay, and Veteran Rock. We particularly liked Center of the World Rock, since for us, when we were there, it truly was.

Slipping by West End Rocks at the tip of Abaco, with puffy little fair weather clouds marching along above us and the wind holding steady, we were off Great Sale by 1400, no time to quit on such a delightful sailing day. Onward we swept, making Mangrove before sunset, having covered 73 miles, the longest daylight sail I have ever accomplished while cruising.

We anchored on the west side of Mangrove, and this time the lee held over the night and the cushions stayed aboard. The breeze was still a moderate easterly in the morning, and we celebrated the last leg of the cruise by making it a spinnaker run to West End.

The Exumas

For 22 years, from 1957 to 1979, I don't think I missed a calendar year in getting to the Bahamas. Some years it was just for the Southern Ocean Racing Conference races, but usually there was some cruising involved. This great spread of islands that starts 50 miles off the Florida coast is an endlessly fascinating cruising area from the Abacos in the north to far off Mayaguana and Great Inagua, and we managed to cover most of the areas at some time or another. Such is the extent of the Bahamas, though, that there are as many places to which we have not been as ones to which we have been. It is the only area where we have had all three of our cruising boats, Mar Claro, Tanagra, and Brunelle. In addition to the Abacos, treated just previously, we have done the Bimini–Cat Cay area, the Great Bahama Bank, the Berry Islands, Eleuthera, the Exumas, and the islands on the way south to the Caribbean: Long Island, Mayaguana, and the Caicos. The Caicos are not politically in the Bahamas, but they are physically of a piece with them.

Of all these areas, each of which has special charms, the Exumas have to be rated at the top. This 90-mile chain, which runs southeastward starting 30 miles from Nassau, has some of the most beautiful water colors, best anchorages, and most delightful sailing breezes of all the areas I have cruised. We have gone back there as often as possible over the years. Since 1979, when we took Brunelle through on the way to the Caribbean, we have not been back, as she is based in the British Virgins. Since then there have been unfortunate inci-

dents of piracy, drug action, and murder, scaring many peo-
ple away. I have no personal knowledge of the latest
developments, but from all reports, things seem to have calmed
down. Exumas cruising has so many facets that it will take
accounts of two cruises to cover it all.

Although the lower Exumas from Staniel Cay at the center of the
chain to Great Exuma at the lower end are less familiar as a cruising
ground, we actually had our first glimpse of the Exumas in covering
the Out Island Regatta at George Town in 1958. Flying down the
chain in an old converted PBY, we had a marvelous view of the varying water colors over the banks and the intricate jigsaw of little cays
and larger islands.

Over the vast Great Bahama Bank that separates the islands, the
water was a translucent green, paling to white in the shallower areas
near beaches. Between the islands, a cut in from the deep indigo of
Exuma Sound would send a bright blue finger slashing across the paler
colors, and here and there shallow coral made tan or greenish brown
hues. I had seen water colors throughout the Caribbean and South
Pacific in earlier sailing and navy sea duty, but this magic chain opened
new perceptions in the delicate clarity of the water and the relationship
of the islands and the cuts lacing through them.

Nobody had told Jane that the PBY was an amphibian. We had
taken off from the solid land of the airport in Nassau, and she had a
moment of sudden panic when we touched down at George Town and
the pale waters of Elizabeth Harbor winged up past the windows.

The native workboats made a stirring spectacle in the regatta, as the
assault of colors on the eye continued to astound me, and I had one
great day of crewing aboard the sloop *Charity B* when she won a race.
So clear was the water that there was a sense of flying through space
rather than sailing in something solid as the big white sloops skimmed
over Elizabeth Harbor. It was an exciting introduction, but it was a
dozen years or so, after many cruises in the northern Exumas, that we
had a chance to cruise the southern end. This was in a Pearson 390

216

named *Pelagos* operated by CSY when they had a base at George Town, Exuma. The Pearson 390 was one of the early well-thought-out center cockpit full-cruising boats, and she was extremely roomy and comfortable, and a capable if not exciting sailer.

George Town was a fine base in itself, with the remembered brilliance of Elizabeth Harbor right there and plenty of room for local day sailing and gunkholing, but it had a flaw that eventually led to its abandonment for bareboat purposes. From it, there is a 20-mile stretch of open water in Exuma Sound to the nearest cut into the rest of the Exumas. With charterers having to keep a schedule and turn boats in on time, a tough slug through those last 20 miles against the prevailing southeaster could mean an unpleasant session for the average bareboat crew, and so it proved.

Also, the cuts through the Exumas are very difficult to identify, and we proved this on our first day's run to the recommended entrance at Rat Cay. My crew and I were sure we had it right, but we had actually negotiated a completely anonymous cut one cay away. By careful eye-balling, we made it all-right, as it was fortunately a clear one, but I could see that the problem was real. Later a boat was lost by making a not-so-fortunate error in trying to make the same cut.

Our lucky error put us onto the bank and its beautifully pale, clear waters. The wind was in the southeast, and we were able to sail up the zigzag of channel with the help of the indispensible *Yachtsman's Guide to the Bahamas* to a peaceful overnight stop at Children's Bay Cay. Another good day of sailing took us to a not-so-peaceful spot just inside Farmer's Cay Cut. The wind had come northeast and was sending enough of a slop through the cut to kick up a surge and bounce inside. An interesting feature of the Pearson 390 was a glass port in the bottom in the after cabin; you could lie in your bunk and watch the undersea life in action. The only problem was that it had a magnifying effect, and when the bottom was only a couple of feet below the keel, as at this anchorage, you would swear that the boat had to be aground.

The northeaster developed into a squally one the next morning, and we had a fast reach in the lee of the cays in lowering clouds and rain spits up to Staniel. Just short of Staniel, off Harvey Cay, a driving rain

Pipe Creek

squall cut down visibility so far that we anchored in the lee, along with a native sloop, to wait it and its 30- to 35-knot gusts out. The marina off the pleasant little out-island club at Staniel, which has steadily been expanding since we first went there, was snug in an easterly (but is exposed in a norther), and we sat out a nasty morning of gusty squalls after a pleasant buffet and steel band evening at the club.

In clearing weather after lunch we explored the Pipe Creek area, one of the prettiest in the Exumas, and used Sampson Cay, a few miles north, as the next overnight and the turnaround spot.

Unfortunately the breeze veered around to the southeast with clearing weather and blew with some authority, and there was nothing to do but power all the way to George Town to make sure of our scheduled return. The gorgeous colors were there, as were the vistas across the wide expanse of the bank to port and through the cuts in the cays to the deep blue of Exuma Sound on the other side, but it was all to the tune of the engine's hum. Once back in George Town, we had time for a final night in one of the inner ponds on Stocking Island. This is the 5-mile-long sliver of hills and white beaches that almost landlocks Elizabeth Harbor, and the complex of ponds that cuts into its western side makes wonderful hurricane holes and a perfect anchorage in any weather, with vast white bonefish flats stretching off from the pale blue of the anchorage.

This cruise had filled in the gaps for us south of Staniel, and the northern part of the chain was a lot more familiar to us from any number of visits. Perhaps our best cruise of all these was back when we had *Mar Claro* in the Bahamas for the winter of '62 to '63. She had been sent down from New York on her trailer by ship and based in Nassau's Yacht Haven while we commuted to her as often as possible.

For an April cruise during Jane's vacation from teaching school, we picked *Mar Claro* up at Rock Sound, Eleuthera, where friends who had been using her had left her, with the aim of heading for the Exumas. At the time we had only been there in large, professionally crewed yachts that had to anchor well offshore, and the gunkholing and exploring had to be done by dinghy. With her 2-foot-4 draft, *Mar Claro* did not even need a dinghy. We could poke in any where we wanted, eyeballing our way, until we ran aground, and we would then shove her off a few feet, anchor her, and wade ashore to explore. There is no better area for this kind of cruising than the Exumas, and all we needed was a break in the weather.

That we got, right from the start. A rare westerly was blowing when we boarded, and Rock Sound Harbor was wide enough to kick up a chop that bounced her light displacement hull for our first night of sleep, but the breeze was around to the northwest by morning, and we could thread our way through the shoals off Powell Point and reach swiftly down the Eleuthera shore to Davis Harbor, a good jumping off point for crossing Exuma Sound to the Exumas.

In proper fashion, the breeze veered to north during the night, and we had a bright blue, crystal day for the 35-mile leg across to Highborne Cay.

It was one of those sails you remember for a lifetime, where everything was just about perfect. The sun got rid of an un-Bahamian nip in the air as it rose, and we swept out toward an empty horizon, moving as fast as she would go. A U.S. Navy buoy 12 miles out gave us a good check on course and speed, and after that we were alone on the blue for several hours. It was not hard to imagine that we could be halfway from the Canaries to Antigua, or perhaps somewhere near the Marquesas, and I was seized by complete euphoria.

"This is the best sailing I've ever seen," I cried.

"Quiet," Jane said, "you'll scare it away."

"I don't care what happens after this. This makes it all worthwhile."

Our 1100 ritual of a cold Pauli Girl beer right off the ice helped to keep the euphoria alive as we continued to surge along, and it was not until after lunch that we spied company on the northern horizon, identified as the converted trawler *Empress*. She was a charter yacht owned by Bill Norton, one of the colorful characters among charter skippers, with whom we had often crossed paths and hoisted a few. In fact, his nickname is "Snortin' Norton," as his usual greeting at almost any hour of morning, noon, or night is, "Hi ya. How about a snort?"

Empress remained hull down, and we saw nothing else until a few lumps appeared on the horizon that had to be an Exuma, but which one? I was familiar with the approach from the northwest from Nassau, but I had never come in from this angle, and the Exumas have a tendency to all look exactly alike until you are practically ready to step ashore. The sun lowering in the west was no help.

The best guess I could make was Saddle Cay, south of my intended landfall at Highborne, and I learned later from Norton that he had found a set to the south from the north wind on his crossing. By the time we closed with the shore, the sun was right in my eyes, plating the water with glittering silver, and, in heading between two little rocks that I thought were the proper entrance to Saddle, we nudged onto sand. Looking straight down, I could see how shallow it was, but there was no eyeballing ahead in the sun path.

I was about to jump over and push off, when a Whaler loaded with men in bathing suits came from behind one of the little cays and headed for us. They were unshaven and hairy looking, and the first words I heard seemed to be in Spanish. The week before, a Cuban group had been arrested while trying to stage a raid on their homeland from Norman's Cay, and I had wild thoughts that this might be some sort of hijacking.

Instead, a very Limey voice called, "You missed the proper channel, mate. It's over there."

With that they jumped into the water and pushed us off in a moment.

"The other side of that rock. That's the ticket," and they were off with a cheery wave. I found out later they were vacationing British office workers with one Latin friend, and so much for my Walter Mitty fantasy.

We managed to nose our way into the Saddle Cay anchorage, where a friendly native poled out and helped me to settle in the right place and put out a Bahamian moor. This is accomplished by setting an anchor up tide and then dropping back on double scope to set another anchor down tide at a slightly veed angle. The boat is then pulled back to the middle, with even scope on each anchor, and will swing each way as the tide turns.

By now it was almost dark, and we settled down to cocktails and supper, still glowing from the wonderful sailing and the accomplishment of getting to the Exumas in our own boat. In the morning we awoke to the ever-amazing spread of colors around us. *Mar Claro* seemed suspended in air and stayed that way for most of the week. The water around us was bottle green, paling to near-white in the inshore shallows. To the west the shallows changed gradually to powdery blue on the outer bank, and the dark line of Exuma Sound set off by the white of breakers on the reef could be glimpsed through a cut in the cays to the east. Coral showed a dirty yellowish brown when near the surface and dangerous, greeny brown when possible trouble, and black when deep enough not to bother us. Eyeballing this way was easy, but the water was so clear over the sand that it was hard to judge just how deep it was. In *Mar Claro* it made little difference, as she was easily pushed off.

My outburst of the day before had not scared the breeze, and we had it on the port quarter from the northeast for a run south past Norman's to Warderick Wells. When we passed cuts in from Exuma Sound, the deep blue ribbon of sound water would be centered on strips of powdery blue, green, and yellowish white, and the eye was continuously assaulted with the variations. By late afternoon we were off the north cut into Warderick Wells and we hardened up to the channel entrance, an avenue of sharply defined blue between gleaming white flats. We followed its twisting path into the island until it opened into a wider pool, as blue as the channel, where we did a Bahamian moor and settled down to enjoy the perfection of the setting, completely alone. Not a boat or house was in sight, nor a light at night after the sunset glow died. The stars shone clearly right down to the horizon, and all was quiet except for the faint hum of wind in the rigging and the gurgle of tide parting at the bow.

Only one thing marred the perfection. Jane's method of arranging meals was to put a complete menu in one plastic bag when we were away from fresh stuff, and the bag she pulled out on this most delightful of evenings happened to contain spaghetti and beets, two items I can cheerfully do without.

There were a few words and a small silence, but everything was so great that I could not let a little thing like spaghetti and beets ruin the evening.

Our ever-cooperative breeze, still blowing in a clear blue sky, sent us reaching southward again to one of the loveliest stretches of water I have found anywhere, Pipe Creek. This is where our later cruise in *Pelagos* overlapped *Mar Claro*'s path, but we had not seen it before when we came into it via a luncheon stop at Compass Cay. Pipe Creek is really a winding channel a mere 20 or 30 yards wide between a series of small cays on both sides. To windward, the restless surf of Exuma

Gunkholing at Long Cay

Sound batters the rocks, and spray can be seen flinging into the air, while the placid sheen of the bank stretches away beyond the cays on the other hand. To keep the pace slow, we just had the main up, and *Mar Claro* glided silently through the ever-changing perspectives of coves and cuts and tucked-away beaches.

It is 7 miles to Staniel Cay, and we were back in "civilization" amid some friends from the charter fleet, like *Empress*, Art Crimmins' *Traveler*, and Bud Gieselman's *Teresa*, all of whom we had rendezvoused with before. After the isolation of Warderick Wells and the peace of Pipe Creek, this was a complete change, with much visiting between boats and a buffet supper and calypso party at Staniel Cay Yacht Club with close to 50 people from the yachts whooping it up.

It was time to think of turning around and heading north, and the breeze continued to do what we needed. By now it had settled in the southeast, still in gorgeous clear weather, and we had a wonderful sail

A Haitian sloop shared Shroud Cay with us

up the cays in the company of *Teresa* and *Traveler*. The breeze of 16–18 knots was just strong enough for *Mar Claro* to slide along at hull speed, while the 43-foot *Teresa* and 68-foot *Traveler*, heavier and towing dinks, could not go any faster than we did. We could see them adding sail and tweaking sheets and heard later that their charter parties wanted to know why that little boat was staying with them, really ragging Bud and Art.

We did not want to get them in trouble with their customers, but for us it was another memorable sail. In these conditions, we would roll up the sides of *Mar Claro*'s hood so that the cabin was one big cockpit with a navy top and we could alternate sun and shade. We had never sailed any faster for so long a time, averaging 6.5 knots on the 35 miles to Shroud Cay. We were invited aboard *Teresa* for dinner, and the guests continued to kid Bud good-naturedly, asking me, "How do you manage to sail a little boat like that so fast?"

Our last full day in the Exumas was spent gunkholing our way northward via a luncheon stop at Long Cay, where we waded ashore to do some exploring before continuing on to Allan's Cay, the northernmost anchorage in the Exumas. We were pleasantly tired after the great days of sailing and had turned in early when we heard the bump of a dinghy alongside and the unmistakable voice of Bill Norton calling, "Hey, aboard *Mar Claro*. Come on 'n have a snort. We're having a party on *Empress*."

This was a genial way to wind up what we still look on as the most technically perfect cruise we have ever taken. The wind, the weather, the people we met, and the continued days of great sailing could not be topped, and we still had the southeaster for a fast final sail to Nassau.

By now even cautious Jane was not worried when I talked about it being the best sailing I had ever seen.

Part V

THE CARIBBEAN

Transatlantic to the Caribbean

Since the time of Columbus, the classic route to the New World from Europe has been the trade wind passage from islands off the North African Coast, like the Canaries or Cape Verdes. The target can be Antigua, Barbados, Martinique, or any of the Antilles, though Columbus ended up further north; San Salvador in the Bahamas. For years I had read of this passage in many a book and in countless articles submitted to Yachting, *and I had always had a yen to take it someday as the easiest way of accomplishing a transatlantic voyage under sail. The hairy-chested foul-weather-gear types could have the North Atlantic.*

I had the impression that everything from orange crates up had managed the trip judging from some of the vessels I had seen in Caribbean harbors, and this was almost true. When our chance came, it was not exactly in an orange crate, and it did not even qualify as a passage under sail. It was aboard the famous four-masted bark Sea Cloud, *built in 1930 for Marjorie Merriwether Post (Hutton at the time). It was cruise ship living, but there was enough of the romance of sail to it for me to include it here as what might be called an extra added attraction.*

There she was. As I stood surrounded by chrome-trimmed Italian motor yachts and reverse-sheer IOR racers at Marbella's Puerto Banus

Marina on Spain's Costa del Sol, *Sea Cloud*'s 200-foot spars towered into a gray Mediterranean overcast outside the jetty. It was like stepping back 100 years to take the launch away from this jet-set ambience and climb the gangway under the intricate tracery of her rigging, and it was something of a miracle that this great windship was still in commission.

Of course she was a rather special windship. I had sailed in the Norwegian training ship *Christian Radich* and visited aboard some of the other OpSail vessels, and *Sea Cloud*, the largest sailing yacht ever built, is quite removed from their spartan atmosphere. She was luxury and whimsical indulgence personified when she was first delivered to Marjorie Post Hutton as *Hussar* in 1931. She was black hulled then, and only had a few sybaritic cabins for Marjorie and guests. Over the years, she was renamed *Sea Cloud* and painted white when Marjorie became the wife of Joseph Davies, Franklin Roosevelt's ambassador to Russia in the 1930s, and was finally sold to Trujillo, the Dominican Republic dictator in the 1950s. After his assassination she rusted away in various tropical ports, as several attempts to put her in the charter trade ran into legal problems, but she was finally rescued from idleness in a Panamanian harbor by a group of German businessmen (and yachtsmen).

Completely refitted at a reported cost of $6 million, she was put into the cruise ship trade in the late '70s, with modern cabins added to give her a passenger capacity of 79. In the summer she plies the Med and transfers to the Caribbean for the winter, and this November passage from Spain to Martinique was her transfer voyage, scheduled for three weeks. It was to trace the fourth voyage of Columbus via Gibraltar, Casablanca, Lanzarote in the Canary Islands, and then a trade wind crossing of two weeks to Martinique. That and the fact that her sails are square was about the only connection with Chris. He did not have four Enterprise diesels (a legacy from the Trujillo era) capable of pushing her at 17 knots when they were all hooked up to her two propeller shafts. With two engines operating, she could make about 11 knots. Columbus would have been a bit amazed at air-conditioning, at the ornately decorated luxury of the original staterooms, and at the meals

Sea Cloud spreads her sails against the setting sun

that were turned out in her main saloon and for luncheon buffets on deck.

For those of us as passengers, life was very similar to that on a small cruise ship, except for the ever-awesome presence of those four masts and their spars and sails. Any fantasies a passenger might have of skipping to the tops and furling the royals in the teeth of the booming gale were soon dispelled by the word that passengers are very definitely not allowed in the rigging, though they could pitch in and haul lines on deck if so inclined.

Exy and Irving Johnson (of *Yankee* fame) were aboard as lecturers, and Irving, at age 76, managed to climb to the top of the mizzen almost as soon as he came aboard, bringing back his experience of rounding Cape Horn in *Peking*, the ship now at New York's South Street Seaport, in 1929. When he came down, grinning like a kid who had just raided the cookie jar, he was then given the belated word that he had broken the rule.

There was not much sailing to start with. By the time all the passengers had been ferried out from Puerto Banus, it was midafternoon. There were about 60 aboard for the passage as far as the Canaries, half Americans who were going the whole route and half a German party going to Lanzarote only. To make schedule, the four diesels were cranked up and we headed for Gibraltar, 40 miles away, at top speed.

The Rock was an impressive sight as its bulk loomed out of low-flying scud, with the late sun sending an occasional slanting shaft against its steep flanks. By the time we tied up at the ship pier for a quick trip by sight-seeing taxi, it was almost dark. We did have time to see the main gates, closed against all access from Spain because of a disagreement between it and England, a couple of its 30 miles of tunnels, and one ape asleep in a cage. From the highest point of the drive, far up on the Rock's brow, there was a fine view of purple twilight closing down on the Bay of Algeciras.

We were off again in the evening, powering through unsettled weather in the Straits that told of the clash of Atlantic and Mediterranean systems. We found ourselves in the morning on a flat, windless sea, gray under a colorless sky, off the African coast. In midafternoon, we came on a good-sized freighter of Panamanian registry lying motionless on the oily sea. *Sea Cloud* came close and slowed down while our captain, Hartmut Schwarz, a former German naval officer with tall ship experience on the *Gorch Fock*, called across to ask if the rather rusty and run-down-looking ship was in trouble. The answer was negative, and we steamed away, leaving her still lying there until she dropped from view. Schwarz said that this was a deep part of the ocean where "insurance cases" often developed. Who knows?

Casablanca's commercial port was incredibly dusty, cluttered, and busy as we came alongside early in the morning. While we waited for clearance, with the passengers lining the rail, the captain's black Labrador, Bongo, managed to get down the gangplank and run around the pier area, lifting his leg on everything in sight to the encouraging cheers of the ship's company.

This city of 3,500,000 mixes Arab and Western cultures in profusion and confusion, with its contrast of glass and concrete high rises, an impressive modern Catholic cathedral, and the expected ambiance of *souks* (native marketplaces), narrow streets, and veiled women. Its beach-front areas were generally drab and colorless, with a big hotel here and there, and one area of luxury homes in a lush setting, where the Casablanca conference was held in World War II.

Our departure the next morning was through a cloud of industrial pollution so dense that the city was lost to view almost immediately as we plowed over a steely calm sea. Then, after lunch, a line of breeze came over the water from the invisible coast, and there was great excitement as the sails were broken out for the first time. Young men and women of the deck crew scampered aloft to the orders shouted by the mates in a strange mix of German and English. All told, there were 55 crew from 17 different countries, with about half of them in the deck gang, including several girls. They clambered aloft with the others and soon the ship was beginning to gather speed as the breeze built. On deck, gangs hauled on the braces, swinging the yards to the breeze, with much scurrying and shouting, and Irving Johnson was right there with them, heaving away with a will and enjoying himself tremendously. Most of the other passengers seemed to prefer to watch, gaping aloft as the sails fell free and filled.

The awakening life of a ship under sail brought a new camaraderie aboard in the mutual interest of watching the operation and being at last under sail on a square-rigger in a fair breeze. Until now, the German and American contingents had done very little mingling, and there had even been some rather churlish confrontations over dining room seating, and bus seating in Casablanca. A set of silly games billed as the Mid-Atlantic Olympics, with potato races, passing of oranges chin to chin, and the like found the Germans intensely competitive, taking each event seriously and winning every one, while the Americans played it for laughs.

Now, with *Sea Cloud* surging along, and with a special Bavarian Night dinner and singing program as a farewell to the Germans, there was a general thawing and mixing. It was a gustatory and social success, with much reading of poems, telling of jokes, and a lot of singing.

Lanzarote, where we tied up at the end of a long jetty enclosing an inner harbor jammed with fishing boats, small freighters, and a few

Fishing boats at Lanzarote

yachts vying for a toehold in the jumble of colorfully decorated work boats, is the northeasternmost Canary Island, 80 miles off the Moroccan Coast in latitude 29° N. Its main port, Arrecife, is a rather typical European resort town, with modern hotels, shops, and restaurants mingled with reminders of earlier times in old forts, churches, and residences. It has pleasant greenery along the waterfront, all of which gives no hint of the landscape of the rest of the island. Immediately outside town, it is like being dropped on the moon, as the whole island is volcanic, with many small cones and a few larger ones, and barren, pockmarked desolation of brown and black lava and desert areas of sand.

Sandstorms often sweep across from Africa when a strong east wind is blowing, but the inhabitants manage to produce crops of grapes and onions in certain areas where the lava dust is fertile enough. The grapes are grown on stunted vines crouching in hollows in the sand, and a flourishing local wine industry is the result, supplementing tourism. It was all in strange contrast to the sea-blown atmosphere aboard *Sea Cloud*, and it was from here that we took our departure for Martinique.

On a lazy afternoon of light breeze, Captain Schwarz gave the tourists on hotel row along the beaches of Arrecife a show by setting all sail. Behind the gleaming white high-rises, the jagged profiles of the volcanic cones made a strange backdrop as we drifted slowly along. Wind surfers came out and flitted around us, gawking up, and water-skiers made patterns across our bow and stern. One boat brought a great roar of rage from Schwarz, with much fist shaking, when it cut across the fishing line he always had streaming from the stern.

With the "show" over as evening calm descended, we heard the now-familiar creak of blocks as the sails were doused, all from on deck, in a loose furl, and the rumble of the diesels shook the deck. We would be slanting southwestward to end up in Martinique's latitude of 14°30′ and would have to make 200 miles a day to arrive on schedule in two weeks. I had not realized how extensive the Canaries were, stretching southwestward over 300 miles of ocean. The lights of Grand Canary off the starboard quarter that evening were the last land we were to see until Martinique.

We had one day of great sailing and normally we should have been in the northeast trades after leaving the Canaries, but there was a large storm center southwest of the Azores several hundred miles to the northwest of us. It showed as a great ring of trouble on the ship's facsimile weather map, and we could tell of it by the large, long swells moving down from the north and a southwest wind, fairly fresh, sucking around the storm system and curving into it, killing the normal trades.

The sails were put in harbor furl, tightly stopped up in contrast to the usual nightly loose furl, and the yards were slanted to give the least wind resistance while we powered further south than had been originally planned to get out of the storm system's influence. While we were keeping a cruise ship schedule, it was interesting to contemplate what our passage would have been like before the days of auxiliary power. I had the feeling we would still be wallowing between Gibraltar and Casablanca, and this wind would certainly have been a bothersome one for our route.

After a couple of days, we moved out of the system, the wind came around to the east, where it should be, and we settled into a wonderful routine in the langorous warmth of the trades that lasted all the way to the West Indies. This was the classic route so many voyagers have taken from the days of the explorers to the modern-day explosion of long-voyaging yachts, and it was great to experience it in this unique vessel. En route, incidentally, we sighted four sailing yachts in the two weeks.

With another great flurry of activity, the sails broke into the sun again, the thump of the diesels was stilled, and *Sea Cloud*, heeling alightly, built her speed up to close to 10 knots. There was a grin on everyone's face as we stood with necks craning and watched how they "corkscrewed" the yards to meet the wind twist aloft. This was what we had come for.

There were now 29 of us as passengers; all but 4 were Americans. Four Germans, two elderly gentlemen and two women, sisters off on a holiday, and the life of the party, had become familiar friends by now. There was always the fascination of watching the ship's work, but there were other amusements too. Meal times, open seating, with lunch always a buffet on deck, were pleasantly congenial, and the food was generally good except for one disastrous attempt to give us lobscouse, a form of fish stew from the old sailing ship days that missed the mark with modern taste buds by a wide margin. The Johnsons gave wonderful lectures on their cruising, with Irving's movies from *Peking* a classic highlight, and other passengers chipped in with talks on their special fields of information. We had several "sea story" sessions, with everyone swapping yarns in an informal manner, moderated by me with as much tact as I could muster. The open-air bar on the top deck was a midday rendezvous point, the library got a good workout, and there were even a couple of joggers circling the main deck. It was nine times around to the mile, and some of us walked it instead as a way to work off the meal hours.

The crew members were easy to talk to and informative on their work. Most of them were young adventurers who considered it a great experience for a few voyages but were not ready to settle into a long-term arrangement. This attitude was fortified by the fact that the purser, who administered the crew's routines, was evidently a holdover from Nazi mentality and endeared himself to no one.

The days went by in a pleasant blend, and there were some especially good ones near the end of the passage. As we neared the West Indies, the trades had a little more heft, the flying fish were more voluminous in their shimmering flights, two sei whales came alongside to play around us for most of an afternoon, and each night the sunsets, made more dramatic when viewed through square-rigged patterns, grew more colorful.

One day we had a bottle-throwing party. Everyone put messages in bottles and tossed them overboard, and at least one, launched by Mrs. Robert Foster of San Diego, was picked up and responded to by a visitor on Barbuda.

Once, with the wind lighter than usual, we had a photo-taking session. While *Sea Cloud* lazed along, a few of us were dropped off in a lifeboat and circled around taking shots. Aside from the chance to get pictures, it was a memorable sight to see her there, backed by puffs of trade wind clouds in her natural setting on the deep blue of the open sea, and as we chased her into the lowering sun, her silhouette was magnificent against the western horizon.

Then the breeze piped up, and there was one glorious 36-hour period when the trade was strong enough to keep us sailing without power. With a bone in her teeth, she surged over the whitecapped seas, and

The beauty and symmetry of a square-rigger from the bowsprit

at night, with the moon almost full, we all gathered on the fantail to savor the feeling of sailing through the night with the sails drawing beautifully.

It was during this spell that I had a chance to go out on the bowsprit for picture taking (with crew escort), and it was a great place to get the feel of a full-rigged ship at sea. Some 40 feet below me was the deep blue of the sea, then the rise and fall of the bow cleaving the waves into white wings, and behind me the lovely symmetry of the ship, all straining curves and controlled power against a blue trade wind sky.

The dawn arrival off Martinique's steamy, tropical mountains came all too soon.

Belize

The world's second longest barrier reef, exceeded only by the monumental Great Barrier Reef of Australia, lies off the coast of the Central American country of Belize, just south of Mexico's Yucatan Peninsula. Belize was formerly British Honduras, adopting the name of the capital city of the country when it gained independence.

The reef stretches for more than 100 miles along the coast and has several satellite reefs outside it in the Caribbean. It encloses a smooth water lagoon that varies from about 2 to 10 miles in width between the reef and the mainland, and the mainland shore is jungle country.

A latitude line drawn eastward from Belize would go south of Jamaica and Hispaniola in the Caribbean and pass just north of Antigua. The climate is typically Caribbean, with the expected trade wind, and the seas have had a good distance to build up under the trades before meeting their demise on the reef.

My cruise there was in June 1975, when there was very little yachting development in the area. Since then a bareboat charter fleet has gone into operation, but the area is generally far behind the Eastern Caribbean in facilities, resorts, and the character of its civilization. The cruise was also different, as it was the only "dude" cruise I have ever been on. For "dude," read a cruise on which passengers book individually, rather than as a group, just paying for a ticket (our English barge cruise was on the same basis). Actually, this was a special junket for press and travel agents to board a

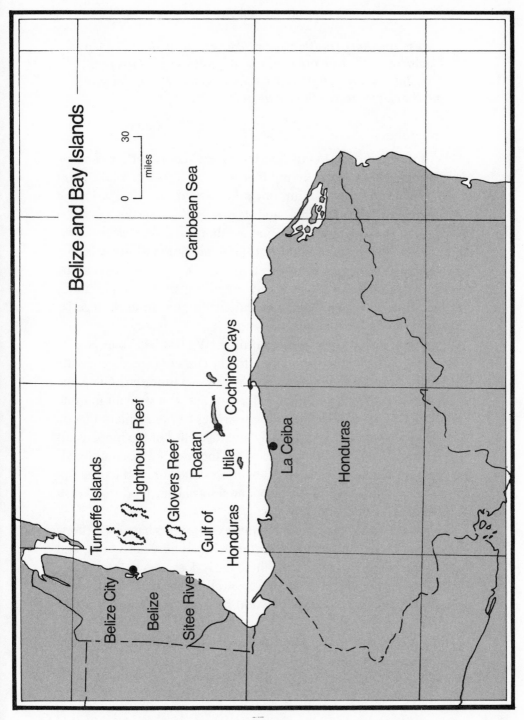

Belize and Bay Islands

0 ____ 30
miles

Caribbean Sea

Turneffe Islands

Lighthouse Reef

Glovers Reef

Roatan

Utila

Cochinos Cays

Gulf of
Honduras

La Ceiba

Honduras

Belize City

Belize

Sitee River

rather ungainly Baltic trader conversion called Golden Cachalot, *a 90-foot three-master. Unfortunately the operation did not take and was soon abandoned, but it did give me the chance to visit a unique area.*

The initial approach to cruising the Belize reef is not a promising one. Belize city is a dump, to put it accurately, a grubby tropical port of ramshackle houses and a run-down business district on a river that is an open sewer. It is low, hot, and steamy, with no scenery, and the harbor is an open roadstead, so shallow that even the *Golden Cachalot*, with a 9-foot draft, could not come alongside a pier or quay. With each ebb tide, a great brown stain seeps out of the river into the roadstead, spreading its odiferous waters in a giant fan of pollution, and the schooner's crew had to be careful to pick an anchorage far enough out to escape this daily visitation.

Our group arrived early in the morning. We had left Miami on an 0700 plane of TAN, the national airline of Honduras, and, since the flight was 1 hour and 55 minutes and there was a time zone difference of 2 hours, we arrived 5 minutes before we left. We were all in quite a good mood, since TAN had started serving complimentary Bloody Marys and screwdrivers immediately after takeoff, but the mood gradually simmered down while we sat in the lobby of a waterfront hotel, Belize's best, but possibly a class C by most standards, and looked out across the brown miasma of the harbor awaiting a launch ride to *Golden Cachalot*.

I might add that I have heard that intervening years have seen efforts to clean up the river and harbor, that new hotels have been built, and that the bareboat service operating there today does not use this harbor. At the time of my visit it lived up very well to Somerset Maugham's sarcastic remark that, should the world be given an enema, it would be applied in Belize City.

This introduction made it perhaps even more fascinating to escape to the unspoiled, primeval world of the reefs, where the waters were the usual startling colors and clarity of the tropics and the trade wind

Golden Cachalot

blew clean and free from the open sea. As soon as *Golden Cachalot* weighed anchor and cleared the roadstead, which, in character, seemed to have collected more than its share of the world's semiderelict, rust-streaked freighters, there was a complete change in atmosphere. For the rest of the week, except for occasional native conch smacks, we saw just one powerboat with a dive group aboard, and not another vessel or plane.

Golden Cachalot would sail when there was a reaching breeze, and she breathed old-time ship atmosphere in her sails and rigging. Instead of turnbuckles, her rigging was adjusted by lanyards and deadeyes, and her sails were heavy and old. We actually had one fine sail on a reach when the trade was up to 25 knots, but most of our progress was by power. Her appearance had not been helped by an ungainly "castle" on her fantail that contained the six passenger cabins (doubles) and the lounge, as well as the bridge, but she was comfortable to be aboard, and the food was good.

Rather than a sailing experience, this was a nature tour. The cruise director was a professional naturalist who led shore expeditions, and there was diving, snorkeling, bird watching, reef walking, iguana spotting, Sunfish sailing, and jungle-river exploring. Since none of the passengers knew each other beforehand, it was an interesting exercise in adaptation. After preliminary fencing and sounding out, cliques soon formed. The ship's comic emerged, as well as the ship's horse's ass, who set about contradiciting what everyone said right from the start, and people with like interests gravitated together. I fortunately had a congenial roommate, even though he had mainly come for the scuba diving, which I do not do.

After a first night quietly at anchor in a lagoon on a nearby section of the reef, we headed offshore for Lighthouse Reef, 30 miles beyond the main barrier. Lighthouse, which is lined with wrecks on its seaward side, some of which could be seen as we skirted inside the reef, is the site of a strange anomaly of nature called the Blue Hole. This hole is perfectly circular, about 200 yards in diameter, and more than 400 feet deep, inky dark blue, in a setting of reefs and pale pastel flats. To get there, our young English captain went to the crow's nest and called down wheel orders as we snaked through a maze of reefs and shoals and their brilliant colors, with our 9-foot draft just scraping by. We anchored in the only break of the reef surrounding the Hole, swinging out over the dark blue depths. Captain Cousteau had come here in *Calypso*, but very few vessels have managed the tortuous route in through the reefs.

The scuba divers had a banner day. They reported fantastic conditions along the walls of the Hole, which are lined with stalagmite-filled caves, and the companionship of numerous hammerhead sharks. I manned the ship's Sunfish and sailed around the area, and it was a rare experience to come planing in off the shallows onto the blue depths as distinctly as stepping off a curb. Around the perimeter, I could see the dorsals of sharks and the occasional flick of a tail in the shallow reef waters, and I made very sure not to capsize.

By way of contrast, our next expedition took us to a mangrove island called Half Moon Cay in a lagoon of Lighthouse Reef, where red-footed booby birds hatched, and my first visit to a booby hatchery was memorable. The birds have no fear of man, and it is possible to walk right up to their nests in the low-lying bushes and eyeball a nesting mother at about 2 feet. Iguanas up to several feet long lurk under the lime-encrusted trees—the whole island is white—and stand immobile when they know they are being watched. Nearby was an island where frigate birds hatch, and the atmosphere was entirely different from the free and easy booby hatchery. The frigate birds, dark and fierce looking, with a pronounced vee in their big wingspread and a long forked tail, have no intention of letting anyone come near their nests. A small boat approaching would be dive-bombed with ferocity, and no one landed there.

Crossing the main lagoon to the mainland, we anchored off the mouth of the Sitee River, a slow-moving jungle stream that wound into the interior through dense growth and few signs of man. In the ship's launches, bird-watching expeditions headed upriver, and I found the shoreline and the jungle growth more fascinating than the birding, of which there was very little. When someone got all excited because they saw a starling, I offered them a trip to my yard in New Jersey, which often swarms with them. We did see a few exotically colored birds making bright spots in the denseness of the jungle.

At an idyllic-looking little island called Tobacco Cay, a native fishing settlement located next to one of the passes through the big reef, we donned sneakers and walked for a quarter of a mile across flats to the edge of the reef. Surf creamed onto it further out, but we could walk past small tidal pools teeming with fish of all colors—walking snorkeling I called it—and the coral took many forms, shapes, and colors. Shell collectors were happy there as well.

By now, everyone except the demon contradicter had become quite good friends, and the young crew members, mostly American, had become distinct personalities. Most of them were adventurers who would try anything once to get to see the world and were not particularly professional as sailors. The naturalist, a young Californian, was well trained in his field and a helpful guide as well as a competent cruise director.

The night off Tobacco Cay, with everyone feeling quite adventurous from having climbed around on the reef, there was a special party on deck at which hair was let down as it had not been before, and there was a new feeling of relaxed intimacy that had been previously lacking. A bunch of strangers had shared a common experience and had become friends, even though we would all be going our separate ways very soon. I had been a crew member in ocean races, had occasionally been a guest on friends' cruising boats, and had had a few trips with professional charter crews, but I was mainly used to being my own skipper while cruising, and this had been a different and interesting change of pace.

It was also a change of pace to come in from the rich blue of the sea on the wings of the trade and move into the brown scum of Belize Harbor. The brilliant world of the reef already seemed a million miles away.

The Bay Islands of Honduras

The Bay Islands are a small Anglo-Saxon enclave in a Hispanic world. They belong to Honduras, and they sit in the Gulf of Honduras, southeast of the Belize Reef, south of Mexico's Yucatan Peninsula, and north of the big peninsula Honduras makes sticking out into the Caribbean. They were ceded to Honduras in 1861 by Queen Victoria, but the inhabitants, still largely of Anglo descent, have never adapted to Spanish ways. When we were there in 1978 to "case the joint" preliminary to CSY opening a charter base there, there was a concerted effort to bring them more in the orbit of mainland Honduras, with compulsory Spanish schooling, but the inhabitants were being stubbornly individualistic in staying with their long-time life-style (and they have never forgiven Victoria).

The atmosphere was reminiscent of the more familiar Eastern Caribbean in prewar days, and the lay of the land was very near to ideal for the charter operation CSY was contemplating. Roatan, the main Bay Island, is on an east–west axis and is a 30-mile-long cigar-shaped island with a profusion of excellent harbors. Most of these are on the south coast, which means they are protected from winter northers, which can be a problem. These occasionally sweep down across the Gulf of Mexico from the western plains of the United States with wintry blasts and cold rain, but the south shore is well *sheltered. Most of the north shore is a long barrier reef with only one or two breaks. In addition, there are three off-lying sets of cays—Utila, Guanacca, and Cochinos—that are a distinct dividend for local cruising. Our boat there was a stock CSY 44,* Basilisk, *and we had her for the week after Jules Wilensky had been gathering material in her for CSY's local cruising guide.*

Getting there was not, like the advertising slogan, half the fun. We (Jane and our friends Helen and Ted Tracy) had taken the same pleasant TAN flight from Miami that I had in going to Belize, complete with Bloody Marys and screwdrivers from 0705 on, but once TAN had deposited us at the airport at La Cieba, Honduras, our fortunes deteriorated. A whole chapter could be detailed with what we went through to get on the DC-3 to Roatan, but suffice it to say that it took us more than 4 hours of un-air-conditioned discomfort and language difficulties before we found ourselves on a wobbly DC-3 winging away from La Ceiba across the blue Caribbean.

Roatan is only 30 miles offshore, which sounds like a simple flight, but it was not that simple. The airplane's acronym, incidentally, was SAHSA, which is something to do with Honduran aviation, but we were told by disgruntled Roataners that it really meant Stay at Home, Stay Alive.

Without a common language to tell us what we were in for, we thought we were flying nonstop to Roatan, and there was a moment of near-panic when we looked out to see mangroves under the wing on one side and shoal-water reefs on the other and then felt the plane bounce along a dirt runway with loose stones assaulting the underbody. It turns out that this was Utila; at least the peeling sign on the overgrown outhouse that served as a terminal said so. Finally, after a bouncy takeoff that just missed dragging a few mangroves along with us, we were airborne again, quivering like a sensitive dog, and in no time at all were plunked down on a dirt strip that was enveloped in

248

clouds of dust. We and our bags were thrown out into the dust, and, while there was no visible evidence, we figured this must be Roatan. Such is travel in Latin America.

Things improved after that. Out of the cloud of dust, a young man emerged and introduced himself as Compo, who was to be CSY's local manager. He obviously had some Hispanic antecedents, as he was olive skinned and dark haired, but he spoke with the Roatan twang, a lilting accent reminiscent of Bermuda or the Bahamas, and, the more we got to know him, the more we realized he was a true Roatan native with the ingrained attitude of suspicion toward mainland Honduras. If anything goes wrong or doesn't work, a Roataner will tell you it's "Sponish." He took us to a private house overlooking Brick Harbor, where the CSY base was to be established, and where we were to gird our loins for the coming cruise.

The house was set well up on a hill with a fine view of the harbor, the fringing reef, and beyond, the deep, whitecap-flecked blue of the Caribbean. The trade was blowing briskly, and it was a heartening scene. There was no boat in the harbor, but the scene grew more heartening when a sail appeared running down the coast from the north, and she could soon be identified as a CSY 44 when she entered the dogleg channel into Brick Harbor. Wilensky was turning the boat over to us, and he and his crew also spent the night in the house while we compared notes. We were to have the same local seaman, Charlie Osgood, as guide.

Compo had the boat provisioned the next morning, and we moved aboard at midday and met Charlie. He was a professional merchant seaman in his early 30s who had grown up on Roatan, was married and had a young child, and whose family had been on the island since the eighteenth century. He knew every rock and coral head in the area and proved an infallible guide, no matter what the 1876 charts said. He was engagingly friendly, hated everything "Sponish," knew every-one in every harbor we went to, and was generally a very pleasant shipmate. He had a great weakness for country and western music, and much of his time was spent with a portable radio in his lap or by his side. One of his buddies was the country and western disc jockey on the Roatan station, and every so often he would dedicate a song to Charlie.

"Haven't seen my old buddy Charlie [drawled out as "Chaaarlie"] Osgood around lately, but I hope he's where he can hear the next number," the voice would boom, and Charlie would chuckle and slap his thigh as the song came on. The theme song of the program was a country ditty called "I was Lookin' Back to See If She Was Lookin' Back to See If I Was Lookin' Back to See If She Was Lookin' Back at Me," which became the theme song for the cruise. By the time the cruise was over, we had all learned the words and would sing it in unison.

There was a fine trade blowing when we were ready to take off the next morning, and we thrashed into it enthusiastically on a beat to French Harbor a few miles to the east. We came in there to have a look at the shrimpers, with a large fleet nested along the town piers. Shrimping is one of the main industries on Roatan, but this seemed to be between-seasons time, and the fleet was in port. Everywhere we went Charlie knew someone, so that we could nest with a shrimper or tie up at a private dock, and we hardly anchored at all during the week. The south coast of Roatan has a harbor around every point, and we made a short jaunt, again beating into a lively trade, eastward to Oak Ridge, another shrimping center. Here we had a berth at the private pier of an American couple who had lived there for years, and everywhere we went Charlie was able to put us in the middle of local life. Typical of people who moved to some out-of-the-way Caribbean island before it was discovered, this couple was already bemoaning the way Roatan had changed, although to us, in comparison with Antigua, British Virgin Islands, and other cruising centers in the Eastern Caribbean, it was light-years away from being spoiled. Their house was right at the water's edge, with the terrace off their porch actually the quay where we were tied, and it had a fine view of port activity and the little houses crowded along the shore.

Another stop eastward was the sprawling harbor of Port Royal. A long reef, with an opening in the middle and at the western end, separated it from the open Caribbean, and there was room to anchor all the bareboats in the Caribbean in its well-protected expanse. The pirate Henry Morgan had based here at the height of his Caribbean operations, and remnants of his fort still stand on the cay at the break in the reef. This used to be the main maintenance base for his ships, which he had careened along the shore, and the remains of some that were wrecked or abandoned can still be found along the reef. This has attracted divers from all over the world, and the wreck of one of their mother ships was a prominent fixture on the reef. She had been caught in one of the two hurricanes to strike through here since World War II and was stranded on the coral.

Several privately owned yachts on extensive cruises were anchored here, but in general we saw very few visiting yachts in the whole Bay Island area.

Perhaps the nicest harbor we found on the south coast of Roatan was at Caribe Point Bight, a deep indentation behind protective reefs, with graceful hills around it. We tied to a small pier here, the beginnings of a planned resort and marina, in a setting of complete isolation. I climbed the hill above the pier to take pictures, and the setting was idyllic, the epitome of a tropical hideaway, with the ever-impressive display of colors across the reefs in light greens and pale blues giving to the royal blue of the open sea beyond. The harbor itself was deep enough to be a rich blue, not as deeply hued as the Caribbean, but a thorough contrast to the pale shallows on the reef.

Backtracking along the shore, we went westward to Coxen Hole, Roatan's main port and tumbledown metropolis, to do a bit of shopping and so that Charlie could check with his family before heading "offshore." This was to the Cochinos (*hog* in English, but more romantic sounding in Spanish) Cays, 20 miles to the south, halfway to the mainland. The high mountains of Honduras had been a distant backdrop to our sails along the coast of Roatan, and now we were headed for their blue bulk. The trade was on the beam, and *Basilisk* took off with a bone in her teeth, covering the distance in under 3 hours on our best sail of the cruise.

At first we could not pick out the Cochinos against the high background of the mainland, but they gradually took shape and popped into greater detail as we surged toward them, and when we rounded into the bight of the largest cay to anchor for the first time, they opened out as a picture-book group of cays and islands that had the aura of the South Pacific. The Cays were owned by a Scottish family named Griffiths. The father had been a caretaker and inherited the islands from their Honduran owner, and now he and his son and their wives presided over this unusual domain, planning its gradual development. A few houses dotted the hillsides, and there were fishermen's shacks on some of the smaller cays. Golden beaches lined most of the islands, and reefs inshore meant fine diving. A tiny grass airstrip took up most of one of the little cays.

This had to be the highlight of the area in scenery and atmosphere, but there was more to see. In our alloted week there was not time to take in both Guanaja to the east and Utila to the west, and we decided that Utila, which was a bit closer, would be the choice. For these first few days the weather had been classically Caribbean, but now, as we set sail for Utila past the beaches and palm trees of the Cochinos, we ran into one of those "it never happens like this" conditions. Instead of building during the day as it usually does, the feeble morning trade wind disappeared completely, and we were left wallowing on an oily, windless sea. When a breeze did appear, it was a whisper from the west ("it never blows from there") and the temperature shot up into the 90s. We were thankful for the cockpit Bimini, and we finally ended up powering into the remote little community of Utila Cays. This is a base for shrimpers, and we tied alongside one whose skipper was a friend of Charlie's.

The whole town, built on a couple of minuscule cays, is a bunch of small shacks on stilts over the water, with a boardwalk connecting them, and most of the traffic is by canoe and other small boats. The entire town came down to gawk at *Basilisk*, still a novelty in the area, and to visit with Charlie, who knew everyone. We were the main entertainment in town. From there we spent a lazy day drifting around the outer Utila Cays, dots of sand and coral on a wide pale-green lagoon, each with a palm tree or two and some with a single house.

Anthony's Cay

We beachcombed on a deserted one, picking up shells along the white fringe of beach, and swam in the limpid shallows, isolated and alone in the world. Only native canoes were visible, and just one or two of them, as we drifted over the calm waters on the way back to Utila Cays.

A young family friend of Charlie's had asked to hitch a ride with us. He was Joey Cooper, a dark, intense, and very attractive lad who wanted

253

to see relatives in Coxen Hole. In his 14 years, he had only been the 20 or so miles to Roatan twice and had not been anywhere else. He was an engaging shipmate and pitched in enthusiastically in all the ship's chores.

He loved to take wheel tricks, and when Charlie negotiated some lobsters at a good price at East Harbor, the metropolis of Utila, on our next stop, Joey attacked them with vigor, picking the meat expertly for us. Our last stop was a move back from the isolated world of Utila. On the north shore of Roatan, Anthony's Cay is a well-established resort specializing in diving, and we drifted over there on the still light and vagrant westerly while porpoises played around the bow, much to Joey's delight (and ours).

The entrance is a narrow one, and I could see how the north shore of Roatan would be bad news in a winter norther. The reefs loomed at us through the glass-clear water, close by on both sides, as Charlie piloted us in. Dinner ashore was a step back to the world of tourists and resort amenities, and, in turning the boat back the next day, we almost felt as though we had been cruising in two separate centuries.

The Grenadines

The Grenadines are a 60-mile chain of small islands, none longer than a few miles or higher than about 1,000 feet, that stretch between St. Vincent on the north and Grenada in the south. Bequia, northernmost of the Grenadines, is 5 miles from St. Vincent, and the smaller southern Grenadines south of Carriacou almost touch Grenada. The chain is split politically between the two big islands, with the dividing line north of Carriacou.

In the 1960s we cruised the Grenadines three times, and I was convinced that no better cruising area could be found. Since then we have been back four more times, but no more recently than 10 years from the present writing, and the reports that have come back from friends who have been there lately have been disquieting. First of all, the "rowboat Mafia" menace of teenaged boys hawking services and "protection" has grown to unpleasant proportions. Also, as has inevitably happened in the great spread of private and charter cruising in the Caribbean—and all areas—since the '60s, the popular spots have been overrun, losing their unique charm of isolation. Grenada has in the meantime gone politically sour.

We first saw the Grenadines from the old schooner Mollihawk, the original charter yacht in the Caribbean, when operated by V. E. B. Nicholson Co. of Antigua. This was in 1962, and we were alone in such choice spots as the Tobago Cays, an impossibility today, and there were just two other yachts in the harbor of St. George's, Grenada. We bareboated there in 1968 and 1970 and had a crewed charter in

255

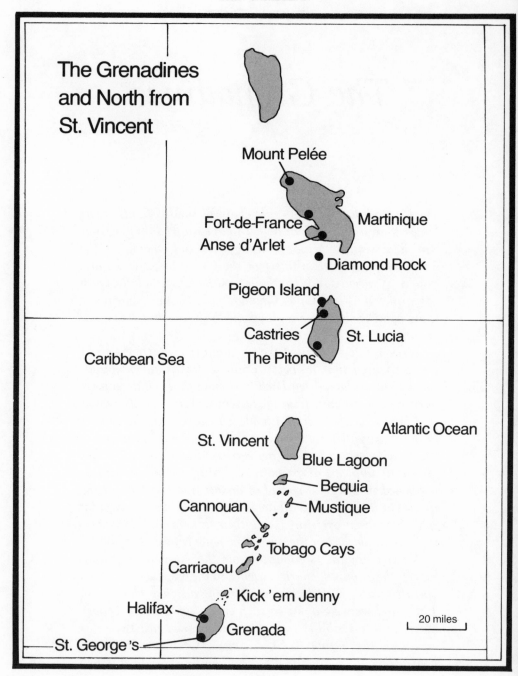

The Grenadines
and North from
St. Vincent

Mount Pelée

Fort-de-France
Anse d'Arlet

Martinique

Diamond Rock

Pigeon Island

Caribbean Sea

Castries
The Pitons

St. Lucia

St. Vincent

Atlantic Ocean

Blue Lagoon

Bequia

Cannouan

Mustique

Tobago Cays

Carriacou

Kick 'em Jenny

Halifax

St. George's

Grenada

20 miles

1969, and our last visit was in Talonega *in 1973 (see the next chapter). Circumstances have kept us away since, although we got to Bequia Channel in* Brunelle *in 1980. Perhaps we shall try again, but meanwhile it is pleasant to remember the Grenadines as we saw them in the '60s.*

Our first bareboat cruise in the Grenadines was an exciting challenge. The one taste of the area when we had come through in *Mollihawk* had left memories of gorgeously clear water, perfect trade wind sailing on a perpetual reach, and untouched anchorages where we were alone with the stars. To take this on by ourselves seemed a wonderful opportunity, for at the time *Mollihawk*'s professional skipper had been so worried about doing something wrong with a *Yachting* editor on board that he had kept the auxiliary turning over the whole time we were sailing, took sails down if a cloud darkened the sun momentarily, and anchored so far out in most of the harbors that they all looked alike. We were immobilized passengers and had forced ourselves to sit back and enjoy whatever happened. Now, I felt, we could really get our teeth into it, operating on our own.

Things did not start propitiously, however. When we arrived at Grenada's slightly terrifying airport, where you seem to be flying straight into a mountainside in making the approach, we found our luggage had somehow gone astray during our plane change in Barbados. We travel with a large red duffle bag, and we were told that someone had thought it was a diplomatic pouch and sent it to the U.S. Embassy in Trinidad.

We were to board the 36-foot Van de Stadt sloop *Merlin*, a fiber glass cruiser/racer, at St. George's, the snug little city at the other end of the island from the airport, and the taxi ride over the crazy zigzags of Grenada's mountain roads, with banana trucks careening wildly at you around curves and blind corners, was almost as exciting as the airport approach.

Merlin was fine for our purpose, though a bit small and crowded for 36 feet. She was well equipped and was a fast sailboat, and her only real drawback was a very small companionway, with a fixed, contoured top on the coach roof instead of a sliding hatch, giving the opening something of the shape of an Edsel grill, and not much bigger. Our cruising companions were Julia and Mason Gross, and Mason, a large ex-oarsman, found negotiating this arrangement so difficult that he would only go through it once a day. If he wanted something from below thereafter, someone else had to fetch it.

The boat was fine, but, in the manner of charter services in those early days of the trade, she was not ready when we arrived at Grenada Yacht Services, the busy marina on the newly opened lagoon off the main harbor of St. George's, a great development since our 1962 visit. It seemed she had a battery problem, but Rudi, the mechanic, would take care of it. Rudi, beefy, with a thick German accent, exuded confidence and "don't vorries" as he hooked up a charger. In our travel-tired city clothes, we hoped he was right, and the hum of the charger accompanied our snoring through the night.

In the morning, there was consternation and much head scratching when Rudi, arriving cheerfully to disconnect it, found he had hooked the charger up backward: "Ach du lieber!" But after all, we could not leave without our luggage and it was as yet unreported. On came the hum again, correctly hooked this time, we hoped. Jane and I were considering buying bathing suits and T-shirts the next day as we were having a nightcap in the cockpit, when the dock attendant came to say that there was someone at the gate to see me. I could not believe it when this proved to be an airline truck with the red duffle bag, dusty but intact, sitting in the back in lonely splendor. Eureka!

We could now provision and head for sea, and the chief thrill of shopping via dinghy across the harbor in St. George's was in buying a case of Mount Gay Rum for $7.00 in bond, and Scotch for $16. This was to be for consumption on board only, and we vowed to do our level best to comply. By the time we were loaded, it was too late to head for Carriacou, 30 miles away in the Grenadines, so we made a leisurely departure, aiming for the little harbor at Halifax, halfway up the 17-mile west coast of the island. It was that time of day when the lowering sun casts a glow of gold on the island peaks, soaring 3,000 feet into a heavy cover of cumulus, and our fortunes seemed to have taken a symbolic turn for the better when a silvery curtain of rain misted down the sun-dappled hillside and a rainbow's arch spanned the entrance to Halifax in perfect symmetry.

As is so often the case in leeward-side harbors, there was an underlying surge in Halifax that kept *Merlin* ranging fitfully around her anchor while it rumbled and hissed on the beach, a more satisfying lullaby than the hum of the battery charger. In the morning we were faced with the price of getting to the Grenadines: the passage by Kick 'em Jenny. This is a craggy pile of rock, halfway between the north end of Grenada and Carriacou. It is officially on the chart as Diamond Rock and looks very much like the one off Martinique, but everyone calls it by its nickname. This is supposed to come from the name given to it by the French in the days when clumsy square-riggers had a hard time fighting by its strong breezes and currents from the Atlantic and Caribbean that clash here. They called it *quai qu'on gêne*—worrisome island— and it has naturally been corrupted into the colorful, meaningless, but somehow expressive, Kick 'em Jenny.

Kick us it did, as we had a rough day of beating past it once we came out from the protection of Grenada. It was a wet, hard thrash. *Merlin* sailed well, but she had low freeboard, and the size of the short, confused seas off Kick 'em Jenny seemed designed expressly for slashing her cockpit with spray.

The waves were big and bright blue, and the crests hissed and swished as they tumbled toward us. There was a pronounced westward set, and the closest we could come to Carriacou was 3 miles off, when we finally came under its lee and flipped over to port tack for a hitch into Tyrrel Bay. This deep indentation at the south end of Carriacou is a welcome haven after being kicked by Jenny, and we settled into the bonded stuff as quickly as possible in an effort to cut the all-pervading salt. Little boys in the scruffiest of rowboats were selling limes and the local phenomenon, tree-growing oysters, even in those days, although with none of the insistence that is the style today. The oysters, though a novelty, are really watery and bland and not very good.

Jane and I once beat into Tyrrel Bay when we were cruising by

Native workboats at Bequia

ourselves on an even wetter thrash by Kick 'em Jenny, and as we dropped the hook in its blissful calm around 1700, we agreed that if every cruising day was like this one, we would not cruise very much. After a couple of belts, we were in the sack at 1730, sleeping the sleep of the exhausted.

From Carriacou on we had no more beats in *Merlin*. The trade remained evenly in the east as we crossed up and down the chain. In some areas the islands and reefs give protection and it is fine, smooth water sailing; then you suddenly come into a patch of water that is

260

opposite a break in the reefs, and the seas build up to offshore proportions in no time.

Bequia was our northern turnaround point. It is the most civilized and interesting of the Grenadines. The main harbor, Port Elizabeth, is a colorful mix of yachts and native boats, and in the '60s there was still native boatbuilding. Bequia schooners traded through the islands under sail, since replaced by powered vessels, and a big, husky-looking gray schooner riding at anchor was the newest, and probably one of the last, products of local sailboat building.

This was one of the places we had dinner ashore, at the Sunny Caribbee, and it had been the only place for this in 1962 in all the Grenadines. Leaving Bequia, we had a pungent reminder that whaling still goes on there, passing to leeward of Isle de Quatre, where the whaling station is. At noon we picked a tiny cove on the west side of Canouan, barely detectable on the chart, for a lunch stop. It was our only day that lacked bright sunshine, and there were spits of rain in the air when we decided to anchor for a while. There was just room for us between the rocky cliffs in the cove, and there was an extra added-attraction sideshow while we had cocktails and a salad: Hundreds of pelicans dive-bombed the inshore reef in wave after wave, splashing down in a continuous assault like the wild action of a naval air attack in wartime. Since there was no name on the chart, we decided to call the place Pelican Cove.

The sun came out again as we moved on to Palm Island. This took us right by the much-touted Tobago Cays, and we no doubt should have stopped, but there was a forest of masts in the anchorage, and we decided to keep on going. It was the only Grenadines cruise in which we have not stopped there, and it is truly one of the prize cruising anchorages anywhere. The water seems clearer and more brilliantly multihued, the beaches are whiter, and the reefs are more colorful than almost any anchorage to which we have been. It was the first place I ever snorkeled, and unfortunately I have never found a better place since—a climax too soon.

Palm Island, née Prune Island, had recently been taken over by world voyagers John and Mary Caldwell, who had performed prodigious feats in converting this deserted spot into a resort. As we anchored off its talcum-white beach, we were treated to the startling sight of what looked like about 300 native workers catching the "rush hour" native sloop back home to Union Island, 3 miles away. One more lunch pail aboard would have capsized the whole caboodle, but John reported that they made it that way every day.

It turned out that this was the first night the restaurant was to be open at the new resort, and dinner was to be a special event. We came ashore for a preprandial swim and were just changing after a shower in one of the beach front cottages when a shout of "come quick" from John summoned us out to the beach, wrapped in towels and still dripping. We were just in time to catch that sometime phenomenon, the green flash, which can only be seen when the ocean horizon is absolutely devoid of clouds at the moment when the sun's upper limb sinks below it. Then a molten glow of green tips the last of the sun, and, as on this night, a flash of green shoots into the sky momentarily. John had been right to see it coming, and everyone cheered.

At Union, which is marked by a distinctive pair of peaks that form a very definite U, a landmark that can be seen all over the Grenadines, we again ate ashore at another newly opened spot, a so-called "yacht club" at the little port of Clifton, and it was a short sail from here back to Carriacou. Here Linton Rigg, a former yacht broker from the States who had lived in the Bahamas for a while and started the Out Island Regatta at George Town, Exuma, had settled in as proprietor of a small guest house and restaurant called Mermaid Tavern, and we stopped for a visit and a family-style dinner with all the inn's guests.

Linton, who had grown quite deaf as the years caught up with him, had a booming voice, and his most intimate side remarks were immediately heard by everyone for yards around. I asked him how his health was, and his confidential answer, in the booming voice of a hog caller, was, "Well, Bill. I'm doing as well as could be expected. Just have a little trouble with my prostate, that's all."

Two elderly ladies among the guests looked up, mouths agape and soup spoons halted in midair, and then quickly bent their heads to their soup again.

262

The Grenadines

We had been keeping in touch with home base in Grenada twice each day via the "Children's Hour," then in effect on AM radio. Usually it was just a cheery confirmation that everything was OK on both ends, but the next morning in Tyrrel Bay, the very British voice of the charter manager came on with, "*Merlin, Merlin, Merlin:* traffic for you. Cable for Dr. Mason Gross [pronounced "Grahss" with a British broad *a*]." He then went on to read a message about a fund-raising effort at Rutgers University, of which Mason was president, ending with the phrase, "All this is to be kept completely confidential." We howled with laughter at this: confidential to us and everyone else on the "Children's Hour"!

Carriacou had also given us a special treat the evening before in a taxi ride to one of the highest hills, where there was a magnificent view across a panorama of reefs and cays. The sun, almost down, spread a path of gold, with the bits of land outlined blackly on the glitter, and this time there were clouds and a breathtaking display of colors, but, naturally, no green flash.

We were out among the little islands the next morning headed back for Grenada with the wind fair on our quarter on a bright, blue day. With decks dry and the sun warm on our skins, it was a surging sleigh ride over the big, blue rollers around Kick 'em Jenny, and we lifted a glass to it and laughed at the memory of how it had been going the other way.

North from St. Vincent

The "big islands" of the Lesser Antilles south of Antigua—
Guadeloupe (and the Saintes), Dominica, Martinique, St.
Lucia, and St. Vincent—offer a different kind of cruising
from Antigua itself or the Grenadines. They are mountainous, with relatively few harbors, and the runs between them
are 30 to50 miles of open sea. This is almost always on a
reach in the prevailing trades, and, in contrast, sailing on
the leeward side of these islands is often frustrating and con-
fusing, since their peaks create a large lee. Sometimes there is
flat calm in the lee, sometimes the trade breaks through in
fitful puffs and sudden williwaws, and there can even be a
reverse thermal wind from the west on occasion. We have sailed
in a fresh westerly for as long as 3 hours in the lee of Guadeloupe, even though the trade was steadily in the east on the
windward side.

Scenery and sight-seeing are more important there than the
kind of short-order gunkholing so easy to do in the Grenadines, Antigua, or the Virgins. The towering peaks, some volcanic, are impressive, and the variety in cultures between
islands 30 miles apart is astonishing.

Our first Caribbean cruises in 1961 and 1962 aboard Viking
and Mollihawk took us to Antigua–St. Lucia and Martinique–Grenada, respectively, an exciting first acquaintance
with the kind of cruising I had enviously read about for years.
Our adventures in taking Brunelle down the chain to St.
Vincent and back were chronicled in my last book, South to
the Caribbean, and the cruise in this chapter was on a Carib

264

41, Talonega, *an Alan Gurney-designed bareboat operated by CSY out of St. Vincent.*

The airport at St. Vincent is on an open hillside with a magnificent panoramic view of the Grenadines off to the south. We arrived in late morning via a taxi plane CSY was then sponsoring for the San Juan–St. Vincent connection, and we were happy to be there, since the pilot had identified Dominica as Martinique on the way down, and I was glad he had eventually found St. Vincent.

The main shore road of St. Vincent actually crosses the airport, and it was an odd experience in the taxi taking us to the CSY base to wait at a stop light and traffic gate while a plane zoomed off in front of us. Wandering goats ignored the stop light, but they were evidently plane-wise enough to stay off the runway when it was in use. The view of the Grenadines basking in sun glitter stirred the adrenaline and had us ready and eager for sailing by the time the taxi nosed down the steep drive to CSY's base on well-named Blue Lagoon.

Blue it is, and a lagoon it is, with a narrow entrance channel that has been blasted through the fringing reef, and it is the perfect picture of a tropical harbor. Its only drawback is considerable depth in the center and iffy holding ground, so that its capacity is a bit limited. In contrast to other charter areas, where Americans or Englishmen had conducted the briefing session, a very knowledgeable Vincentian did it smoothly and well here, and the people working on the boats were also very sharp. I have found over the years in the Caribbean that Vincentians, and to a lesser extent Antiguans, are the most expert local boatmen.

After a day or two of playing around in the Grenadines, the main thrust of our cruise was to be northward through the big islands, and we used the first days to become familiar with *Talonega*. The design had been developed expressly for Caribbean bareboating, with a roomy center cockpit lay-out. She would be considered underrigged in most areas, but she was just right for these waters, as she could easily handle +30 knots under full sail. Our only unhappy experience was a collapse of the hibachi, when the butterfly nut on its extension arm had not been tightened enough, and four beautiful filet mignons were contributed to some lucky groupers in Bequia's Elizabeth Harbor. Ted and Helen Tracy were with us for this cruise, and Ted was in charge at the moment of disaster. At this writing, 10 years later, he has still not fully recovered from the dismay (and the memory of the canned spaghetti that had to be substituted).

Our northward swing started with a short run westward along the bottom of St. Vincent to Young Island. This is practically next door to Blue Lagoon and merely served as a change of scene. Young Island is a luxury resort taking up all of a small island just off the shore, with a perfect beach facing the anchorage. Its buildings are set unobtrusively in palm trees in back of the beach, and a craggy hill rises behind them, capping the graceful scene. The narrow stretch of water between Young Island and the big island is a popular one, although there are currents that make a boat ride uneasily across the wind at times.

From here we took off on a brisk run past Kingstown, the commercial port, where freighters and a cruise ship were at the piers, and the town rose in clusters of buildings on the foothills of the island's higher peaks. For a while we spun along swiftly, but, as so often happens, when we turned up the leeward side, the wind became puffily uneven, and we made erratic progress into Cumberland Bay. This half-moon of palm-lined black sand is a good leeward-side harbor and at that time, 1973, was used extensively by bareboats and charter yachts. On entering, though, we were exposed to the kind of welcome that eventually developed into a real problem, culminating in the murder of a prominent American yachtsman by an intruder on his boat. For quite a while afterward Cumberland was "off limits" to charter yachts, and we bypassed it in *Brunelle* in 1980, but I understand that efforts have been made to improve the situation and that some boats do use it.

We were greeted by a swarming fleet of rowboats manned by shouting boys fighting each other for the chance to take our line to a tree on shore and offering all kinds of services and, with veiled threats, protection. This treatment has become the scourge of the islands. It was particularly virulent in Dominica when we were there in 1980, and, as mentioned, has reportedly grown to annoying dimensions in the Grenadines.

Things finally settled down, with our anchor over the stern and a line to a palm tree, and the boys had drifted away to annoy latecomers when we had another form of invasion. Jack Van Ost, the New Jersey dentist who founded CSY and pioneered in many bareboat innovations, had preceded us by a day cruising through Cumberland, and, knowing that we were due to follow, had hired a native band to come aboard to give us a party.

We were just catching our breath over quiet martinis when the band drew alongside and announced, "De Doctuh sent us." Somewhat taken aback, we nevertheless let them swarm aboard and were soon enveloped in calypso rhythms. At first it seemed like great fun and a nice gesture on Jack's part, but as the evening wore on, the gesture began to backfire. The physical presence was overwhelming enough to actually frighten the ladies, and soap and water seemed to have been a seldom-used commodity at Cumberland. They became more and more insistent and overbearing in asking for drinks and cigarettes, and the more they had to drink the more importunate they became. They also claimed that they had not been paid, which we later found out from Jack to be untrue, and it was not until I told them that I would pay them if they left that we were able to get rid of them.

There is a fine line between pleasure and annoyance in this sort of confrontation. On other occasions we have had a delightful and very friendly time with native musicians aboard, but this bunch was bad news, and I was not surprised to hear later reports of the troubles at Cumberland.

In the sun and wind of the morning the incident was all soon forgotten as we took off for St. Lucia. We had to power through the cone of calm under 4,000-foot Soufrière, the volcano at St. Vincent's northern end that erupted with such devastating effect in 1979. When we sailed by it in *Brunelle* in 1980, the satanic smell of sulfur was strong on the wind, but in 1973, the peak was green to its cumulus-capped top.

Clearing it, we felt the full heft of the trade and began a typical open-sea reach toward St. Lucia. It was purple and misty under its

267

Trade wind clouds over St. Vincent

covering of cumulus, and the distinctive twin peaks of the Pitons were dim shapes. Behind us, St. Vincent's cultivated slopes were still a bright green, and, as always happens on this kind of sail, the colors of the islands gradually switched while we surged northward.

Trade wind clouds marched in from the eastward horizon, making dappled shadows on the blue of the sea, and the waves built to a steady pattern of advancing whitecaps. Rushing in on the beam, they would rear up to windward, threatening to tumble aboard, but, with the hiss

Approaching landfall in the Lesser Antilles

and roar of their approach in our ears, the boat would rise to the onslaught, and the back of the wave, streaked in foam, would race off to leeward. There is a hypnotic fascination to this kind of sailing, an envelopment in sound and motion, intensified by the glitter of the sun path on the water and the warm rush of trade wind on the cheeks.

269

Now and then a maverick offshoot of a wave would slap the hull instead of passing underneath, sending a burst of spray across the cockpit, just to remind us that we were very close to the water.

As we approached the Pitons in afternoon, the leeward calm took over. We coaxed her along as far as we could, but finally gave up and powered into Marigot Lagoon, one of the most picturesque of Caribbean harbors. Halfway into its length, a palm-covered point makes out from the north shore, almost cutting off the channel, and there is perfect protection behind it in the inner harbor. The story goes that ships were hidden there in the days of piracy and colonial warfare with palm fronds tied to their mast tops so that they blended in with the trees on the point.

Castries, a few miles further north, is the commercial port for St. Lucia, with yacht services in Vigie Cove hard by the airport on the north side. Castries has little feel of colonial days, unlike so many Caribbean towns, since it was wiped out by an earthquake and fire and rebuilt in twentieth-century style. As a concession to yachtsmen, a special customs office had been opened on the waterfront, easing that perpetual nuisance of these islands, entering and clearing.

An attractive but expensive restaurant called the Coal Pot on pilings at the edge of Vigie Cove was a pleasant place for a shore meal. Sticking to St. Lucia for another day, we went the few miles north to Pigeon Island. In 1961, in *Viking*, we had found this a unique spot, with a small out-island resort run in very individualistic style by a retired Gilbert and Sullivan actress known as Madame Snowball. I'm sure she had played Katisha and Buttercup, judging by her figure and manner, and the place was one of the offbeat delights of the islands. Now we found it closed, and the little offshore island, where Admiral Rodney had a lookout post on top of its highest hill, was connected to the main island by a long causeway. The character of the place was completely changed, and I found this a depressing manifestation of "progress," although one result was a new dredged lagoon off the inner end of the bay that has since become an active yachting and chartering center. We saw a green flash at sunset there, but Ted Tracy did not and is still convinced it was a "snipe hunt."

The sail across St. Lucia Channel toward Martinique was an even brisker replica of the passage from St. Vincent to St. Lucia. Jack Van Ost had suggested we explore the windward side of Martinique, where there is an intriguing maze of little islands and cays inside the fringing reef, but one feel of the trade, slightly north of east, which would mean we would have to tack around the southeast corner of Martinique, convinced me that the windward coast would better be left for summer exploration. If we did go out there, it would mean coming in from the open sea, with the full scend of the seas behind us, trying to find an unmarked opening in the reef with the afternoon sun in our faces. When we caught up with him in Martinique and "thanked" him for the St. Vincent calypso band, he agreed that I had made the right decision about the windward side.

Martinique, capped by the infamous volcano Mount Pelée, was an impressive pile of peaks and cloud cover looming over the rolling seas. The trade was a good 25 knots and *Talonego*, driving on a close reach, went to it with a will. Big flying fish, glistening in the sun, broke away from the bow to dip and soar over the waves, and there was more spray aboard, with the wind further north, than on the previous sail. Gradually the gray blob of Diamond Rock separated from the dark hills a few miles behind it. This is the distinctive hunk of stone that the British took over, scaling its seemingly unsurmountable sides with mountaineering techniques to keep watch on the movement of French warships in and out of Martinique during the colonial wars of the late eighteenth century. With Admiral Rodney perched on Pigeon Island, the Diamond Rock lookouts could send heliograph signals to alert him on what the French were doing.

At the end of this exciting sail, the S.S. *France*, there on a cruise, was an awesome sight off Fort-de-France. We anchored in the bay off the Savanna, a large park along the waterfront of Fort-de-France, and checked in with the newly established customs office on the quay. The official was smiling and courteous, and this was a distinct advance over the old commercial port office in town.

The anchorage was a busy place, full of yachts and crisscrossed by ferries, ship's launches, and local workboats. Music blared from loudspeakers at the Savanna, and there was a bumper-to-bumper stream of traffic honking its way along the waterfront boulevard. Fort-de-France is a cosmopolitan city of about 70,000, with a European ambience in its shops and restaurants and the look of the crowds on the street. Local women, in all skin shades, beautiful, with erect carriages, dress as well as Parisians, and there was even the Paris *Herald Tribune* on sale.

Although the restaurants have come and gone over the years, we have had excellent meals worthy of note on occasion, and the shops are well stocked and stylish. Food shopping here is a special adventure in fighting your way through the open-air market and its myriad odors and in trying to fathom French brand names and packaging in the *supermarché*.

The French islands, especially Martinique, seem to have an entirely different feeling from those that were British and are now independent. There is no sense of racial separation and tension, and the attitude toward visitors is a sophisticated, matter-of-fact one. (It is only on the water, in the way they handle their boats, that the French display a distinctive truculence and hostility.) In Fort-de-France, there are light-years of difference between the atmosphere of this civilized city and the crude, primitive ways of Cumberland Bay or Dominica.

If there had been more time, we would have continued on north-ward to Dominica and Guadeloupe to complete the big island group, but the boat was to be turned in at Martinique in two days, so we remained there. We had been fascinated by the rugged scenery of Dominica in 1961, when we stopped there in *Viking*, but not by its lack of good harbors. A taxi ride high into the mountains to a resort called Springfield Plantation had shown us a wildly exotic jungle rain forest. Guadeloupe had only been a stopover on the way south, though there are enough harbors there to merit a separate cruise, and we had found Les Iles de Saintes, a small rocky group between Guadeloupe and Dominica, an intriguing bit of Brittany dropped in the Caribbean. (A return in 1980 proved highly disillusioning in the way the quaint fishing town had been junked up in the name of tourism.)

We had had enough of the bustle of Fort-de-France after one day, and it was a radical change to cross the bay 3 miles to the little beach

A native schooner off Dominica

resort of Anse Mitan. We anchored off a broad white beach, where children frolicked in the water, squealing and shrieking as children do on beaches everywhere. Families lazed under bright umbrellas, and water-skiers and Sunfish sailors skimmed around us. (This was before the advent of the windsurfer, now ubiquitous in Caribbean resort harbors.) In the evening, we had a live-it-up evening ashore at the Bakoua Hotel. This is a modern white building perched on a promontory overlooking the bay, where the view of the city lights across the way was dazzling, the food excellent, and the steel band lively.

On our final day we eased down the coast 5 miles to Anse d'Arlet, a broad, beach-lined bay that seemed to be the favorite Sunday target of the local folk in Fort-de-France. All sizes and types of local boats were there with everyone having a fine time in the bright sun, and we had a fine time ourselves on our last sail back across the Bay of Fort-de-France, where the trade wind gave *Talonega* a rail-down thrash by way of farewell to us.

Antigua

Antigua was the first Caribbean island to feel the post-World War II boom in yachting, partly by accident and partly for natural reasons. The major natural reason is English Harbour, the best natural yacht harbor anywhere in the West Indies. Also, Antigua is located at the turn of the Antilles, where the arc of islands that has been running east and then southeast all the way from Florida swings due south, across the trades. With English Harbour as a base, it is easier to reach south from Antigua, and back up to it, than to beat there from the northwest, which fit in well with the developing charter activity.

The accident was the arrival in the late '40s of the 1903 all-teak schooner Mollihawk from England. She was manned by Commander V. E. B. Nicholson, a retired British naval officer, his wife, and two teenage sons, and was supposedly on her way to a new life in Australia. She came into English Harbour's deserted ruins for a few days of catching up, and Nicholson was asked by a hotel proprietor to take some guests for a sail. This he did, and Mollihawk stayed on as the first charter yacht, and from this start the Nicholsons built a charter business that is still thriving today under the second generation. We had our introduction to Caribbean cruising in 1961, courtesy of the Nicholsons, in the converted North Sea trawler Viking and we had seen Antigua grow over the years to the crowded, active center it is today.

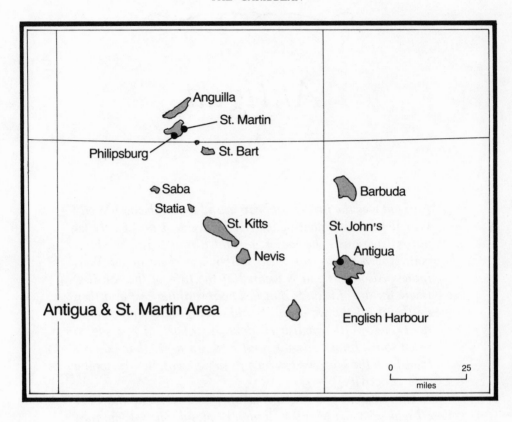

Anguilla

St. Martin

Philipsburg

St. Bart

Saba

Barbuda

Statia

St. Kitts

St. John's

Nevis

Antigua

Antigua & St. Martin Area

English Harbour

0   25

miles

There are very few single islands of modest size that offer enough in the way of harbors for a complete cruise, and Antigua is unique in that respect in the Lesser Antilles. More than once, we have based there for several weeks at a time, and we have started several cruises there, dating back to our very first Caribbean cruise in the converted North Sea trawler *Viking* in 1961, and it is always rewarding to take a few days and poke around Antigua's many bays and coves.

There is perhaps a special incentive to enjoy what Antigua has to offer, because getting there is usually a challenge. In the three times we have taken *Brunelle* there from the north, we have met with completely different sets of conditions for the straight pull of about 80 miles from the St. Martin area. It is possible to island-hop down in a big semicircle via St. Kitts and Nevis in two 50-mile legs, but the joker here is that Nevis is almost always dead to leeward of Antigua, and 50 miles of beating into the trades is not relaxed cruising. This is a much better route when returning northward.

We were lucky the first time, leaving St. Bart at dusk in a fresh northeaster. With a reef in the main and both headsails set, we averaged 7 knots on a swift, steady reach, finishing up under a late moon that made those usually dragging hours before dawn a memorable sailing experience.

More often, it is hard to lay Antigua on the course of 140° M, as the wind is usually a bit south of east, and morning will find you sagging off toward Montserrat 20 miles southwest of Antigua, with a long tack to come back. This was the case on our second passage, which made the trip almost twice as long. The wind was not as strong, and it was not a hard thrash, just time-consuming and bouncy. In a hard southeaster, it is a real plug to make it.

On our last visit we left St. Martin in a light southerly and took several hours to get by St. Bart, where the wind quit completely at sunset, and we had a dull night of powering over a rolly, windless sea. With us at the time as temporary crew was Leslie Powles, who was voted yachtsman of the year in England in 1981 for having completed two solo circumnavigations, one in each direction. The second was nonstop for 329 days out of sight of land around the five southern capes: Good Hope, Leeuwin on Australia, Tasmania, New Zealand, and the Horn. Les, sandy haired, lean, and wiry, was the first circumnavigator to do this, and his time at sea set a record I would never want to equal.

We lured him off his boat, *Solitaire of Hamble*, a 34-foot sloop he built himself, for the first time since 1975, and he was like a mother hen worried about her brood while separated from his vessel. Used to the life of a solo sailor, in which he spends his hours reading below, doing his navigation, and listening to the radio while his steering vane does the work, he found the long night of two-hour wheel tricks plugging along under power quite arduous, and, in kidding about it, wondered whether he might not deserve the Cruising Club of America's Blue Water Medal for such a tough trip. (We were on our way to join the Cruising Club of America's Winter Cruise, starting in Antigua.)

On his second circumnavigation, he all but ran out of food and existed on half a cup of rice a day for the last two months, even resorting to flavoring it with toothpaste to break the monotony. When Jane started to prepare supper, I asked him if he would like rice and got the expected reaction.

When he started on his first trip, he had never done any sailing except for one 2-hour lesson from a friend, which ended with him asking, "How do you stop the bloody thing?" He bought a sextant and an instruction book on navigation and set out from England for Barbados, intending to learn navigation as he went along. He did all but one thing right, which was to change the sun's declination from north latitude to south latitude after September 21. He continued to figure it as north and ended up in Brazil, 1,500 miles from Barbados, aground on a reef and suffering from sun poisoning and fatigue. A low, swampy coast lay off his starboard side, which by his navigation he thought should be Martinique, and he had a hard time figuring why there were no mountains. When native boatmen came out to him speaking a strange tongue that obviously was not French, the confusion was complete. It was not until he ended up in a hospital, which happened to be a maternity one, the only kind in the little village, that he found out where he was.

English Harbour; Freeman Bay in the foreground and Falmouth in the rear

Undaunted, when released after a two-week stay, he continued on around the world, obviously picking up experience, and it was a strange fact that we were the first people he had ever been shipmates with after some 70,000 miles of sailing. He was anchored in Philipsburg Harbor doing temporary odd jobs in a boatyard and writing a book about his experiences when we kidnapped him overnight.

Antigua is sticky about entering and clearing. When you come in at English Harbour on the south end, you must anchor in a quarantine area until boarded and cleared, and this sometimes takes half a day or more. Worrying about his untended boat, Leslie wanted to catch the first plane back, so we powered into St. John's, Antigua's capital and commercial port on the northwest corner, to enter. The port office is at the deep-water port, where the bulkhead is so high that it is impossible to get ashore from a small boat, but we have learned to tie up to one of the big tugboats based there for handling ships using the port and clamber ashore via her high bow.

It was exactly noon on a Saturday, there were no ships in, and the place was deserted. I finally heard the echo of footsteps coming around a corner in the big shed, and a young policeman, hearing my story, called the security guard from the outer gate of the port area to come enter us (for an overtime fee of $25 E.C., or $10 U.S.) and clear Leslie so he could catch his plane. Both were very polite and helpful, which is not always the case with officials here.

There was still very little wind, and what there was came from the south, so it was on with the engine again to power down to the south end. We had new crew coming to the dockyard at English Harbour the next day and wanted to get there, and St. John's, a grubby commercial port city of 25,000, is not the most attractive place to lie. It is hot, situated as it is on the leeward side, and the town's open gutter sewage all drains into the harbor.

Sunset found us entering Falmouth Harbour, a big, open, but well-protected bay just west of English Harbour, for a quiet anchorage off the little Antigua Yacht Club. Once again we had had a new experience in reaching Antigua.

The restored dockyard, just a 5-minute walk from the yacht club,

The Dockyard, English Harbour; *Brunelle* in the center

though 5 miles by sea, is one of the most fascinating yachting centers imaginable. The first time we had seen it, in 1961, the buildings were mostly open ruins and about a dozen charter yachts were based there, along with the occasional long voyager dropping in. The charter boats were all traditional vessels like *Viking*, Brixham trawlers, old Alden racing schooners, and plumb-stemmed British yachts with a nineteenth-century look. Over the years the buildings have been restored to become the attractive Admiral's Inn, a museum, a snack bar, and various shops and service facilities, but the old cannons are still upended in the dirt as bollards and the big windlasses used to careen ships are still in place. It is a world crossroads for cruising yachts, and I once took a census of hailing ports and found 20 countries and a great many U.S. and British ports.

In basing there we have found the dockyard a noisy, crowded, but stimulating place to be, with its sense of history and the constant activity in boats moving, tourists wandering through, gawking at the boats and buildings, work going on amid the continuing hum of generators and the buzz of sanders and electric tools, and a steady ebb and flow of people moving about the boats. We have enjoyed the sense of being involved, and the chance to visit back and forth with other sailing people, swapping experiences and trading cocktail visits, but over the years we have come to appreciate Falmouth for its better breezes and quiet atmosphere. This was somewhat dissipated when a disco was established on a barge near the yacht club, with its overpowering beat amplified to distraction, but complaints evidently took effect, the noise has been toned down, and comparative peace has been restored.

Falmouth now has a fuel and water dock, with coin showers and a laundry as part of the installation, and there is even less reason to fight your way into English Harbour for those services. Ever aware of the dollar, the Antiguan government has put in a schedule of anchoring fees for Falmouth. They are less than those for anchoring or dockage at English Harbour, and still very reasonable, something like 2¢ U.S. a foot per day. Antigua has become fairly realistic about how to get revenue from one of its major "industries," yachting, without driving away the goose.

After our new crew, Carl and Shirley Boll, arrived, we spent a first night settling in at Falmouth, after a Cruising Club of America cocktail party ashore, while they unpacked and adjusted to the climate. Another advantage in Falmouth is that it is clean enough for swimming, which is definitely not the case in the dockyard, and the Bolls were soon in the limpid green waters washing away travel fatigue.

Normally the trades blow steadily from the east in Antigua, as in the whole Windwards and Leewards area, but this was one of those times that "never happens," and the wind was light from the west, with a resultant rise in temperature. Strange as it was, this was ideal for heading for Green Island, which we had picked as our first anchorage, with some private time to spend before the next CCA affair. This is a lovely, unspoiled spot tucked in behind the reefs on the eastern side of Antigua, and it is usually a stiff beat of a dozen miles to thrash your way there against the trades in the sizable swells of the open ocean. Here we had the unheard of rarity of a run to Green Island, and we took advantage of it until the wind quit completely.

Turning on "the noise," we powered by the impressive mansions of the Mill Reef Club, a large enclave lining a considerable section of the shore, and threaded our way behind Green Island to an anchorage on its north side, off a pretty little scimitar of a white beach. Just as we anchored, the breeze came back to normal, riffling in from the northeast, and it increased during the evening to build up a lively chop, but no serious problems.

By morning it was normal trade wind weather again, and early clouds gave way to a beautiful day. The Bolls snorkeled off the Green Island beach, which had been excellent in years past, and reported little to see, so intervening hurricanes must have destroyed the shallow-water reefs.

With the wind back in its usual quarter, our idea was to head back for the bays on the western side of Antigua, and we ran westward past English Harbour to Johnson Island at the southwestern tip of Antigua. We had been wing-and-wing with the staysail, and now we broke out the jib for the reach up the western shore, aiming at Five Islands Harbour or Deep Bay. These are indentations on the leeward coast that we had often used with perfect protection in trade wind weather. As we squared away to sail north up the shore, the wind, following the coast, came more on the bow, making it a close-hauled fetch, and we began to realize that there was a large, underlying swell coming in from the west. Johnson Island, a tiny bit of rock, was awash with breakers, and *Brunelle* began to lift and fall noticeably as we headed into what should have been smooth water.

Past Morris Bay and the Jolly Beach Hotel, we could see a big swell lifting up great humpbacks far off the beach, and as they began to break, curtains off foam flew backward off their crests in the wind. This was something entirely new to me, although I found out later that this condition occurs once or twice a winter. Five Islands, our first potential anchorage, had a froth of breakers riding in to its beach, and a blowhole on the rocky point protecting the beach was spouting like Old Faithful. No chance of going in there for the night.

A 40-foot yawl from the local bareboat fleet was keeping us company at the time, and we gradually began to get the feeling that they were making a contest out of it. Carl was at the wheel, and the challenge suddenly made itself apparent to him, so we trimmed the sails well and paid attention to what we were doing as we charged upwind over the great swells sweeping in from leeward. The string of small cays outside of it that give Five Islands its name loomed up ahead, and I conned Carl through the narrow cut between numbers 2 and 3 of the five, as he kept asking me if I were sure this was OK. With the surge smothering the little cays in blankets of white, we charged through in great style, leaving the yawl well off to leeward, and Carl exhaled noticeably. A day that was supposed to be relaxed cruising had suddenly erupted into a very exciting sail.

Surrounding reefs, usually subdued in the leeward-side calm, were kicking up great white horses, revealing their position, and the shoreline was a froth of lacy foam sweeping far beyond normal limits on the sand. Deep Bay, another potential anchorage, which is usually a placid pond, was a seething cauldron of surge on the beach and the kickback of undertow, and the only thing to do, now that it was well on in the afternoon with no chance to get back to eastern-side harbors, was to head into St. John's, grubby or not, and hope the surge had not penetrated.

This turned out to be so. A large Russian cruise ship, the *Leonid Brezhnev*, flaunting the hammer and sickle on its stack, was at the deep-water pier when we powered on by and came to anchor as close as possible to the town. My guess was right, and the surge did not come in this far, though friends who anchored a half mile further out said it was quite rolly all night, and the 40-foot yawl did go into Deep Bay. We later heard that they spent a wild night surging around their all-chain anchor rode and fetching up with a bone-jarring shock every few minutes. They came into St. John's the next morning looking for a place to get some sleep.

Taking advantage of being there, we rowed ashore and did some supermarket shopping and bought ice, the chief advantages of being in St. John's, trying in the meantime to ignore the foul, sooty-gray waters seeping out into the anchorage from the open sewers of the town. But better foul waters than a bone-jarring surge, as long as no one fell in.

After shopping, we had a brisk reach back down the western shore, with combers still stirring things up in Deep Bay and Five Islands. Rounding Johnson Island, we felt the surge diminish, and it became negligible as we beat eastward inside Cade Reef in calm water and anchored in the little cove off the Curtain Bluff Hotel. Jane and I had stayed there several times, and we consider it one of the most attractive, best-run places at which we have ever stayed. We had become friends with the managers, Howard Hulford and Ed Sheerin, and I had crewed with them in past Antigua Race Weeks, and it was a fine reunion to come ashore for a sumptuous buffet dinner and some steel band jump-up music. The Curtain Bluff anchorage often has a surge when the trades are south of east, and we rolled around a bit, but not excessively.

With the trade at its most boisterous the next morning, we had a bouncy, challenging kind of beat into Falmouth. I put full sail on her and then began to wonder if it was too much as we elevatored over the steep seas, but she seemed to be taking it well, so we kept at it. Two hours of this kind of sailing is great fun, where all day would beat your brains out, and it was a relief to anchor again in Falmouth's peaceful surroundings. We took advantage of the fuel and water dock, and later in the afternoon enjoyed the excitement of the regular Thursday race from English Harbour through Falmouth and back again. The fleet ranged from the old 12-meter *Chancegger*, now fitted with a deck-house, to ancient gaff yawls and swift modern boats like Ohlson 30s, and it was great entertainment to watch them thread through the anchored fleet and around the racing buoys.

Our farewell to the area was a good dinner at Admiral's Inn as part of the CCA program. We had far from covered all the anchorages Antigua has to offer, but we had had a fair sampling, and our last one was Deep Bay, now calmed down to its normal aspect. From there we took off in the morning, headed north on the CCA itinerary, for a fast reach across to Nevis in a fresh southeaster, and the same breeze carried us by St. Kitts' graceful cane fields and cloud-capped peaks for a final even faster reach across to St. Bart. Going in this direction was a lot easier than the trips down to Antigua normally are.

The St. Martin Area

Until recently, the islands between the Virgins and Antigua have been something of a no-man's-land for cruising yachts because of lack of facilities and the problems of getting to and from them. The "in-betweens"—St. Martin/Sint Maarten, Anguilla, St. Bart, Saba, Statia, St. Kitts, and Nevis—cover almost 100 miles between Anguilla and Nevis. To get to them from the Virgins requires a rugged 80-mile push to windward across Anegada Passage, a notoriously nasty, unpredictable, and downright rough body of water where the Atlantic and Caribbean throw their waves, currents, and winds together. At the other end, it is almost always windward work to get on to Antigua.

When the Virgins and Antigua were the only yachting centers with facilities, these were important considerations, but since the mid-1970s there has been marked development in local facilities, and many boats, both private and charter, base here. St. Martin, unique in its binational split between France and Holland, is the most developed, but St. Bart, a "secret hideaway" until perhaps 1975, is jammed full. I first saw Philipsburg, Sint Maarten, in 1958 as a completely empty bay, but now it is continuously filled with boats.

The main drawback of the area is a lack of an adequate all-weather harbor like English Harbour, Antigua, as all except tiny Gustavia on St. Bart have an open bearing subject to surge that makes them untenable at certain times.

Brunelle has cruised here in three separate seasons, making four round trips of Anegada Passage under conditions that *have earned it the family nickname of "Oh-my-God-ah" Passage. In the process we have become thoroughly familiar with most of the islands and have visited Statia and Saba by plane. Our last experience was in basing in Philipsburg for two months, during which we developed a pleasant cruising routine.*

Every Caribbean harbor has its own special collection of noises, but somehow Great Bay at Philipsburg on the Dutch side of St. Martin (which therefore makes it Sint Maarten) has a few more than most. As in all harbors, there are the eager roosters who start greeting the dawn from midnight onward. There is also a large Catholic church right on the beach that summons parishioners to mass with a tremendous clashing of bells at 0525, and, in case everyone in the harbor isn't awake by then, sends them off to work a half hour later with an even longer set of peals. Jane woke up one morning wondering why they happened to ring the bell 41 times for this purpose.

Then there are the dogs. Philipsburg householders must turn their dogs out for the night, and they then form street gangs and chase each other up and down the beach, snarling and howling like wolves on the Russian steppes. One night there was a fusillade of shots from the beach, forever unexplained, and the shore road is close enough so that hot rod drivers and their squealing tires are a part of the sound effects. Add to this jet planes operating out of nearby Juliana Airport, and the sum is something else besides your idyllic tropical hideaway.

Another interesting phenomenon is the surge, which is just about ever present and can measure from a few inches to one horrendous one of waves more than 6 feet high breaking through the anchorage. If you are at anchor, it is bad enough, but should you be tied up stern-to one of the marinas, it is a shattering (literally, sometimes) experience.

So why are there more than 100 yachts in Philipsburg at any given time, along with freighters, Japanese fishing boats that look as though they had just been raised from several years of being sunk on a reef, big white cruise ships almost daily, and a large collection of day-tripper excursion boats?

The answer probably lies in the fact that this is "where it's at." There are two marinas; a boatyard with a big Travelift; all the service and repair facilities, though they do take some chasing down around the town; good, convenient food markets; duty-free shopping for electronics, watches, jewelry, and all those things; several fine restaurants, and, if you feel so inclined, casinos. Direct air connections to New York, Miami, San Juan, and Europe are also a help, and there is no incoming customs, only immigration. If you want to wait long enough, you can call overseas at the communications center. The whole atmosphere is that of a very Americanized resort.

Although the drawbacks take some getting used to, once you are resigned to never being completely still at anchor or in a marina, it is a handy operating base, and the surrounding cruising area is fine, again given the lack of a safe all-weather harbor. To get into the only one, Simson Lagoon, arrangements have to be made in advance to transport the bridge tender from his home to the bridge to open it for you— if you can find him home. Other than that, it is playing hide-and-seek with the surge. If it is bad on one side of an island, you move around to the other side in hopes that the surge has not reached there.

Once the roosters, dogs, and church bells have roused us in Philipsburg and it is time to go cruising, we have developed a fairly set routine that takes advantage of the prevailing breezes and gets us to the most attractive harbors. The first leg is a run down the south side of Sint Maarten, passing the big hotels in Little Bay, Simson Bay, and Mullet Bay and watching the airport activity at Juliana, until it becomes St. Martin off the French border near the western tip of the island. Here the fanciest hotel, La Samanna, sits above a lovely curve of beach leading to a wrecked landing craft that stands in rusty disintegration near the western point.

We have been on a dead run when the wind is in its normal quarter, sometimes jogging along under main, sometimes with the staysail wung out too, but once around the point, we break out the headsails and round up hard on the wind for a beat into Marigot, the main port on the French side a few miles in along the north shore. Here the water is generally smooth in the lee of the island, and the sailing is brisk until a couple of tacks take you into the wide bay of Marigot.

Off to starboard is an incredible sprawl of Mediterranean-looking buildings lying by themselves on the west side of the bay. This is a broken dream called La Belle Créole, started in the '60s by Claude Phillipe, former maître d' of the Waldorf Astoria, but never finished because of financial difficulties. Abandoned and forlorn, the complex sat there for years like some ghost town of the Old West, and there have been persistent rumors of operators like Club Med and Rock Resorts taking it over. Someday it may all come to life again.

Marigot's bay is wide and shoals gently toward the shore, and it is a fine anchorage if there is no swell or breeze from the north. Then it becomes virtually untenable, but it is a delightful place in normal trade wind weather. There are not as many boats as in Philipsburg, but there are usually 20 or 30 anchored off the town. There are no docking facilities except a commercial pier for interisland freighters, and a tiny, crude haul-out facility; otherwise, access ashore is by dinghy to the concrete quay fronting the town or to a special spot we like to use a bit to the west of the main quay. There is a break in the reef, a small beach, and an alley between the school and the Methodist church. This leads to the shopping area, particularly the *patisserie*, which is right at the end of the alley. Whenever we are in Marigot, which remains France personified, my first duty in the morning is to row ashore, beach the dinghy, and buy fresh, hot croissants at the wonderfully aromatic bakery, talking French to Madame la Proprié-taire while she talks English to me. I cannot think of a better way to start the day, and waistline be damned.

A little later, the open-air market sets up in a collection of crude stalls along the quay. This is a vibrant scene, with row after row of displays of fruit, vegetables, and fish, where dark, fork-tailed frigate birds hover just off the quay, waiting for entrails. The ladies tending the booths chatter among themselves, tend small children they have brought with them, and shyly try to attract you to their wares as you walk through. Jane shops carefully here, comparing the quality of tomatoes, bananas, cristofine, celery, lettuce, cucumbers, and cabbage. In the regular markets and shops in town, there are wonderful cheeses and patés and other goodies, and all the packaged goods and brand names are from France, not the United States, as they are in Philipsburg. Marigot insists on being French, and little English is spoken in the shops, though the dollar is thoroughly acceptable.

It is an experience to make a phone call in the post office–communications center, a standard French arrangement. To make a local call one day, I had to wait behind a tourist to whom the phone operator was painfully slow in selling one of each kind of stamp they had in stock. Prepaid phone calls to the States go through rapidly, but credit card calls are unheard of and collect calls take 3 hours via Martinique.

Marigot's streets are narrow, lined with whitewashed buildings of some age, but fancy tourist-trap shops have moved in here and there, and restaurants abound. One could eat in a different one every day for a couple of weeks and most of them are good, standard French restaurants and fairly expensive. If you order a martini, be sure to give explicit instructions, or, as so often happens on the Continent, you get vermouth on the rocks.

From Marigot, it is 6 miles across to Anguilla and another world. This is the little island of 6,000 inhabitants that reverse-revolted into the British Empire in the late sixties. Tired of being odd man out in the associated state of St. Kitts–Nevis–Anguilla, a poor orphan 60 miles away from the other two islands, Anguilla opted to come back to mother as a colony and had a hard time convincing the British what their intentions were. After some comic opera doings involving an "invasion" by British paratroopers and London bobbies all decked out in winter uniforms, the whole thing was straightened out, and Anguilla is happily a colony.

Unlike most Caribbean islands, it is not mountainous. Long and narrow, 17 by 3 miles (its name means eel), it is low, and its main attractions are beautiful beaches and dramatic cliffs striated in yellows, browns, and reds, where tropic birds, graceful white fliers with red heads and long forked tails, nest and swoop out across the water.

Road Bay on the north side is the main port, and it is always a brisk

beat over the 5 miles there from Anguillita, the little island off the
western tip, past the succession of cliffs and beaches, with considerable
new construction testifying that progress is finally catching up with one
of the last unspoiled outposts. Road Bay still has the look of a sleepy
Caribbean village of the thirties, with a clutter of houses along its long,
golden beach, a couple of beach-front restaurants, one rickety pier for
landing dinghies, and a commercial pier for freight boats. These are a
nondescript lot, all seemingly listing one way or another, and there is
usually some semiabandoned vessel caught there by legal difficulties.

Most picturesque of them all is the handsome schooner *Warspite*, a
78-footer built as a 62-foot sloop in 1907, "stretched" to a schooner in
1918, and used now, after a long career as an island freighter with
some remarkably fast passages to her credit, as a resupply vessel for
Sombrero Light, a lonely manned beacon in Anegada Passage, farthest
out bit of land in the northeast Caribbean and first landfall for vessels
bound in from the north and east. *Warspite*, beautifully maintained
in her glossy black paint, has been in the Gumbs family for all her
career. The Gumbs have been on Anguilla since arriving from England
in the eighteenth century, and many of the islands' blacks now carry
the same name as a reminder of slavery days, pre-1834. Emile Gumbs,
who spent many years as *Warspite*'s captain when she traded around
the islands, was recently Chief Minister of the island. An ardent small
boat sailor too, he takes part in the local dinghy races in distinctive
deep-keeled native sloops that make a fine picture lined up on the
beach at Road Bay.

The only drawback to Anguilla is a rather capricious customs system, not improved by the rude, overbearing manner of the man in
charge at Road Bay, a true autocrat of the rubber stamp. He was so
difficult to deal with that I would check with the immigration office,
where you first checked in before going to customs, and would wait
until I heard he was not in duty before going over to that office half a
mile away.

There are some fine anchorages on Anguilla once permission is gained
from the customs people to visit them, which does not always happen.
Crocus Bay, to the east of Road Bay, has a lovely little cove off a

postage stamp of a white beach surrounded by wild, steep cliffs, with tropic birds swooping gracefully about. Offshore, the Prickly Pear Cays are an idyllic example of tropical glamor, with brilliantly colored shallows and perfect beaches, but beware when the northerly swells come in across the reef. Yachtsmen who elect to spend the night there often end up in a panic situation as the surge develops, and boats have been lost in these conditions.

From Road Bay it is a fast run back to Anguillita and then a beat back to St. Martin. Often we would head for Grand Case, just east of Marigot, where a tidy village lines a long curve of beach and several of the best restaurants on the island can be found. Here again it is a fine anchorage if there is no northerly swell or breeze, and the same goes for Anse Marcel, the last bay to the east on the north side of St. Martin. This is a deserted shoreline, with a long clean beach at the head of the deeply indented bay, and you could be far off in the South Pacific until the day trippers from Marigot and Grand Case come in on snorkeling and beach party expeditions.

The same applies to Ile Pinels, just around the corner on the northeast coast of the main island. To get there from Grand Case or Marcel, it is an invigorating beat around the point inside the flat, lonely island of Tintamarre, which is rumored to have been a German supply depot for U-boats in World War II, and more recently has had a bizarre private airstrip with a collection of old planes. The open ocean swells have authority here, but once you come into Orient Bay, riding the big crests as they build up in shallowing water, it is easy to eyeball in behind Pinels into a beautiful half-dollar of a harbor that has room for about six or eight boats. It is a perfect tropical setting, marred only by the fact that natives who picnic here on week ends leave a monumental amount of trash on the island.

Evening here, with the moon rising over Pinels' palm trees, is a delightful time, but it is wise to move out before midmorning when three day-tripper boats from Philipsburg take over the scene. Green Cay, at the south end of Orient Bay, is another anchorage. The chief entertainment here is nude windsurfers.

From this end of St. Martin, given the normal trades, it is a fast,

Ile Pinels, St. Martin

close reach 12 miles to St. Bart, past a collection of rocks with names like Table Rocher, the Groupers, and Barrel of Beef, and a five-peaked island named Ile Fourche that has one good harbor on its west side, a favorite lunch stop.

As late as 1975, a guide book description of St. Bart talked about the lonely little harbor of Gustavia, occupied only by native sloops engaged in the smuggling trade. The word was that you could go in and tie up anywhere stern-to the seawall and would probably be the only yacht there.

How times have changed. Gustavia, which gets its name from the fact that Swedes settled the island and sold it to the French for 11,000 pounds in the 1870s, has a tiny, well-protected inner harbor and an outer roadstead that is subject to surge and capricious backwinds. The inner harbor is so full of boats that seem to have been dumped there for the ages that it looks impossible for even one more canoe to squeeze in, yet we have managed to anchor there on almost every visit by anchoring fore-and-aft, cheek to jowl with boats on both sides. Five feet either way seems to be acceptable clearance. I have never been here in a bad blow or a strong crosswind, but it might be interesting.

The situation is made even more interesting by French anchoring habits and techniques. I am not being prejudiced in commenting on this, since Loulou Magras, the marine maven of Gustavia from his chandlery on the waterfront, posted a critical article about the anchoring peccadillos of his countrymen on the front door of his shop. St. Bart is French, in fact very French, and 95% white, which sets it apart from all the other Caribbean islands.

The French, who have moved into all Caribbean harbors in great numbers, seem to favor boats painted in odd pastel hues, with combinations like a mauve deckhouse and a chartreuse hull, and oddly angled sheers that make it hard to tell in which direction the boat is headed. Decks are cluttered with old crates and boxes, disintegrating life jackets, stray cats, and unmatched pieces of bicycles, and seem to have been covered with leftover material from a gravel pit. When they come into a harbor, someone in a string bikini, or perhaps nude, standing on the bow, swings the anchor shot-put style over the bow while the boat is still moving forward and then turns without another glance and heads for the wine bottle. Sometimes there is no scope at all, and there can also be about 200 feet in some cases. When they start dragging through the anchorage and are informed of the same, they shrug, take another sip of wine, and say that she will eventually fetch up some-where. When they happen to fetch up across your anchor rode, it is a different ball game, complicated by language difficulties, since they refuse to speak anything but French. (All this is really not very exag-gerated.)

And yet St. Bart is charming, extremely atmospheric, and well worth a visit and some shore exploration, and the croissants are as good as in Marigot. Gustavia is even noisier than Philipsburg, with hymn sing-ing, power saws, and fisherman taking off through the anchorage at 0500 with 50-horsepower outboards added to the usual roosters, dogs, autos, and church bells all very close at hand. It is lively and exciting, but getting to be self-defeating in its clutter, and it is almost a relief to run back to the familiar tohobohu of Philipsburg and those 41 church bells as a completion of the cruising round in these waters.

The British Virgin
Islands

Many of the preceding chapters are on cruises based on one visit to an area, but now we come to something different. I have saved the best for last, as I truly believe the British Virgin Islands combine more good cruising features than any one area. Single cruises in any of the places I have been writing about could perhaps be more successful than a single cruise in the BVI, as circumstances over a week or two could make a difference. I have already explained that ideal cruising as written about here does not mean long, hairy-chested passages out of sight of land, or explorations through a Greenland tickle. The British Virgins offer no such challenges. They may not be as exotic as Tonga, as historic as the Aegean, as blessed with as wide a choice of harbors and gunkholes as Maine or the Chesapeake, or as cosmopolitan as Europe, but they put it all together in a way that no other area does.

For consistency over months at a time of good sailing weather, plus the choice of harbors, the scenery, the ease of operation, the availability of services, facilities, and supplies, as well as the opportunity to branch out to wider horizons when the call comes, I rate this area number one.

As for describing the best cruise here since bringing Brunelle down from the States in early 1979 and basing there thereafter, it would be hard to pick any one cruise as best out of the weeks on end of cruising over several years. The solu-

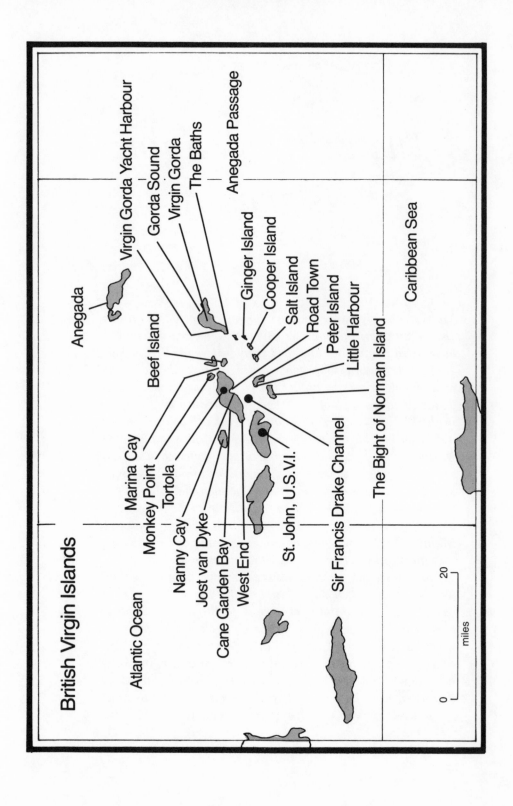

British Virgin Islands

Atlantic Ocean

Anegada

Virgin Gorda Yacht Harbour
Gorda Sound
Virgin Gorda
The Baths

Anegada Passage

Ginger Island
Cooper Island
Salt Island
Road Town
Peter Island
Little Harbour

Beef Island

Marina Cay
Monkey Point
Tortola
Nanny Cay
Jost van Dyke
Cane Garden Bay
West End

St. John, U.S.V.I.

Sir Francis Drake Channel

The Bight of Norman Island

Caribbean Sea

0   20
|_____|
miles

tion, then, is simply to write up the last cruise, just com-
pleted, as this is being written in a berth at Brunelle's *home*
base at Village Cay Marina, Road Town Tortola, capital of
the BVI and heart of its cruising operations.

This cruise was completely typical of our operations here. It took in
most of our favorite harbors, the weather was not the best we had ever
had here, while still being delightful, but was far from the worst, and
it was a fine week of excellent sailing and comfortable relaxation.

It started from Village Cay, where *Brunelle* spends the summer, and
to which we come back periodically during the cruising season for
supplies, maintenance, and a visit to the metropolitan delights of Road
Town. This is a sleepy village strung along the western shore of Road
Town Harbour, which is twice the size of when we first saw it in 1964.
Then there were very few shops, no marina, one water pump at the
town dock, an icehouse that operated on a very hit-or-miss schedule,
and no locally based yachts. Now it has five marinas, a large boatyard,
between 300 and 400 locally based yachts, hotels, restaurants, markets, boutiques, chandleries, and a complex of marine services based
on an area that was desolate swamp when we cruised in here in 1964
and 1966. Still, the ambience is sleepy, the pace is slow, and the
pressures of civilization seem quite far away.

We have a professional boat maintenance service that tends to *Bru-*
nelle when we are north for the summer. They open her up to air her
out and run the engine to charge the batteries on a weekly basis, make
sure her dock lines and fenders are OK, and do routine maintenance
work for hourly rates that are much easier to live with than those in
yards in the States.

There is a certain charm to the arrangement, as the general approach
is a bit casual and absentminded, but things do eventually get done,
and when they are done they are done properly. The boat keeper, Peter
Clarke, an amiable South African who has an English partner and
several Tortolans working for him, has to have his memory jogged now
and then, as when he took a boat to be hauled at Tortola Yacht Ser-

vices and failed to pick her up for a few days after work on her was completed. Finally the yard called and asked him when he was going to take the boat away.

"Oh, that's where that boat is. I wondered where she had gotten to," was his answer.

Actually, he is very conscientious when it comes down to the nitty-gritty. When Hurricane David swept through in the fall of 1979, he managed to bring a dozen or so boats safely through the blow in their slips at Village Cay, which is protected by a high seawall, by personally going aboard each one, sometimes having to swim to get there, to check out her lines.

We had to have some upholstery repairs done after several years of hard use of the equipment, and I asked Peter about getting someone to do the work. His answer gave some idea of the local life-style.

"Well, let me see," he mused. "I can't call Mad Sam this week. He does pretty good work, but you can't talk to him when the moon is full; he's completely unreliable then. Maybe Little John can do it. He's the only other one, and he's all right if you can find him."

All in all, it has worked well, and *Brunelle* has been maintained in tip-top fashion. The hunt for dead cockroaches when we first come back in the fall and the annual summer fumigation has taken place can be a bit traumatic, but it is an accepted part of the routine. A boat cannot be left at a pier for a long period of time without acquiring these persistent visitors, and fumigation is a must before the new season begins.

At Village Cay, we have become part of a community that sees each other spasmodically and in fits and starts over the year, as the owners of the boats that base there come and go, and it makes us feel at home to come back from a northern summer and find familiar faces around the piers.

And so it was from Village Cay that we set out on this recorded cruise on a day of blustery trade wind from the east. We were to head for Trellis Bay, 10 miles away at the eastern end of Tortola, or, more specifically, at Beef Island, Tortola's almost-connected eastern satellite. This is where the airport is, and we were to meet friends arriving by plane that afternoon. The airport is a 200-yard walk from the government dock at Trellis Bay, and it is handy and fun to meet arriving guests right there.

It was a good, stiff beat, with *Brunelle* just able to carry full sail of main, staysail, and roller-furler jib as we charged eastward into a short, steep chop, with rain squalls playing around us over the hills of Tortola and out in the open Caribbean to the south, but none of them hit us. The plane was due to arrive at 1543, and we dropped anchor off the pier at 1540, so I headed ashore as quickly as possible, knowing that it takes a while to clear immigration and customs, even when the plane is on time. As it turned out, there was no sign of it when I checked with the Crown Air counter, and they finally advised me it might be in within 30 to 45 minutes. Eventually it did arrive about an hour late, which is more or less normal for connections here, and it had made a side trip over to Virgin Gorda, 6 miles more to the eastward, on the way. Arriving were old friend and neighbor Julia Gross, who had cruised with us many times, and her college friend of 50 years standing, Dolly Minis, and husband Phil. They are experienced cruising hands. naturalists, and bird and whale watchers who have traveled over much of the globe, including the Galapagos, the Chilian archipelago, the Straits of Magellan, and the Silver Bank off the Dominican Republic in these pursuits, but they were first-timers in the Virgins.

They were in the normal culture shock of a winter day's trip from New York, via the steamy hullabaloo of the San Juan airport, to the Virgins, and theirs was the normal reaction of sighs and exclamations as they felt the softness of the breeze and admired the play of clouds and the glow of the sun setting over Tortola's hills behind the fringe of palm trees that grace the western shore of Trellis Bay.

The breeze held strongly through the night, making them aware they were on a boat sashaying restlessly to her anchor. It was still blowing that way on the bright clear morning that followed a dawn rain squall, which had caused the usual stumbling and fumbling of hatch closings. In the Virgins we never start a day with a rush or set a departure time, unless there is a specific appointment to keep, which there seldom is. Everything is very close, and the choice of harbors is vast.

One of the delights of the day for me is breakfast in the cockpit while gauging the promise of the day from the look of the sky and the feel of the breeze. Then there is dish washing and the usual morning duties of head visits, application of sunburn cream, location of the paperback book currently being read, and straightening out of the cabin. While all this is going on, we usually run the engine for the hour needed to charge the refrigerator and batteries and heat the water for dish washing.

With the chores done, we try to get underway by using the last of the engine hour to assist in getting the anchor up and moving out of the harbor while we make sail.

Speaking of chores, I was responsible for a couple of laughers in trying to be helpful. While Jane was cleaning the boat before the guests arrived, I had volunteered to do the shopping. One of my purchases was a package of frozen chicken, which seemed a great bargain for $1.09. I did not have my glasses on, and I thought it was a package of varied chicken parts. When Jane broke it out for dinner the second night, it turned out to be chicken backs, and there was some consternation and a lot of rude remarks about my ability as a shopper. As it turned out, we ended up getting a chicken salad and a pot of chicken soup out of the much maligned backs, so my $1.09 was not so badly spent after all.

My other gaffe was in serving martinis one night before dinner. This was our first cruise after the summer lay-up, and the water tanks are always a bit musty tasting with their first refill of the season. It takes a couple of run-throughs to get them to normal, so I had filled several bottles on shore at Village Cay for making coffee and tea. I made martinis all around and handed them out, to appreciative murmurs, and we settled down for happy hour.

After a few moments, Julia touched my arm and inquired politely, "Bill, what do you think is in this martini?"

With thoughts of having mistaken some other green bottle for the vermouth, I took a sip, pondered a bit, and had to make the surprised admission that it was water with a touch of vermouth.

"Well, I wasn't going to say anything," Dolly then chimed in, "but I think I have water too."

I had used a gin bottle in getting the water supply from shore, and somehow it had gotten in with the legitimate booze bottles. From then on, whenever I made martinis, the admonitions flew fast about making sure I was using gin.

Since the Virgins lie roughly east and west on the axis of the normal trade wind, it is a wise idea to get all the way east early in a week and then have everything downwind of you thereafter. Though we have had westerlies, southerlies, and northers at some time or other, the percentages, like about 90, are with the wind being somewhere in the east, usually due east. It was that way this bright and breezy morning, as, with all chores accomplished, we made sail at about 1030 and started beating our way to Gorda Sound. This is an "inland sea" some 2 by 3 miles at the eastern end of Virgin Gorda, the easternmost island of the chain, 12 miles away.

We started out under main and staysail, since there was enough heft in the breeze to move her under that conservative rig, and I like to get the feel of things as we start out. She was moving well in the first tack over to Marina Cay, but she could obviously handle full sail, so we "unrolled the window shade" (set the roller-furler) and charged upwind toward the Baths at the southern tip of Virgin Gorda. Once there we flipped to starboard tack and swept along the shore, with its spectacular boulders and dazzling beaches, in the shifty, gusty wind of about 20 to 22 knots. We made excellent time, with our guests reveling in the sailing, the sunlight, and the play of trade wind clouds over the island hills.

When it came time for lunch as we moved under the wind shadow of the highest part of Virgin Gorda, the mountain that gives it the name of Fat Virgin, we cut back to what we call the "cocktail rig"— main and staysail. This keeps her moving, is easily trimmed in vagrant puffs, as in the wind shadow here, and keeps her on an even keel in winds up to 30 knots for such delicate operations as mixing drinks and making lunch.

A norther's swells breaking on Virgin Gorda

With all this accomplished and the fluky winds under the Fat Virgin properly negotiated, we set the jib again and charged out into the open sea past the Dogs, small rocky islets lying between Beef Island and Virgin Gorda. *Brunelle* loved feeling the lift of open-water seas under her, and we took delight in tucking away various questionably sailed bareboats on a long starboard tack offshore. I said "next stop Bermuda" as the bow aimed at an empty blue horizon, but actually low-lying Anegada, less than 20 miles to the north, would have come first.

When the northern entrance to Gorda Sound, marked by buoys between the reefs on each side of it, opened up to starboard, we flipped and charged shoreward as the seas diminished under Necker and Prickly

Sunset at Beef Island

Pear Islands, seaward guardians of Gorda Sound. The sound, completely landlocked in its ring of hills, is the loveliest part of the Virgins. We first saw it in 1964, when we had the entire place to ourselves, and the only houses on the shore were at the native village of Gun Creek, sprawling upward on the south side of the sound. Now it is mecca for most of the boats cruising the Virgins, and there are several resorts and a real estate development, but the charm is still there.

We could see the reefs on both sides as we slid into the flat water of the sound, and the concentration of boats off the Bitter End Yacht Club opened up to port when we cleared Prickly Pear. Bitter End is a complete, nautically oriented resort on the very northeast tip of Virgin Gorda, reached only by boat from the end of the road at Gun Creek 2 miles away. It has all sorts of boats for its guests to use and caters to a nightly crowd of visiting yachtsmen in its meticulously run restaurant. Reservations, including menu choice, must be radioed in by midafternoon. It is one of the casual amusements of cruising in these waters to listen to menu discussions going on, with such questions as, "How is the native-style chicken cooked?"

A special feature of Bitter End is a small marina club called the Quarterdeck Club, where, as a member, I usually tie up, though overnight moorings are available for $10 (credit cards accepted, with free launch and garbage service), as we enjoy the chance to explore ashore, the showers, and the prettiest dockmaster anywhere, an English girl named Jenny.

Exploring ashore includes a fine swimming beach and a walk around the point on the beach with a great view across the reefs to Anegada Passage, plus a beautifully tended rock garden on the hill where most of the hotel cottages are sprawled. There was also bird watching for Dolly and Phil. Dinner at the restaurant is a pleasant ritual ending with spiced rum on the terrace while looking across the beach to the anchored boats.

On our way out of Gorda Sound, we usually take the passage at the west end that is verboten to charter boats, because most of them have 6 feet of draft. It is a picturesque slide over pale-green water in the cut, narrow with hidden beaches tucked away on each side and one wicked reef to starboard that breaks in a swell and has claimed its share of unwary boats. It is a straight run through from Bitter End, and we then reached down the Virgin Gorda shore to a luncheon anchorage at The Baths, a strange collection of tumbled boulders as big as three-story houses, with pools in among them and palm-fringed beaches. There is always something of a surge here, not a place for overnighting, and there are times when the surge is too much to permit dinghy landing on the beach. As a "must" stop, The Baths, at the height of the season on a good day, can resemble Cuttyhunk on a Saturday night.

A mile away is Virgin Gorda Yacht Harbour, run by the Little Dix Rockefeller resort, a handy place to shop, with several markets right at the marina, plus other stores, fuel, ice, and water (10¢ a gallon), and several restaurants nearby. We tucked in there for the night after our stop at The Baths and were glad of a snug berth on a breezy night, with rain clouds sweeping in early in the morning. Big black clouds would build swiftly over the hills to the eastward, heralded first by a quick increase in wind and then curtains of slashing rain that swept off to leeward against a backdrop of purple clouds in a matter of moments.

We ran before them down Drake Channel under main alone, with *Brunelle* rolling freely in swells coming in from the north, donning and doffing foul weather gear as the squalls caught us and swept by, to end up at a favorite stop, Little Harbour on Peter Island. This is a picture postcard palm-lined cove, with the Chubb family's winter home perched on the hilly point forming its north side. The late Percy Chubb established a mooring here for Cruising Club of America members, and we use it often as a chance to explore the little reefs lining the shores of the cove, excellent snorkel country, and as a secure mooring in a harbor that presents anchoring difficulties despite its snug protection.

The hills around it cause the prevailing easterly to backwind in from the west and "toilet bowl" around the harbor unpredictably, and it is a three-ring circus to sit safely on the mooring and watch the goings on as the bareboat people attempt to figure out what is happening to them when they try to anchor. Sometimes this ends in an 0300 session of scrambling and shoving as the boats swing around at different angles. Sure enough, even on this night of mild wind and only an occasional gust, two boats rafted together near the beach dragged their short-scope anchor and drifted out to tangle with a boat anchored next to us. No harm done, but a lot of flashlight beams swooping around and shouts and cries on the night breeze before things settled down.

On a morning of in-and-out clouds we took in the reefs via a glass-bottomed bucket from the dinghy ("sissy snorkeling" again) and explored ashore. This requires permission from the caretaker, as visitors without an introduction are not supposed to land. The profusion of oleander, hibiscus, frangipani, and unidentifiables, along with limes, grapefruit, mangos, and the peculiar rough-skinned West Indian *limone*, is overwhelming, and Dolly found a bird or two of interest.

After a swim and lunch, we took a sight-seeing sail over to Norman Island, next island to the south, with its string of caves along the stark red cliffs of its western shore. These are supposed to have given Robert Louis Stevenson the idea for *Treasure Island*, and it at least makes a good story and adds a touch of interest. After a swing through the big cove known as The Bight to look at the anchored boats, we headed on to Road Town. The Bight is a popular stop because of good protection, but I seldom anchor there because of deep water, not the best holding ground, and the profusion of drag-prone boats.

Our ongoing 5-mile sail to Road Town across Drake Channel was at hull speed in a lively easterly, and we settled into our home berth at Village Cay for some next-day shopping chores. For dinner, Jane cooked cristofine, a West Indian form of squash, with ginger root as seasoning, a special local treat we enjoy.

We didn't finish Road Town activities until 1600 the next afternoon and just had time to reach across to Little Harbour, again at hull speed plus, to pick up the mooring and admire a sunset of glowing copper over the distinctive pattern of hills made by St. John and the western end of Tortola.

It was still blowing the next morning, with a rain squall to wake us up, and we beat our way eastward under full sail, which was just about at the limit of what she should take, to a luncheon stop at Cooper Island Beach Club. This beach-front bar and restaurant is a relaxed place to have a meal ashore, though the anchorage is an uneasy one because of vagrant backwinds, surge, and not-too-good holding ground. There are a couple of clear patches of white sand I always try to aim the anchor at when we stop here. Despite supercilious service from a young English lad, who seemed to resent our interruption of his reading of *I, Claudius*, it was a pleasant interlude before weighing anchor for a brisk reach across to Marina Cay.

This is another popular anchorage, with a hotel and restaurant on the tiny cay, scene of a book and movie called *Our Virgin Island* about a young English couple building a honeymoon cottage here in the thirties. Their building is still the central one of the hotel. The anchorage is protected, except for a surge coming across the fringing reef at high tide, and I always anchor in shallow water on a clear sandy bottom, in among the resident boats, as the water further out is deep, with a cross tide.

This was the first night without rain squalls since the cruise started, a good one for star gazing, since the moon was now in its last half and rising late. As for star gazing, I can always find Orion, and the Dipper if it is up, but at this time of year the Southern Cross was below the horizon. I really enjoy seeing it opposite the Dipper when it does poke up in the Northern Hemisphere skies on occasion.

For a last day for the guests, we had a gorgeous one, a "typical" Virgin day of breeze from the east at 14–16 and white, puffy trade wind clouds, with no rain squalls. For the first time, we could set the Flasher, our poleless spinnaker, for a short drill on how it works as a demonstration for Phil, and then made our way through Camanoe Passage, with the lift of Atlantic swells under us, to a favorite spot, Monkey Point at the south end of Guana Island. This is a colorful day anchorage where pelicans dive-bomb the perimeter all day long and showers of silvery fish, chased by torpedo-bombing jacks, sweep across its surface. Swimming and snorkeling are fine, and there is an interesting notch in the shoreline that gives a view through to the eastward across a little beach. Who the monkey was, I don't know.

As a wind up, we circumnavigated Guana, coasting close in along its steep shores for a look at the century plants and other flora, with a few birds for Dolly—by now pelicans and boobies didn't count. On the seaward side, a fast reach brought us back to Camanoe Passage and our last anchorage off the airport in Trellis Bay. Ordinarily, when in Trellis, we go ashore to the Last Resort Restaurant for dinner and the inimitable comic songs of the proprietor, Tony Snell, but it had not yet opened for the season, so the last night was a quiet one of star gazing.

We had not seen all the places the British Virgins offer. Northerly swells from some mid-Atlantic disturbance had kept us from the north-side harbors like Cane Garden Bay. We had not had any wild adventures or extra thrills, but nothing had gone wrong. It had just been a delightful week, spiced by fast sailing every time we moved, and a good example of why I call this the best area of all the favorite places we have cruised. In this typical week, similar to so many others, we had simply experienced the essence of what cruising is all about.